Sausage in a Basket

SAUSAGE IN A BASKET

The Great British Book of How Not to Eat

Martin Lampen

BLOOMSBURY

First published in Great Britain 2007

Bloomsbury Publishing Plc,
36 Soho Square,
London W1D 3QY

A CIP catalogue record for this book is available from the British Library

ISBN 978 0 7475 8918 1
10 9 8 7 6 5 4 3 2

Typeset by Palimpsest Book Production Ltd, Grangemouth, Stirlingshire
Printed in Great Britain by Clays Ltd, St Ives plc

Bloomsbury Publishing, London, New York and Berlin

The paper this book is printed on is certified by the © 1996 Forest
Stewardship Council A.C. (FSC). It is ancient-forest friendly.
The printer holds FSC chain of custody SGS-COC-2061.

www.sausageinabasket.com

www.bloomsbury.com/martinlampen

FSC

Mixed Sources

Product group from well-managed
forests and other controlled sources

Cert no. SGS-COC-2061
www.fsc.org
© 1996 Forest Stewardship Council

To Mum and Dad. For the life, the love and the free food.

Introduction

I'm hungry.

These days I'm always hungry. I'm hungry because I can't find anything I want to eat. In fact, it's difficult to find anything to eat – in shops, restaurants, pubs, glossy recipe books, takeaways, my fridge or at the back of my cupboard among scattered sugar from a half-eaten packet of Nice biscuits and salty black dribble from that leaking bottle of soy sauce – that doesn't make me feel slightly queasy.

Last Saturday evening I spent two hours wandering around an out-of-town supermarket the size of an airport hangar, putting food in my trolley, taking it out again, returning it to the wrong shelves in the wrong aisles.

I still couldn't find anything to eat. I'm sure I caught a chest chill by the frozen gateaux. I'm practically positive that someone from senior staff was following me, returning all my rejected choices to the correct shelves. Had I been wearing the 'Get Fit' pedometer I'd found free that very morning at the bottom of a box of freeze-dried fruit-and-nut flakes I would surely have clocked more than ten miles, burnt several hundred calories and reduced my body-fat percentage by several points while searching for a suitable Saturday-night meal.

Nuggets; bites; fish fingers; chicken pieces in pre-prepared sauces; red-pepper halves stuffed with couscous, soft cheese and unidentified herbs; canned chunky soups; wheat-free macaroons that sounded like they might be healthy even though I had no idea why I might want to start avoiding wheat. I glided my trolley past all of them, waltzing up every aisle and back again to a clanging wall-to-wall pop soundtrack: the in-store CD of the week, the third *Hairbrush Divas* compilation.

Packets of pricey pasta stuffed with field mushrooms and garlic feta cheese; Greek-style stuffed leaves with a side pouch of low-fat hummus dip; luxury salmon fish-cakes; minced-beef-and-onion crispbakes; a microwave-able Cantonese takeaway selection in an octagonal cardboard box assembled to resemble a Tang Dynasty temple. Six wafer-thin slices of Scottish beef in tartan-trimmed packaging with a black-and-white photo of a sunlit loch next to the weight and nutrition information (sixty per cent water – interesting). Remove film before eating and consume within three days of purchase on pain of death. I briefly considered them all. I even picked some of them up, but I felt my stomach turn so I put them down again – in the Top Twenty DVDs rack.

The female pop singer on the PA system sang, over synthesised drum beats and a cynical Heaven 17 sample, 'I want to feel your energy/I want to explode/Tonight is the night . . .' Boom. Boom. Cha-Boom.

I wanted to cry. I needed to eat. I could eat a horse. It was 8.15 on a Saturday night and I was the only person shopping in a supermarket. Boom. Boom. Cha-Boom.

I *could* really eat a horse. I draw the line at those chicken bites that are shaped like drumsticks and are in fact reconstituted rooster moulded into fuzzy drumstick shapes.

Time ticked on. It was 8.45. I came close to buying a two-pack of those luxury chicken pieces that you have to pour a small plastic packet of honey-and-herb glaze over five minutes before they're finished. No matter what the meal's supposed theme – Cajun, Thai, Indian, Chinese, Italian or French – those sauces always taste like maple syrup; but the action of adding the gloopy mess to fatty breasts or oily chops does at least simulate the preparation of something from scratch.

I passed the wine aisle. Is it acceptable to buy a bottle with a screw cap or to drink a German dessert wine with a small tub of microwave apple crumble?

I have to admit, the chicken-in-syrup two-pack looked reasonably appetising. However, I just knew I wouldn't be able to open the sachet because the only scissors I can ever find are the ones on my Swiss Army Knife. I use them to trim my houseplant and, by the time I'm able to scrape the bark off and dip them in soapy water, the chicken is burnt and I'm waving a tea-towel under the smoke alarm to stop it from beep-beep-beeping.

I put the chicken pieces back – in the wrong aisle, along-side the rice cakes and those hard brown crispbreads for crash dieters, homesick Scandinavians and subscribers to *Family Circle*.

In the end I gave up, bought some dental chewing gum

and a scratchcard and drove home to eat bran flakes with raisins and semi-skimmed milk.

I have another pedometer, if anyone wants one. I have six of them now. I'm still hungry.

I've lived in Great Britain for every one of my thirty-three years. At a rate of three meals a day, that works out at more than 35,000 servings of breakfast, lunch, dinner and the occasional pickled-onion-and-cheese supper, all eaten in the land of the Sunday roast, the warm, frothy pint, the Yorkshire pudding, the spotted dick, the tub of coleslaw and the powdered cheese sauce.

Yet, in thirty-three years of living and dining in Britain, I don't think I've ever eaten a truly satisfying meal.

Convenience dining has been with me since birth. My dad wasn't present at my delivery. He didn't pace the floor in the waiting room. He didn't hold Mum's hand, cut the cord or hand out cigars to passing porters. He wasn't even in the hospital. He was a mile and a half away in British Home Stores' cafeteria, eating bacon, egg, stewed tomatoes, mushrooms and beans and a glass of fruit squash from one of those fruit-squash dispensers where a stainless-steel propeller in perpetual motion stirs orange or lime green liquid.

It was Plymouth, Devon, in November 1973: the land of the cream tea in the era of the £1.20 cafeteria dinner.

My dad was a Royal Navy artificer and my mum was a school dinnerlady. My mum's Irish; it was compulsory for Irish women marrying Englishmen and moving to England between the rise of the rock opera and the fall of Margaret Thatcher to find employment as school-kitchen staff. Maybe it had something to do with Enoch Powell and Internment, but probably not.

There have been rare occasions – a first date, perhaps, or a three-week anniversary – where I've imagined that I've eaten a great meal only to realise later that I was fooling myself: in fact the date droned on about her ex for two hours, the house white made me hallucinate and I splattered summer fruits coulis all over my trousers.

Being single, I rely on pre-packaged foods: watery pastas, cheese-topped pink-meat patties coated in breadcrumbs and watery ready-meals, swimming in preservatives and prepared with 900 per cent of the daily salt allowance for men. At the time of writing I haven't eaten anything for six weeks that wasn't a shade of orange and topped with cheddar.

Lunch isn't much better. The thirty-minute gap between pretending to work in the morning and pretending to work in the afternoon allows for only a quick trip to the super-market and a flimsy bread-based snack: chicken or ham, salad or cheese, glued together with a honey-and-mustard mayonnaise and flung into a dusty white bap or a tasteless tortilla wrap. All washed down with a £4.00 mango-and-carrot energy drink as the clock ticks down to 5.30 and the crumbs from the roll harden in my keyboard.

Maybe the lack of a sophisticated, balanced diet in my life can be put down to the time restrictions of a busy urban lifestyle. Maybe it's a result of the dominance of the supermarket chains and the over-processed, over-branded food that they sell. Maybe bad food is genetic – an Anglo-Saxon attitude imbedded in our DNA, right next to the genetic code that makes us so fond of spitting in the street and Tuesday-evening TV documentaries about plastic surgery and shark attacks.

So, what is British food, and why is so much of it joyless, flavourless and stodgy? Why is the way we eat – balancing plates of lukewarm, turkey-flavoured, cheese-topped mini-waffles on our laps as we try to follow the omnibus edition of some serialised soap where stage-school graduates drop their consonants and pretend to be poor – so graceless? Why does eating out in Britain offer such bad value for money? Why must everything we scoff down be marketed as fad or fashion, sold to us on TV by hungry tykes, harried-yet-savvy mums or puppets from the Jim Henson Workshop? Why is everything we eat coated in a golden batter or covered in crumb, given a snappy, alliterative name, conveniently slotted into a Winter Warmers or Summer Bites assortment and sold to us from a greasy laminated menu?

Here's the lowdown on inadequate eating in the UK since the seventies: from my mashed-turnip upbringing through to the butternut-squash years; from the individual fruit pie to moist almond frangipani; from the school curry to the lamb shank via the cheese board and the sausage in a basket.

These are the dishes, the food rituals, the dining habits and menu options that have defined my life so far. They filled me up but they let me down. Dig in.

All You Can Eat: £5.99

Have you no shame?

No? OK. No problem. Maybe you're a cash-strapped second-year science student coming clean to your long-term boyfriend, over sticky pasta shells in a scarlet-coloured sauce, that you've become an escort to pay your tuition fees.

Maybe you're one half of a happy couple called Keith and Kirsty. It's your first wedding anniversary and you're saving up for Orlando and a dormer extension.

Maybe you're furiously fighting an addiction to French onion soup from a murky, black communal cauldron, plastic scoops of damp sweetcorn, vinegary three-bean salad and a thin, over-sweet, not-quite-defrosted slice of 'New York' cheesecake.

Maybe you're a tourist with aching feet, out on the Heritage trail taking out a map from your lime green and battleship grey bum-bug, marking out the march to the old mill and lured in by meatballs, macaroni cheese, mock gables, a serious lack of decent dining alternatives in the immediate vicinity and a money-off coupon clipped from a leaflet you picked up in the Butterfly Farm gift shop.

Maybe you're a pushy line manager with a pink shirt

and greasy hair, treating your team to a post-project cele-
bration dinner of potato salad, golden fish bites and puny,
pink-in-the-middle chicken legs in a watery chasseur sauce.
Your team just wanted to go to the pub; you insisted on
an *activity*. You cleared a space on the white board and
asked if anyone had 'issues' with the all you can eat. You
used to eat here on Friday lunchtimes with your ex and
there's always a chance she'll be here today.

It doesn't matter why you're here. I'm not here to judge.
Save your excuses and pile up your plates.

Ambience

Restaurant ambience – it's an intangible quantity: loca-
tion, décor, service, lighting, external views and softly lit
lobster tanks. No plastic fishing nets hung from the
ceiling, no strobing lights, hen-night rabble indulging in
food fights or easy-peasy puzzles printed on the paper
placemats.

You need quality condiments and bone-handled knives;
leather-bound menus with red-velvet placeholder ribbons;
waiters who call you 'sir' and 'madam' rather than 'mate'
or 'pal' – or even 'squire' and 'm'lady' like they did at the
Medieval Barbecue you went to before Christmas.

You'll be offered warm seeded bread rolls from linen-lined,
hand-woven wicker baskets; laundered cotton napkins
rather than rough paper serviettes; an in-house pianist inter-
preting Chopin rather than Bruce Hornsby & the Range
echoing through a tinny tannoy or Peabo Bryson through
a substandard speaker system; comfortable upholstered

seats rather than moulded plastic stools or bumpy metal perches; wine lists on parchment handwritten in calligraphy scripts.

I once set fire to a linen napkin in a top restaurant. I was fidgeting while a female friend was telling me about her dad's cancer.

It wasn't my fault – I fiddle and fidget in female company, and they shouldn't have put such a large candle on so small a table.

I had to throw the burning napkin in the water feature.

Thankfully, none of the koi carp were harmed – which is more than can be said for relations with my friend, whom I haven't seen since.

Apples

I don't like apples. They're hard work – I lose interest after five or six bites. They're sometimes sour. They attract wasps. They pop up unexpectedly in side salads – always an unwelcome, out-of-place appearance, much like Ted Danson's jarring cameo in *Saving Private Ryan*.

Apples wither after a week, their skin gets stuck in your teeth and they make your hands sticky. The pips are a choking hazard and I found a worm in one once. Actually, there's a strong possibility that I just saw that in a cartoon . . .

I keep confusing real life with cartoons. It's been happening for months – ever since an army of red ants made away with my picnic.

Attentive Waiters

'Is everything all right, sir?' 'Can I get you anything else, sir?' 'Another bottle of the house white that tastes like Mr Sheen, sir? Or how about the Pinot Gris? It's from Alsace. It smells like damp dog.'

'Everything is fine, thanks.'

'Is everything all right, sir?'

[Repeat every three minutes, from the chilled fish soup to strawberry mousse and farmhouse cheeses.]

Waiters of the world, relax. Keep your slicked-back ponytails on. Everything is, indeed, all right. Everything is Jim Dandy until I say it isn't. Until you see me impaled on my steak knife or choking on *mon petit pain*, let it go, stop pacing the floor, quit hovering and asking whether everything is to my satisfaction. Everything is just fine. Go back to the kitchen and spit in the soup or do whatever it is you do when you're not carrying trays.

Avocado

Avocados confuse me. They're classed as fruit but used like vegetables. They're apparently good for you, yet contain more calories than a deep-fried, chocolate-glazed almond croissant. They're full of fat – more, in fact, than a Zinger Tower burger – but it's the 'good' kind of fat, like the kind found in walnuts and doting Italian grandmothers.

Avocados disturb me. They have a hard, lizard-like skin over their green mushy flesh and a big brown stone in the middle.

That stone is the mental object my mind conjures up whenever I hear the word 'ovary'.

Bailey's Irish Cream

A unique spirit made from a mixture of fresh cream, sugar and the finest triple-distilled Irish whiskey.

I had a mini-bottle on a plane once. The steward poured it over ice in a plastic glass and winked. I hid behind the in-flight *Skymag* and read anodyne features on Bali, the Broadway longevity of *Les Misérables* and expensive automatic watches. I drank six more mini-bottles and winked back.

My head hurts just thinking about that flight. Creamy whiskey liqueur shook in my stomach and foamed in my mouth as we made our bumpy descent into Dulles International.

I'm not sure who Bailey was, but surely he's been responsible for more human misery than Sinn Fein's Martin McGuinness and Ulster Defence Association leader Johnny 'Mad Dog' Adair put together.

Baked Potato

There's a self-denial aspect to the whole baked-jacket-potato phenomenon. It's like a hairshirt; an edible sackcloth, only with twice the fibre content, an unimaginative tuna-mayo and sweetcorn filling and/or scalding-hot baked-bean topping.

Unless, of course, you just eat the fluffy potato filling and leave behind the brown, leathery coating.

I'm always disturbed by the way baked potatoes are presented, preserved and sold in cafés or canteens. There they sit: shrivelled and unloved in that huge heated glass incubator. They're shrinking faster than Michael Keaton's head in *Beetlejuice*, or Paul Gascoigne's since he gave up the booze.

The case is framed with black *faux*-wrought-iron. 'Hot Baked Potatoes' is printed on the glass in a florid, gold-leaf *faux*-Victorian font.

I could never really enjoy a dish that uses, as its unique selling point, the fact that it contains massive amounts of something called roughage.

Baking for One's Colleagues

I used to work with a woman – we'll call her Anne – who spent her evenings baking. She'd bake tiered sponge cakes, gooey-fruit and choc-chip cookies, raspberry pavlovas that melted in the mouth, and moist five-fruit flans, then bring them to work the next morning to share with her colleagues, the motorcycle couriers and even that surly freelancer who sat by the fire exit listening to country & western on his headphones, nodding his head and thinking about what he was going to have for dinner even though he'd only just eaten lunch.

(Yes, that would be me – in a quick-pan cameo as irksome as Ted Danson's in *Saving Private Ryan*. Ted can play me in the adaptation – I don't mind.)

I'd always politely refuse her treats, claiming that I was 'cutting down'. That wasn't the real reason. The real reason was that she swore too much. If something was a hassle or looked like it would be difficult she'd say it was 'a complete ball-ache' or 'a complete shitter'. Call me irrational, but I could never eat vegan damson flan made by someone who used such crude idioms.

Homemade cakes remind me of the cake stall at my primary-school summer fête. They remind me of the opening ribbon being cut by Gus Honeybun, the mute rabbit puppet who read out birthdays after the regional news summary; and of the second-rate, sawdust-stuffed lucky dip and pencil prizes with brittle leads and flaky metallic paints. They remind me of the parent-teacher cake stall, with all those scones made with hard sultanas and the Victoria sponges of unknown origin sweating in the sun. They remind me of the white-elephant stall and the fifteen-pence Marvel *Superheroes* annual from 1976 with another child's name scribbled on the inside cover and a snotty smudge over the wordsearch.

Balti

A Balti is a communal curry dish, cooked and served in a big pot. Diners use greasy flat-bread as a spoon and tuck in, dipping floppy folded naan, dirty thumbs and shandy spillage. Fucking disgusting.

Yes, I know the Balti was invented in Birmingham. I really do not care.

Barbecue

As a physical entity the British barbecue is that small black biscuit tin on rusty roller-stilts that sits in a cobwebbed corner of the garage for fifty-one weeks of the year, on top of an oil-stained square of bathroom tiling and next to the orange mini-football (chewed up by next door's dog), that seldom-used Breton boules set with the missing jack, the deflated and folded paddling pool that no longer fits in the box that it came in and your sister's buttercup-yellow Raleigh Sunbeam bike (the one she hasn't ridden since she started talking back to Mum and Dad, buying black clothes, make-up and cassettes by the Spear of Destiny). The biscuit tin on wheels sits there – filled with spiders and last year's dusty charcoal – blacker by far than your sister's jeans.

The British barbecue is no place for the squeamish. It's where cheap meat goes to die: bright-pink flesh tossed on a smoky pyre – like a Viking funeral with white spirit, charcoal briquettes and greasy metal spatulas with slippery varnished handles.

The British barbecue as an outdoor dining experience is all about half-cooked chicken and half-arsed potato salads, runny speciality marinades, charred-wood BBQ sauces as sold in American airport gift shops, metal tongs with opposing grip teeth that don't quite mesh together, cruddy blackened banana and melted-marshmallow desserts roasted in tinfoil.

For a refined barbecue flavour, my dad would add a blend of mesquite and hickory woodchips to the charcoal and carefully prepare a tray of assorted sauces, seasonings, rubs, glazes and marinades for the meats.

'Yes, lovely idea, Dad. Those herb-soaked woodchips along with that special-reserve Tennessee-whiskey rub and the rosemary-and-garlic marinade make such a difference to the Wall's pork sausages and multipack beefburgers you burn to buggery every summer.'

The British barbecue hot dog is unlike any other in the world. The sausage is tiny. The sausage is barely there. The sausage is covered in Freddy Krueger-style burn scabs. Feel free to pick the scabs off and flick them at flies. The sausage is hidden under a thin red stripe of sauce and a single sassy French-mustard wiggle. The bun is huge. The bun is white and spongy. There's butter in the bun.

'Mum, you've buttered the buns. You're not supposed to butter hot-dog buns.'

The melting butter from the hot-dog buns drips between the straps on my plastic summer sandals and on to the bare, pink flesh of my feet.

You won't believe how large the bun is. The tiny, burnt sausage makes the bun look even bigger. The overall visual effect is of a scorched betting-shop pencil nestled gently betwixt two soft, white, thinly buttered feather pillows.

It was family tradition to hold our barbecues on the front patio. The patio was all empty terracotta plant pots, plastic trellis supports (with no vines on them), sloping rust-coloured hexagonal paving slabs and woodlice.

Millions of woodlice.

Unfortunately, the patio was also visible from the main road. Men walking their dogs stood still to admire a perfect panorama of our patio and coal-smoked snacks while Shep and Toby did their dirty dog business in the gutter. Gangly kids on BMX bikes slowed down, using their feet as brakes, then stood up on their pedals and craned their necks to goggle and gawk at our burnt banquet. Gangs of older youths sucked on cans of fizzing cider, jeered and barracked our smoky picnic and, in my feverish, charcoal-hot imaginings, taunted me thus: 'Look at him. I know that lad. Doesn't he go to St Boniface's Roman Catholic College for Boys? He's a fifth-former. He's in the army cadets and the chess club. He's seventeen and still schleps a satchel to school. It's Saturday night. It's summer. It's sunny with a slim chance of squally showers. He's sitting on a deckchair, talking to his parents and eating a scalding-hot pork sausage – protecting his fingers with half a roll of floral-patterned kitchen towel because they've run out of buttered buns.'

The black biscuit tin on wheels sent up to the sky the perfume of blistered pork and thin, second-rate smoke signals that whispered: 'Come one, come all. Watch us eat. Laugh at us. Laugh at Martin Lampen and the Great British Barbecue.'

We were determined not to be driven inside. We stuck it out through the scabby chops, the flying ants, the woodlouse invasion, the pink chicken legs and the hail storm. We stuck it out until my mum made the move: we'd eat the rest in the kitchen and avoid the wasps and the inevitable stone-throwing by the cider-sozzled gang.

Best-Kept Local Secret

It's the best-kept local secret: a local restaurant that's been serving great local food since 1986. It's jammed in between the boxy 1967 Town Hall and Feathers, a 'private club' with blacked-out windows.

There's no leg room, your chair backs on to someone else's soup and the owner is also the receptionist, the maître d' and the wine waiter. The ashtrays have been whittled out of pine and coated with sticky black lacquer.

Try the Red Leicester risotto with breaded button mushrooms. It's world famous – from Banbury to Birtsmorton.

Hey, look: framed photos of the owner/receptionist/head waiter standing next to Joe Longthorne, Kiki Dee, Linda Lusardi and someone from *Soldier Soldier*.

Birthday Cake

While browsing through some old photo albums at my parents' house, I made a distressing discovery about my childhood . . .

There's no photographic evidence of myself or my sister between the ages of five and sixteen.

There are no photos of us playing in sandpits or frozen in moments of innocent, snot-nosed, short-trousered *bonhomie* on family holidays. None of us posing, pink faces braced against the elements, in front of model villages or miniature ponies on half-term day-trips.

There are, however, eight leatherette-bound albums filled entirely with Polaroids of birthday cakes. I counted three chocolate hedgehogs, a sponge and strawberry-fondant Womble, a misshapen and off-model but well-meant Millennium Falcon and an unbroken nine-year sequence of M&S chocolate-sponge caterpillars – captured for ever on the business end of a plastic camera shaped like a choc-ice.

Actually, I lie. Those photo albums aren't entirely filled with photos of birthday cakes. At least two of them are filled with blurry snapshots of the Red Arrows.

Mum and Dad, come clean. You loved the Red Arrows more than you loved me.

Birthday cakes are shoddy affairs these days. I nearly bought my nephew a Superman sponge and Jelly Tot cake for his birthday. It was a standard jam sponge cake with a 'jacket' of sickly icing with a large, edible rice-paper transfer of Superman's 'S' insignia stuck on top at an odd angle.

As an experiment I managed with two swift hand movements to peel off the icing, exposing the bleached white sponge underneath.

I didn't buy the cake. I put it back on the shelf and walked away.

The security guard followed. He didn't stop me.

Black Pudding

Black pudding is the pig's blood, pork fat, onion and oatmeal staple that sits on the side of every full English breakfast in the land, turning the stomachs of tender souls nursing fizzy lager hangovers, daring them to bite into a big, greasy black-meat medallion that tastes like nosebleed.

I constantly craved black pudding. I yearned for it. Until last year, when I ate a half-cooked one and, as a consequence, was violently ill and had to spend three days in bed, shaking, shivering, and nibbling on dry toast, plain digestive biscuits and the corner of a *Woman's Realm* while whimpering for the last rites with a washing-up bowl by my bed to catch the sick.

I even blacked out for several hours. It was spring: the birds were singing outside, sun streamed through gaps in the dusty Venetian blinds. I was half a stone lighter, sitting upright and, with swollen hands, assembling a jumbo jigsaw of *The Hay Wain*.

Funnily enough, the rotten black pudding – the source of all my sorrows – hadn't even been served as part of a greasy-spoon full English. It had been made with apple and rosemary, cut into small cubes and served as black, meaty croutons in a pricey, unsubstantial gastropub salad with rocket leaves and a salty blue-cheese dressing.

I haven't touched black pudding or blood sausage since. In fact, I haven't touched any foods that contain spicy 'mixed meats', blood, offal or entrails since the 'Black Pudding in Salad' incident.

This was the biggest food-based conversion since 1977, when Cat Stevens gave up the pork scratchings and changed his name to Emilio Estevez.

Bloomer

I don't care how much French farmhouse Brie, Ardennes pâté and grapes you stuff it with, or if you're presenting it with the sandwich halves face down in rectangular shrink-wrap rather than stacked side-by-side in a plastic triangle – it's still only a very spongy white loaf. Don't try to sell it to me as a luxury item, like mink slippers or the weekend loan of an ivy-covered cottage in the country.

Bottled at Source

Abbey Well, Highland Spring, Glenpatrick, Ty Nant Welsh Spring, Pennine (bottled at source in Huddersfield), Deeside (from Pannanich Wells near Balmoral Castle in the heart of the remote Scottish Highlands), Kentish Hills, Buxton Still, Malvern, Gleneagles Natural Sparkling . . .

Apparently, you can't walk more than a hundred yards in the UK without falling into a natural spring, an Ice Age glacier, a gushing source of healing, sparkling spring water or a 400-year-old magical fairytale wishing well with purifying pixies, adjacent sandstone filter, bottling plant and market-research department.

Bread and Butter

Every teatime in our house, between 1975 and 1994, my mum would say the same thing to Dad and me: 'Who wants buttered bread – and how many slices? Speak now or for ever hold your peace.'

We'd respond with numbers ranging from three to eleven, depending on the dish being served. Fry-ups, plaice in breadcrumbs with tartar sauce or anything with chips warranted at least half a loaf of buttered bread.

In fact, every single meal required several slices of Mother's Pride. Every food fad that took hold of the pebble-dashed bungalow at Cardigan Road – from frozen fishcakes to Mum's late-eighties experimental prawn lasagna and that chicken-and-ginger stir-fry recipe as read out by Chris Kelly on *Food and Drink* and scribbled down in a scrapbook via the blocky computer text on page 609 of Ceefax – was accompanied by at least half a dozen slices of starchy sliced white.

From the time I started eating solids right through to my teenage years, when my train-track teeth braces would clog up with lumps of spongy loaf, I'd take a single slice of bread and fold it in half after piling it with anything from canned chicken curries, tomato-paste and Cheddar-cheese toppings skilfully scraped from mini-pizzas and even ruby-red meat surgically removed from Chinese spare ribs.

The logic that drove my substantial sliced-white consumption? The food on my plate is bland and un-inspiring. The only way to struggle through shepherd's pie, savoury rice or Crispy Pancakes is to smother them with sugary tomato sauce and stuff the lot in a slice of sweet white bread.

Breadcrumbs

They were used as a navigation tool by Hansel and Gretel in the story by the Brothers Grimm (who, when they weren't collaborating on psycho-sexual fairytales of attempted infanticide and gingerbread houses, were arguing about who got the big piece in the chicken Kiev twin-pack).

Here's a recipe for Italian breadcrumbs:

3 cups carefully broken breadcrumbs
2 tablespoons dry milk
1 tablespoon brown sugar
1 tablespoon dried parsley
2 teaspoons onion powder
1 teaspoon garlic powder
1 tablespoon extra-virgin olive oil
salt and pepper

The British love anything cooked in breadcrumbs. If they can't slap a bit of cheese on it they'll suffocate it with breadcrumbs. And not of the light, fluffy, seasoned Continental variety detailed above. British breadcrumbs are small, gritty and yellow. They're yellow in a way that no natural substance is yellow, apart from the sick of an infant and the teeth of that pensioner who loiters around the library, hogging the microfiche and thumbing through the human-anatomy section and the romance novels.

Nothing interesting is ever coated in breadcrumbs in Britain. Sliced aubergine? Provolone cheese? No thanks. We wouldn't know au gratin if it came up and spat in our faces. We'll pebble-dash processed poultry or fish with yellow grit and call it a goujon.

(See also Scotch Egg.)

Breakfast

You're just no fun any more. You've changed. It just isn't working. Give me one good reason why I can't borrow your make-up. I hate your guts and I wish you were dead.

All statements I've recently uttered before 9.00 a.m. The first three were used in reference to the so-called most important meal of the day.

These days my breakfast is all flakes, nuts, grains and cleansing micro-granules; probiotic, antioxidant dishes that aid digestion, provide relief from the pain of trapped wind and help support the body's natural defences.

Just look at me: sprinkling dried cranberries and organic sesame seeds on my Hokitika Spring Blend Muesli and listening to the latest cancer statistics on the *Today* programme. I'm just not the happy-go-lucky thrill-seeker I used to be. When was the last time I got hopped-up on Frosties and just went completely crazy?

For breakfast from now on I want 300 grams of crys-tallised, chocolate/banana/strawberry-flavoured refined-sugar chunks. I want a bowlful of pink synthetic marshmallows as promoted by a grinning anthropomorphic squirrel called Smacky with big buck teeth and a yellow baseball cap with a large 'S' on the front. I want Smacky to star in a series of seizure-inducing thirty-second commer-cials on Saturday mornings with neon strobing effects and animation that references the work of both Tex Avery and Dr Timothy Leary. I want to stare at his toothy face on the cereal box every morning as I dribble pink milk over my fluffy pyjamas and listen to the DJ on the radio exchange chauvinistic banter with the girl from AA Roadwatch as he clumsily segues into 'Joyride' by Roxette, kick-starting my dizzy, day-long sugar high.

And I want decent free gifts. I don't want a twenty-page

booklet on prostate health. I want a Smacky Squirrel ninja secret-agent wind-up whistle. I want seven different kinds of day-glo choking hazard – collect 'em all.

And I want edible Octopussy Shrinky Dinks.

Breakfast Bar

In 1988 my parents had a new kitchen fitted, replacing the shoddy prefab wood-chip kitchen that came with our pokey bungalow. The new centrepiece was a teak-veneered table built around teak-veneer storage units and high chairs with wicker seats and easily tarnished tubular-steel frames.

Continuing their long tradition of renaming everyday items in order to give them a 'Southfork' sheen, my parents insisted on referring to the new kitchen-table-without-legs as the 'breakfast bar'.

They'd previously rechristened the garden shed the 'summer house'; the tiny sink space next to the kitchen was tagged their 'utility room'; and the cupboard under the stairs, where we kept our windcheaters, multipack tins of beans, spaghetti hoops and bottles of bleach, was referred to as the 'larder'.

Bruschetta

Ritz crackers for the barn-conversion brigade.

Bubblegum

I love bubblegum. I love the smell. I love the sugary, fruity tang of the big B. I love the initial sugary crunch, the teeth-tingling fizzle that lasts for five seconds before the cherry flavour recedes and the candy colour fades to a brain-matter grey. I love the bubble-blowing interludes; the popping and spitting. I love the jaw-aching longevity of the bland, blanched chew.

I didn't chew bubblegum regularly until I was eighteen. Mum warned me I'd choke on it. She invoked the memory of a lad in the local paper who died when a shrivelled ball of gum lodged in his windpipe.

And whistles. And boiled sweets. Mum was none too keen on whistles or boiled sweets for the same windpipe-clogging safety reasons.

To my mum, bubblegum-chewing and whistle-blowing were one chart place down from glue-sniffing, marijuana-smoking and running across the road on the kiddie-mortality Top Ten.

The first time I had bubblegum was a disaster. I was seven or eight; had the incident been on TV or film, the quick comic edit would feature me chewing happily on Hubba Bubba before a cut to me being held down while pre-chewed blue gunk is cut from my hair, tears streaming down my face.

I'm not saying that my mum's anti-gum, overprotective stance affected me in adult life. But it's true that my heart beats faster when I unwrap a blueberry Bazooka Joe and the pulse in my neck throbs like thunder when I cross the road at a gap in traffic rather than at a designated crossing.

Buffet Car

Rattle through the British countryside. (Hill. Field. Industrial estate. Hill. Field. Industrial estate. Hill. Field. Out-of-town storage centre.) Enjoy a can of Stella and a large stale cookie in a carriage that smells like a pet shop.

Butter on Biscuits

I used to work with a woman who'd spread butter on her biscuits. Any biscuit: rich tea, digestive. Even on sugar-sprinkled Nice biscuits.

She also had pictures of kittens and Lee from Blue – clipped from fluffy-pet calendars and *TV Hits* respectively – stapled to the canvas desk buffer.

Unfortunately, the buffer didn't block out sound; it didn't block out the buttery-biscuit-munching or the tuneless high-pitched humming of 'All Rise'.

Café Culture

There's been a lot of talk recently about Britain adopting a Continental Café Culture – the naïve belief being that extended opening hours would see Britons eschewing public drunkenness, talking about beer adverts and choosing 'In a Big Country' on the pub jukebox, and taking instead to drinking Chablis Domaine des Isles outdoors while nibbling on delicate filo dishes and reading French philosophy.

Fat chance.

My first experience with drinking outdoors was as a thirteen-year-old pop fan at the 1987 Radio One Roadshow on Plymouth Hoe.

Picture this: it's 12.30. I'm dizzy on a unique Southern Comfort and Lilt mix. The last goodie bag has just been awarded and organisers are trying to placate a restless crowd with paper Radio One baseball caps – the ones with the cut-out spiral bit in the middle that your head fits through. DJ Mike Reed is chastising the young audience: someone is throwing beer cans at the Moody Blues. 'Have some respect!' he cries, before adding: 'Taking us up to "Newsbeat" – Scritti Politti.'

One o'clock and the police move in. The Lady Mayoress is hit in the face with a can of Norseman Bitter. All bloody hell breaks loose.

Canned Tuna Chunks

I hate canned tuna. I abhor 'chuna' chunks. Without coming across as a churl, I have to say that they make my stomach churn. I've christened the manoeuvre the Skipjack Upchuck.

It's a hatred hangover from secondary-school packed lunches: white bread soaked through with brine; damp tuna flakes; two crumbling custard creams bound together in sodium-sodden clingfilm; soggy saltwater condensation on tinfoil; all items rattling around in clammy, fish-scented Tupperware.

The texture and taste of tuna flakes reminds me of damp, corrugated cardboard, and they're sold in those squat, squinty little cans – which remind me of cocky men of diminutive stature pumping weights in the gym.

Those diminutive weightlifters with their puffing-and-pouting tiny mouths and bugged-out eyes also remind me of the natural state of the contents of the can: the tuna fish prior to being soaked in brine and canned.

And there's only so much you can do with tuna fish – it's been stuck in a tired, monogamous relationship with sweetcorn for decades now. Isn't it time for tuna chunks to start experimenting with other partners – maybe play the food field? Perhaps wake up the following morning soaked in sesame oil lying next to a wanton, lightly picked artichoke heart.

Canteens and Work Cafés

I've eaten in a fair few workplace canteens in my time. The canteen food at the BBC was insipid, though it was fairly easy to secrete a lemon and pepper turkey escalope that tasted like Fairy Liquid under a pile of soggy chips and a scoop of bulk-buy baked beans in thin, over-tangy tomato sauce.

The canteen at Channel Four was small, friendly and took great pride in its weekly 'Potato Bar' (one of those wrought-iron life-support machines for dying spuds). Friday was always Fish Day.

One firm I worked for in the summer of 2003 handed out healthy-eating pamphlets. The pamphlets, coupled with the poor company pension scheme and a stationery cupboard that was open only for the hour between

11.00 a.m. and noon, gave the working environment an 'East Berlin in the early eighties' edge.

The canteen at the local council I worked for for a soul-destroying year and a half was disconcerting and antiseptic: every dish they served was bleached white, apart from the Halal meat and pitta portions. There was no heating in the winter. Workers wore ski jackets while tucking into pie, chips or a filled French baton. There was no fish on Friday for religious-sensitivity reasons.

Since leaving school I've had a fair number of jobs and every company I've worked for – from local councils to media multinationals and blue-chip advertising agencies – had a similar set of employee demographics. No matter how forward-thinking the business methodology, no matter how fluffy and friendly the company 'core values', the employee profile was always the same: the senior management were amiable, public-school males with wonky teeth and proper partings in their hair; middle-management were taciturn, no-nonsense, middle-class graduates in blue shirts and cheap yellow silk ties; the catering staff were invariably chipper Irishwomen; and the cleaning staff (the nicest people in the company, with the highest level of job satisfaction) were from Ghana.

Limited office space has made spacious work canteens something of a rarity for many British workers. The alternative is the smaller, caffeine-based work café.

Work cafés are rubbish. Transparent attempts by 'the man' to impede out-of-office excursions between 9.00 a.m. and 5.30, from Monday morning start to Friday finish.

One advertising company I freelanced with ran a small canteen on the first floor, called Café Refresh (though it might have been Café Revive). An office junior had designed a derivative logo with fuzzy edges. The menu was emailed daily along with the corporate newsletter, the *Pulse*. Always a riveting read. Roast chicken with an X sauce or a Y rice is the hot lunch of the day and someone who used to work in HR had a baby of X or Y sex – X pounds and Y ounces.

The café served subsidised sliced-white-loaf sandwiches, floury baps, French batons, greasy olive breads and a wide selection of sandwich fillings. A cheery man from Chile served. He was generous with the fillings, though sometimes forgot to change protective plastic gloves between sandwiches. Carrie, the practising vegan and ethics enthusiast on reception, who had protested the pending Philip Morris account, found egg salad in her chickpea-and-carrot ciabatta and blew her top. She gave Gabriele a severe dressing-down – just stopping short of demanding deportation back to Dichato.

Café Refresh (or it could have been Café Zest) also served takeaway breakfasts. Some stuck-up cow in Marketing complained about the smell of my bacon and fried-egg sandwich and insisted I eat it outside. I finished it in the car park and threw the wrapper in the bin under her desk while she was in a planning meeting. At her expense, I indulged in a little Blu-Tack voodoo: whispered an incantation in Victoria – one of the many meeting rooms that were named after train stations – and beat out a ju-ju rhythm on a flip-chart with a retractable pencil.

Come to think of it, it might have been called Café Zoom. Or Café Creative.

As well as Café Refresh, the company also had a coffee-and-tea kitchen. Teabags were gratis, milk was purchased on rota. They kept a beer fridge, which stayed locked until 5.30 on a Friday afternoon, four grimy bean-bags and a second-generation Nintendo console that no one had dared to use since that fourth round of redundancies and relocations.

Between my morning serving of takeaway porridge from the café round the corner, my mid-morning double latte and muffin, the extended lunch and the mid-afternoon cup of calming herbal tea and limited-edition Walnut Kit-Kat, I never work a full eight-hour day any more . . .

My Current Nine-to-Five Routine

9.48 'Sorry I'm late. Tube hell – I overslept and was stuck between stations for half an hour. I'm starving. I didn't even have time for my Frosties. Ahh-ha-ha.' I then grin at my own joke.

I hold the grin. For twelve minutes. It hurts my face.

12.00 Lunch. Hold the phone while I grab a Brie-and-grape granary fold and frosted-fruit frappé. 'I'm hungry. I'm taking a long lunch. Is that OK? I missed my Frosties. Ahh-ha-ha.'

3.00 Back from lunch. Stare at screen for two hours in a sketchy simulacrum of actual activity. Grrrreat!

Caramel/Crème Caramel

Caramel is the sticky, gooey, sugar-based DNA from which most sugary drinks and snacks spring: pralines, fudges and brittles; colas, malts and other gassy, cherry-flavoured sodas; dulce de leche, butterscotch, confiture de lait and the toffee Trio topping.

I can't eat caramel any more – it makes me want to heave. The first flat I rented in London had a toffee-coloured PVC bathroom with a thick, synthetic, deep-pile butterscotch-hued floor.

There was dried blood and black 'bits' in said yellow-coloured carpet and a thick, caramel-like layer of unidentified gunk between the custard-coloured tiles.

Crème caramels are those vile-looking tubs of dessert they sell in supermarkets; those yellow-and-brown tubs of caramel dessert made from egg, vanilla and vile runny, sugary caramel.

I'd never actually seen anyone buy crème caramel until last Tuesday, when a woman in front of me at the checkout bought a four-pack of the syrupy desserts with the noxious two-tone yellow colour scheme that brings to mind a summer sunset over an Eastern European factory town.

Crème-caramel desserts are like mucky top-shelf maga-zines or *Tubular Bells Vols. 1 and 2*. Nobody ever admits to buying them, yet they sell in their millions each year.

I don't know why supermarkets still sell crème caramel. I think it's just to make the layered yogurts look more appealing.

I wanted to say to her, 'Don't buy the caramel dessert. It reminds me of the grubby bathroom décor in a previous flat. It makes me feel sick. Wouldn't you rather have a yogurt, a mousse or a sherry-free mini-trifle?

'Try a syllabub. Just for me.

'Or maybe a torte . . .'

Caramelised Onions

Onions cooked in two kilos of butter. For fifteen hours.

(See also Gastropubs.)

Carrot and Coriander

In 1985 you couldn't turn on the television on a Sunday night without bearing witness to stone-faced speciality acts. Chinese acrobats; Russian jugglers; police motorcyclists stacked on top of each other like profiteroles; bearded card-trick specialists from San Francisco; fifteen gunners from Portsmouth pushing cannons in midsummer as part of a display of British military might – nineteenth-century British military might. (All through the Cold War, while the Soviets were parading thousands of armed soldiers with furry hats and nuclear warheads on the back of ten-ton trucks through Red Square on May Day mornings, in Earls Court, Britain's troops were lifting field guns over jumps left over from the under-nines Shetland pony gymkhana, while the Band of the Coldstream Guards played jaunty brass versions of 'The Dambusters' and the *James Bond* theme. It's a living miracle that we're not all speaking Russian, slurping beetroot soup and queuing for stale bread.)

In those days, televised entertainment on the Sabbath was ninety-nine per cent plate-spinning, stilt-walking, fire-eating, knife-throwing and police-dog-handling, God-slot choirs singing hosannas and mugging for the in-church cameras, and the occasional French-Canadian cartoon. This was dry television. It was humdrum. It was middling. It was mildly diverting at best. It occupied your attention for twenty minutes and once it finished you could go back to worrying about impending nuclear war with the Union of Soviet Socialist Republics.

Twenty years on and jugglers and Chinese acrobats have vanished from the schedules. On any Sunday evening, the British TV viewer is spoon fed a thin, consommé-like diet of 'real people' called Tamara and Reece converting farmhouses in rural Alsace, *The World's Top 100 Top Hats*, and, in all likelihood, that film that seems to be on Channel Four every week, where Nicolas Cage gives half of his lottery winnings to Bridget Fonda, thus infuriating his wife, played by that Hispanic actress (the one who isn't that J-Lo woman) with the high-pitched voice who was never in anything else.

Twenty years ago, the only soup flavours available for purchase in supermarkets were country vegetable and cream of tomato. They were two completely serviceable soups. Dull-yet-God-fearing broths, ideally eaten during a prerecorded variety show in the presence of Princess Margaret or a televised military tattoo. Today, the only flavours of soup available to buy are carrot and coriander and broccoli and stilton.

My point is: things in Britain were average then and they're average now. Television, music, film, food and vegetable soups – all average. Tamara and Reece are no more entertaining than the Chinese fire-jugglers and carrot and coriander is no tastier than cream of mushroom.

In fact, I think I prefer minestrone and cream of mushroom. Eating broccoli-and-stilton soup is like licking curdled milk from a charity-shop carpet and I've never been a huge fan of coriander. In moderation it's fine, but too much and your dinner tastes like a South American church on All Souls Day (that's one for all the Catholics in the audience).

Chinese Food Facts China produces 274,900,000 tonnes of carrots per year. The leaves of the coriander plant are often referred to as 'Chinese Parsley'.

There are twelve and a half million acrobatic troupes in Anhiu province alone.

Carvery

I've eaten at a carvery only once, during a business stay at a golfing hotel in East Anglia. (A golfing hotel with a complimentary basket of cheap lotions, an extendable shaving mirror and a handy shoe-buff sponge in every bathroom.)

The carvery meats – chicken, beef and pork – were placed on a long table, the table that doubled as the breakfast buffet (they'd forgotten to remove the wicker basket full of Special K sachets) and lit by the world's brightest halogen bulb. The chicken had white paper frills on the end of its greasy legs. I'd only ever seen paper frills on the end of chicken legs in old Tom and Jerry cartoons.

I was one of just four people eating there, the others being three business diners, who, judging by their mournful expressions, were caught up in the last pre-sale business dinner prior to the Apocalypse. Also present was a waiter – wearing the tall white hat and starched attire of a top chef even though his only task was to cut thick chunks of greasy meats for business travellers and hobby golfers – sitting on a tiny footstool reading a local paper (a local councillor was on the take; and someone had been taking airgun pot-shots at family pets). When a carvery customer approached the bar, our 'chef' would set his paper down and carve wedges of greasy meat: wedges that were uneven; thick at one end and thin at the other, like the blocks of baited cheese sitting on mouse traps in old Tom and Jerry cartoons. Three of chicken, three of beef and three of pork. Then he'd pick up his paper and sit back down, the top of his tall chef's hat just visible above the carvery bar.

Incidently, I was staying at the golfing hotel two nights a week for three months while consulting for a Norwich-based insurance company. The inter-colleague banter in the largely white male and over-thirty office environment was based around co-workers accusing each other of being gay. 'You cross your legs so you're gay.' 'Clive watches the *Larry Grayson Show* and is a big fan of Liberace. Hahaha.'

I told one of them about the previous night's carvery dinner. He made a joke about 'meat'. And so on and so on.

Casserole

At last, some proper British food. Hearty, filling, warms-your-cockles meat and veg cooked in that casserole dish you've had for years (the one with the burnt cheese on the edge; the burnt cheese that you'd need a set of professional diamond-cutting equipment to remove).

I prefer my casseroles to be as simple, natural and stew-like as possible: vegetables, meat and spices. No toppings. No powdered casserole sauces, no crown of grooved potato mash, no layered Cheddar-cheese topping and absolutely no tiled roof of shiny scalloped potatoes.

The scalloped-potato roof is the last refuge of the culinary coward who doesn't quite trust their filling. I had an Irish stew with a scalloped-spud roof in a fake Irish theme pub in Southend city centre. It's was revolting. The undercooked scalloped spuds couldn't mask the gristly, grisly meat and soggy vegetables contained within.

The lesson learnt was thus: get several estimates on your savoury roofing. Never go for the cheapest option, the ready-by-Christmas estimate or that all-corners-cut quote from the far-too-easygoing Kerryman.

Cheap Meats

I love meat and I've never considered giving it up. That said, I'd rather eat vegetarian food – stuffed green peppers and breaded aubergines – for every meal than eat cheap meat.

It can't be good for you. Just think of the water content, the preservatives and the by-products. Never buy fast-food bargain burgers, snack-bar sausage rolls, greying minced beef on 'special', slushy family-size chicken pies or those processed frozen cylinders of turkey breast from a fenced-off farm in Norfolk.

The golden rule in pie, pastry, pizza topping, burger

filling or chop: never eat a meat-based snack that costs less than a pound.

The archetypal cheap-meat purchase is potted beef – the meat-stock spread that, during my childhood, I'd slather on white bread for a lunchtime snack while watching *Pebble Mill at One*.

An elderly neighbour was a big fan of potted meats and pink potted shrimp pastes. I'd have to go over and open the pots for him. This was twenty years ago, before increased demand for fresh foods, before widespread concern over poor-quality meat products, before public disdain for grey-coloured meat butters.

It was also a good twenty years before user-centric packaging design: potted-beef producers hadn't quite figured out that the fiddly, tightly screwed tin caps on their jars didn't quite suit the arthritic hands of their core customer base.

Cheese with Fruit in It

It's at this stage in the proceedings that I'm supposed to reveal how cruel my dad was; list his put-downs and beatings and tell you all about the time he locked me in a cupboard for eight weeks, forcing me to retreat into my own invented language/butterfly collection/singing/dancing/over-eating/kitten-strangling.

I can't do any of that, because my dad is a diamond. He has one fatal flaw. Well, two flaws if you count the way he eats spaghetti bolognese (bringing his lips to the plate, rather than the pasta to his lips, and slurping). His main flaw, however, is his love of cheese with fruit in it.

I hate fruit-flecked cheeses. Vile, waxy dried fruit set in sickly soft cheese turns my stomach faster than the phrase 'Exclusive photos of Mick Jagger in Speedos'.

Dad buys a wide selection of fruit-flecked soft cheeses every Christmas. He's the only person in our house who'll eat them. There he sits, spreading pineapple roulade on an over-salted cheese-flavoured cracker as the credits roll on *Lethal Weapon II*. Why can't he take up golf, domestic violence or long, unexplained bouts of impenetrable brooding like every other man his age?

Chemistry

The foods I was given to eat while growing up had nothing to do with flavour. They had little nutritional value. They had sod all to do with working the taste buds or food as a conversation point. They were all about chemistry.

Powdered sauces and desserts; packet mixes and recon-stituted meats; ice-cream toppings that froze solid on contact.

You didn't need to worry about sell-by dates. Mum might have bought it when you were still in primary school, but, rest easy, you'd be revising for your A-levels by the time the best-before date ticked round on that packet of Knorr granules.

We were living in the space age – the age of frozen, freeze-dried, bicarbonate-of-some-shite instant food.

I swear, before the age of nineteen I'd never eaten anything that wasn't coloured red, involved the addition of half a kettle's worth of boiling water and vigorous stir-ring with a hand-held wire whisk.

Chicago Rock Café

Chicago Rock Cafés are a chain of regional 'entertainment venues'. They're found in places like King's Lynn or Stourbridge and their openings are announced with full-page adverts and two-for-one tokens in local newspapers (on page four, right opposite the photo of three small cub scouts holding a large cheque and that perfunctory piece of crusading regional journalism that details the campaign by residents to shut the sex shop by the bus station).

US-style theme bars strive for that all-American *Cheers*-type atmosphere and don't quite succeed. Maybe it's just me and I missed the episode of *Cheers* in which Norm was charged £18.00 for three 'loaded' potato skins or when Sam was accused of serious sexual assault by a woman with a tattoo of a dolphin on her face.

Pretending you're in downtown Chicago when you're actually in Trowbridge drinking jelly shots and shuffling about to 'Ice Ice Baby' is no fun. It's an experience not unlike one of those creepy club nights where stupid people and girls called Kayleigh with thick ankles and a spare bottle of Breezer in their handbags pretend they're at a school disco.

For the record, Chicago Rock Café is a complete misnomer. Chicago Illinois, despite being a hotspot for jazz, blues, deep soul and dance music, has only ever produced one chart-topping rock band – Chicago featuring Peter Cetera – and they were shite.

(See also Entertainment Venues (Formerly Pubs)).

Chicken and Cheese

You never see them together, do you.

And quite right, too. Like oil and water, like meringue and ragu sauce, like Malibu and Lilt, like Woody Allen and his wife, chicken and cheese is a bad taste, stomach-churning mismatch. It's a combination guaranteed to make even the bravest of would-be culinary alchemists – even that Home Counties restaurateur with his snail porridge, egg-and-bacon ice cream, etc., or me with my special chilli-chocolate Rice Krispie bites – throw their hands up in despair or chuck their guts up.

Chicken Caesar Salad

Play my new game: spot the itty-bitty chargrilled-chicken chunk in the bowl of salty, garlic-mayonnaise-sopped iceberg lettuce.

Look! There's a bit. No. It's a soggy, bruschetta-style croûton.

There's a Parmesan shaving with the taste and texture of a toenail clipping.

Take my advice and avoid the chicken Caesar salad. It's a fetid lettuce swamp. It's packed with hidden calories and it leaves, in its wake, a nasty aftertaste, a cheese-coated tongue and three days' worth of bitter garlic belches.

In *Pro Rege Deiotaro*, the Roman politician Cicero revealed that Julius Caesar often felt the need to vomit after dinner (*'vomere post cenam te velle dixisses'*).

I know how he felt.

Chinese Takeaway

I love MSG.

That's monosodium glutamate and not Madison Square Garden or even eighties German heavy-metal 'mammoths' the Michael Schenker Group (heavy-metal acts are generally referred to as 'behemoths', but MSG – featuring ex-Scorpions and UFO guitarist Michael Schenker – never made that grade, stalling, as they did, at the 'mammoth' stage of hard-rock evolution.

For the record, there is a heavy-metal band Mastodon, though I think they're taking the whole concept a little too literally.

Yes, I love the gunky, sticky, artifically coloured and flavoured, MSG-loaded British interpretation of Chinese cooking.

I'd eaten Chinese before – pre-prepared packs from Marks & Spencer and frozen scampi Won Tons – but my first taste of genuine Chinese takeaway came in 1982. (Or maybe it was 1983.) The year of the dog (or was it the pig . . . ?).

Every time my dad took myself and my sister, Sarah, to the cinema, we'd stop for fish 'n' chips on the way home. On one particular occasion, after *Superman II* (or was it *Superman III*?), our regular chippie was closed so we decided on a takeaway from the newly opened Golden Dragon (or was it Jade Fountain?) on the same street.

It was a culinary cultural revolution. It was Mao Tse-yummy in my tummy. I basked in the golden glow of the battered chicken strips prepared *à la* mock Mandarin; adored the deep-fried prawn balls with pineapple chunks in that gooey yellow cod-Cantonese sauce (the same shade of yellow as those luminous novelty socks I was thrown out of Friday assembly for wearing the week before). I chowed-down cheerfully on the refried white rice with frozen peas (this rice was sticky waaaay before legitimately sticky Thai rice); the spring rolls filled with grimy, Ming-era ground beef and brown, stringy shoots made my mouth water; I merrily murmured 'Mmmm', slurped shredded beef and dribbled mud-brown noodles while vocally aping Benny Hill's distinctly pre-PC 'Chinaman' and making junior kung-fu hand movements.

The Golden Dragon – or Jade Fountain – isn't there any more. In its place is an Internet café, supplier of camping equipment made from hemp and an organic muffin bakery. Plymouth's stately Drake Odeon cinema, along with the scale replica model of Sir Francis Drake's ship, the *Golden Hind*, that hung over its entrance for more than fifty years, closed some time ago (it's now a seedy casino frequented by low-rollers and off-duty taxi drivers with six days of stubble) and big-screen entertainment in Devon's largest city is now available only at a soulless suburban multiscreen multiplex.

My parents moved to a spacious new three-bedroom detached house with a double garage in 1999 – the same year in which the Drake Odeon closed its doors and Michael Schenker and his group released a new studio album, *The Unforgiven*. They (that's my parents, not the Michael Schenker Group) moved opposite a Chinese family and the father of the clan ran a local Chinese takeaway.

'Where do you usually get your Chinese?' Mr Chen asked my dad in their first, polite, across-the-street conversation.

My dad paused then answered, 'Marks & Spencer.'

Chocolate

We don't have many pleasures in Great Britain. Marks &
Spencer food hall, barley and orange-cordial drinks, rude
text messages sent after closing time on Friday night and
forgotten about until Saturday lunchtime, unprovoked
violence on the last bus home and luxury cheese-and-cashew
coleslaw. That's about it. Our film industry is kaput –
content with churning out lousy, old-Etonian-directed films
about football hooligans and comedies about teams of bin
men who put on a production of Verdi's *Rigoletto* in a
quarry. The cars we drive are constructed in Cologne. Our
areas of outstanding natural beauty are besmirched by short-
stay concrete car parks, Arndale-style tourist-information
centres and combination gift shop/cafeterias selling jam
scone and cream-tea combos, fold-out postcard 'concertinas'
of stalagmites, flower-press dream journals, twizzle-wrapped
bags of potpourri (lavender-scented and dyed deep purple
in poisonous processing plants) and Beatrix Potter tea-towels
screen-printed in Saipan.

Our pleasures are few and far between, yet our chocolate
is by far the best in the world. We are to tasty point-of-sale
chocolate bars that make your tongue go numb and the roof
of your mouth feel furry what the US is to sticky barbecue
ribs and Japan is to eel served raw in black rice-paper cones.

Some people – Eurocrats and Waitrose stock buyers –
might point to Belgium as the home of high-end cocoa
craftsmanship. Fair enough if you want to shell out £10.00
for a single layer of twelve bitter praline truffles in a box
tied with rayon ribbon and tapered, textured and folded
to resemble a block of bullion.

The pricey cherry kirsch made in Bruges is, indeed, a fine thing. If a chocolate with a liquid cherry centre were ever to take off in Britain it would be sold to us by a cartoon intermediary – a Mr Cherry or a Cherry Monster. Cut out seventeen proofs of purchase and wait twenty-eight days for delivery of your Mr Cherry pyjama case.

The British cherry kirsch would be made from milky, buttery chocolate rather than the bitter dark bean beloved by the Flemish. It would be eighty per cent cheaper, significantly less po-faced, less sombre and less Belgian.

Swiss chocolate is rubbish too. Sickly, foil-wrapped liqueur 'bottles' made in the Alps and vile milk-and-white-chocolate mottled pralines shaped like conch shells. Big deal. So hum 'Rule Britannia', shake your mane and roar like the king of the jungle on the Lion Bar wrapper: British chocolate is cheap, delicious and available to all.

The best chocolate of all is free chocolate. When we were children my sister and I had a fine scam going: writing fan letters to confectionary figureheads, dishing out praise and pleading not very subtly for free samples. 'Dear Milky Bar Kid. We're doing a project at school about chocolate. We love your chocolate. How do you make it? Send us an autograph and a box of your delicious product.'

The ruse worked. Free badges, stickers and chocolate bars winged their way to us. Assorted promotional junk flew through our letterbox. We scoffed the chocs and repeated our ploy with any number of corporate characters, including Freddo the Cadbury frog, the Turkish Delight sheik, the Edwardian lady in the bonnet on the front of the Quality Street tin (for the record, an early crush), the Milk Tray man, that 'dolly bird' on the paradise island who bolted back Bounty bars while simulating sex and glistening in the tropical sun, and the tap-dancing peanut from the Topic commercials – even though he hadn't appeared in Topic advertising for ten years.

(We would have sent a fan letter to the Man from Del Monte, but neither of us were huge fans of tinned fruit cocktail – especially when 'the Man', with his beige suit and overtones of exploitative neocolonialism and the United Fruit Company, included only one cherry per whole can of pineapple chunks, peach segments and sloppy, sugary syrup.)

Yes, our plan worked well. In retrospect though, the letter to the Cadbury Bunny about the 'funny-tasting' bar of Caramel took on an unnecessarily unpleasant tone.

It verged on blackmail and resulted in a police caution.

Chomp!

Cast your mind back: you're nine again – squeaky voice, itchy nylon T-shirt, short trousers and grazed, scraped, scab-speckled knees. You're squinting into the sun, wearing tri-colour sweatbands on your wrists and one of those ineffectual green-tinted sun visors only ever worn by Reno card hustlers, self-consciously kitsch East London club-goers and, in the early eighties, kids, like me, playing Swingball in the garden on summer holidays.

You've just been to the ice-cream van – an ice-cream van with unauthorised, off-model paintings of Mickey and Minnie Mouse, Goofy, a cross-eyed Pluto with one ear shorter than the other and assorted wonky-looking Smurfs on the side. You're munching on a fun-sized chocolate bar or licking an ice lolly. Your dad, on a break from trimming the hedge, pretends to eat it. He bares his teeth, pantomimes a 'Chomp!' sound and snaps in the direction of your Double Decker, Mini-Milk or Flake 99 before pulling back, laughing at his own joke and patting you on the head then getting back to stuffing branches in black bin liners (triple-bagged to fool the bin men enforcing the council's strict 'no clippings' rule).

I do that all the time now. I pretend to eat other people's food. I do it to people I don't know: to strangers chewing toffees on buses, to stressed business travellers biting into 'to-go' croissants in airport lounges. I distract them with the 'Chomp!' mime as they tuck a café au lait and pain au chocolat receipt into their wallet for expense claims once they get back to Bonn.

I've been threatened only once. A German tourist objected to me patting them on the head. Airport security were called. I managed to lose them in the Tax-Free Shopping store by hiding behind a tower of Toblerone bars and a stack of 200ml Paco Rabanne cologne sprays as they ran past, Keystone Cops style.

Chomp!

Chorizo

Pass the Listerine. Chorizo tastes just like salami. It is salami, but just sliced thicker.

You wouldn't touch it if were wafer thin. If it were vaccum sealed and sold six slices to a pack by Mattheson's it would soon lose all association with rustic Italy, the Casentino Valley and the Province of Arezzo.

Christmas

I spend all year dreading it. I cower as the rest of the country counts down. I shake as I peel open the windows on my own personal advent calender of apprehension (there's no cheap chocolate for each day; not even a small drawing of a tin soldier – just panic and a cold blue funk). When December arrives, while high-street shops announce deceptive three-for-two deals on golf- and vintage-car-themed gift sets and coloured lights twinkle in card shops round the country, I fake sore throats. I walk fast through work-place corridors, head bowed, humming summer songs. I daydream and mutter to myself in order to avoid eye contact with colleagues. I don headphones, lower my gaze and feign industry to circumvent that one dreaded question: 'What are *your* plans for Christmas and New Year, Martin?'

I should lie. I should use my imagination and fabricate a glamorous, fun-packed yuletide itinerary. I should claim to be a Son of David – a fan of the original, more violent Old Testament as opposed to the lighter, Jesus-heavy sequel. I should pretend to be a Witness of Jehovah, a robe-wearing Wiccan warlock or any other kind of heathen – Druid, pagan, eco-warrior, devil-worshipper, Australian.

But, no, while everyone else's seasonal schedule involves criss-crossing between friends, family, partners and in-laws, foreign travel and action-packed winter activity breaks, I will be stuck in the suburbs with my parents, a marked-up *Radio Times* and a box of York Fruits. Just me, Mum and Dad, the sugar-speckled jelly fruits, a listings magazine with the cover hanging off and that hated Hummel figurine nativity set displayed over the fake-flame gas hearth.

While my peers are renting electricity-free cottages in Hardy country with a 'half a dozen or so really close mates and some good New World wines'; while my contemporaries are playing beach football on 'the Islands', chewing leaves and licking the backs of psychedelic frogs with Peruvian Indians or indulging in quick-witted adult conversation with enlightened in-laws while feasting on alternative seasonal fare (rumps of glazed lamb, creamed broad beans, game pie, homemade Christmas crackers with ethical prizes); while everyone of equivalent age and status is enforcing strict television embargoes . . . I shall be at home, slouched on the sofa in an overheated suburban house, propped up on a snowman-shaped cushion, recovering from stringy turkey and runny trifle, eating crystalised citrus sweets and burnt sausage rolls, drinking Skol lager, hiccupping back the peach-schnapps vomit, trying to resist the cheese straws and marzipan stollen, glued to the unengaging adventures of a third-string cartoon mouse in *An American Tail 2: Fievel Goes West*.

The mouse has a high-pitched woman's voice. In *All Dogs Go to Heaven* the poorly animated dog has the voice of Burt Reynolds. The lager is gassy and weak – I've had three cans. A whole chipolata and half a semi-digested brandy snap are lodged against my stomach wall. My parents' house is hot. My jumper prickles and burns. That brandy snap A-bomb mushroom-clouds from my stomach to my abdomen. Ouch.

I'm not entirely sure I didn't swallow a plastic cocktail stick whole, along with the chipolata. The plastic cocktail sticks date from 1973; they're washed and reused every year.

Five cans of Skol – it's the volume rather than the strength

– and an undigested pork sausage in my belly. It's getting hotter. The cartoon mouse's voice is getting lower. The mouse grows fangs and a forked tail and a waves a glowing pitchfork through the screen. Knock-off cartoon mice in 3D. All dogs *do* go to heaven. That mouse *is* from hell.

My Christmas, every year from the age of eight to twenty-eight: hard potato croquettes; chocolate buttercream log; spiky icing on dry fruit cake; pastry; sponge; mince-meat and marzipan soaked in eye-watering essence of rum; sporting anecdotes in one pocket-sized volume.

It's 2.00 a.m. Several Skol and slices of stollen later. There are no cartoons, only static.

My Christmas: rum-flavoured marzipan fruits and beef-flavoured twiglets served in sleigh-shaped bowls; the birth of Our Lord; after-dinner mints eaten half an hour after breakfast; and an animated Bambi-esque, orphaned dinosaur looking for his parents in *The Land Before Time*.

Boxing Day, 11.00 a.m.: as I munch on a melting mint Matchmaker I wonder out loud if the doe-eyed orphan dinosaur's quest is a Christ allegory.

No one replies. My parents have gone to the sales – specifically, the Boxing Day sale at Homebase to buy reduced wrapping paper and gift labels for next Christmas.

The inside temperature hits thirty degrees. I eat the last of the stollen.

Back to work in January and I haven't been snowboarding, or backpacking in South America. A Chirstmas gift from a thoughtful partner doesn't sponsor a family of five for a year in East Africa.

Present-wise, I received a jar of winter fruits in alcohol. There's a pretty red bow on top. I'll never eat the contents, but shaking the glass jar and watching the berries bob around in the thick port syrup is therapeutic – much more so than tropical fish or roaring fires.

I also own a set of vintage-car coasters. There's a mulled wine mark on the Model T Ford. I'm a stone heavier. Rum essence, winter fruits compote and the scent of fruit cake induce sweating and shakes – like Pavlov's winter-fruits pavlova.

No, it was Pavlov's dogs. I wonder if Pavlov's dogs went to heaven, like the one voiced by Burt Reynolds and animated in a scratchy style by ex-Disney man Don Bluth.

I hum the closing theme to *Ferngully: the Last Rainforest* and walk fast, head bowed, through workplace corridors in order to avoid the hated question: 'What did *you* do for Christmas and New Year, Martin?'

Cinema Food

I love trips to the cinema and the unique snacks sold there. These are snacks that you can't buy anywhere else: pillowcase-sized bags of toffee-encrusted popcorn; icy, sugary slushy drinks that turn your tongue an electric-blue colour; stale mint Poppets and cheap Cornetto clones with no chocolate chunk at the end of the cornet.

There's nothing better than chomping on all-butter popcorn – half salty, half sweet – and maybe some milk-chocolate Munchies while watching some high-concept trash from Hollywood . . .

Something with ninjas in it – and possibly one of the lesser Baldwin brothers.

I just can't watch independent, arty cinema any more. If I never see another grainy indie flick from Argentina about the surrogate familial bond between a mascara-smeared drag-queen-on-the-skids, a dirty-faced street urchin and his mute single mother it'll be too bleedin' soon.

I love trashy films. I love that audition scene that's been in every film since *The Fabulous Baker Boys*. It was perfected in the *Sister Act* sequel and film students call it 'auditioning misfit females under the male gaze'. It's all quick cuts: the fat woman who sings opera, the dizzy one who tap-dances, the septuagenarian who thinks she's Shirley Temple, the overweight African-American woman with the head-shaking, finger-wagging 'attitude' for extra multiplex chuckles in the Red States, the compulsory movie-man playing a woman and the chick who barely opens her mouth before they yell 'next'. It's almost as entertaining as the 'Put your gun down' 'No, *you* put *your* gun down' scene that follows thirty minutes later, just as your legs are starting to go numb and you've run out of Revels.

I love everything about trashy Hollywood. From Sunset Strip to Cahuenga Boulevard; in monochrome and Technicolor; Cinerama and VistaVision. I love predictable romantic comedies set on cruise ships and animated versions of Bible stories with comic-relief camels voiced by Dom DeLuise and Ice Cube. I love *Night of the Juggler* and *Werewolves on Wheels*. I love Rudolph Valentino, Lou Diamond Phillips and Rae Dawn Chong.

I've just written the 'treatment' for *Crocodile Dundee in Space*.

Cocktails

Alcoholic cocktails are enjoyed the world over by sophis-ticates and *bon vivants* as well as louche Continental men who wear slip-on shoes with gold-plated chains instead of laces and entertain Russian hookers with pointy noses in lounge bars. They're also sipped by elegant, Dior-draped Sophia Loren *manqués* in boulevard bars in the south of France, where the palm trees sway, old women walk fluffy little French dogs and the streets are paved with gold.

Alas, the streets of Britain aren't paved with gold – they're splattered with vomit, piss, chip grease, type O-negative and broken bottles of sugary cranberry-and-pineapple alco-squash.

From Abbey's to Zanzibar's, De Ja Vu's to Strutters, Millionaires to Golddiggers, Samantha 2's (which used to be Samantha's but the name was changed after the heroin deaths in the chill-out room) to Bon Bonnes, it's Saturday night, the air is thick with an eye-stinging blend of Impulse body spray and Joop for men as the last of the staff receive overdose training and the sound system pumps out Ace of Base. Pretty Polly-clad legs are soaked through with a mixture of sweat, Rimmel and glitter. The cloakrooms are ninety-nine per cent filled with puffa jackets. There's a hen do at the bar – they're sporting clip-on bunny ears and henna tattoos – and it's like 2001 all over again. Strobe lights catch whistles, glow-sticks and multiple St Christopher medals, and fruity vodka-based drinks with smutty names are swigged by lads with subscriptions to custom car magazines and lasses whose idea of a fun night out is taking blurry pictures of the genitalia of drunken men in chip-shop queues with the camera on their new pay-as-you-go Sony Ericsson K750i.

The history of cocktail nomenclature is one of lounge wit, geographic reference, *non sequitur* and tart alliteration. Kir Royale, Death in the Afternoon, Cuba Libre, Brandy Alexander: universal shorthand for liquid sophistication and sharp, fruity joy in a dainty fluted glass.

The great American cocktails recall the titles of Tennessee Williams plays or William Faulkner novels. British cocktails are sold on laminated menus and named after sexual positions. They're called Slippery Nipples, Cocksucking Cowboys, Slow Screws Against the Wall, Sodomy with Pineapples and other hilarious names referencing mixed fruit and semen. All containing the same interchangeable mixture of watered-down orange cordial, cash-and-carry vodka and Irish Cream, all available in 'Chicago Rock Café Norwich'-branded cocktail glasses (available to keep for an extra £6.00) or shatterproof plastic pitchers for £12.00.

Coffee

Britain is changing. Everyone's so sodding cosmopolitan. There's a juice bar with a free-standing parasol cover in the newly pedestrianised precinct. They're selling yoga mats in the open-air market – three for a fiver. There's a wi-fi hook-up for my laptop in the local launderette. Little Tamara and Julian are holding their birthday parties in gourmet burger joints and their friends are ordering wheat-grass milkshakes with their organic minted lamb burgers and chunky butternut fritters.

Club 18–30 are offering package deals to Tuscany. (Probably.)

And coffee – coffee is everywhere. Everyone loves coffee; no one touches strong tea or moves within a mile of malted milk. No one sucks concentrated cordials through bendy straws or sips on cans of carbonated lime and cherryades any more.

It's all about coffee. Drink it slowly, snout-down in the froth. Fetishise its purchase and consumption. Sprinkle cheap powdered chocolate on top and pretend you're in a foreign film. Breathe in its aura: classic Continental cool and US slacker sang-froid – from the Beat era to grunge.

You see them everywhere – on their way to work and on school buses; in cars, on trains; in corporate meetings and in company receptions; in long queues for theme-park rides – wide-eyed coffee drinkers, chugging the bitter brown bean from corrugated-cardboard cups.

Choose from grande, tall, tiny, regular, supremo. El blinkin' massive. Rapidamente.

Glug-glug-glugging from tiny slots in plastic lids. Slimmers ordering soy-milk skinny specials. Regular drinkers requesting extra chocolate sprinkles, a dusting of cocoa, vanilla-syrup splashes, foamy whipped-cream toppings from compressed air canisters and extra espresso shots.

Have it *your* way. Coffee says so much about *you*.

But why do we have to slavishly imitate the method of serving coffee that originated in the North Western United States – the method that the Americans stole from the Italians and bastardised?

Why are we so ashamed of our beverage heritage? Why are there no coffee shops that serve the drink the traditional

British way? Cafés that serve milky coffee in glass teacups, with six sachets of Tate & Lyle and a single bourbon biscuit perched on the side of the see-through saucer. And milk delivered each morning by a whistling Bernard Bresslaw. Look, there's Tommy Steele feeding half a sixpence into a jukebox – not a flashy American jukebox shaped like a rocket, but a square, plastic British jukebox with chip grease between the buttons. Irene Handl is upstairs, banging on the floor with her bedpan and complaining about the noisy skiffle beat.

There's a Carnaby Street-themed café across the road. In Café MOD, men in nehru jackets play pan-pipes, elfin women in miniskirts and Twiggy hair blow bubbles in a multicoloured light show. Help, there's a girl in my soup! There are also amphetamines fizzing away in my milky coffee and someone's spiked my custard cream with powerful hallucinogens. O' what a lovely war.

And another thing . . . Apart from the core methods of serving coffee (espresso, latte, mocha, and the ridiculously named Americano) and fair-trade options, no one really cares about the origin of the drink and the provenance of the bean.

That coffee you're sipping. Where is it from? What's the blend?

No one knows. Everyone's a coffee consumer and no one's an expert.

I've started inventing coffee facts in order to impress people and highlight the inferiority of their coffee knowledge.

Like one of those medical Walter Mitty types who pose as hospital consultants, I masquerade as a coffee expert, swig on a machine-bought powdered brew and proclaim that it's a rich mix of beans from a high-altitude volcanic range in Santa de Los Maracas. I mix myself a flask of freeze-dried milky instant and wax poetic on the full, almost wine-like taste of the Nueva Segovia blend. Did you, for example, know that in Italy it's vulgar to drink cappuccino after 11.00 a.m.?

Actually, the last fact is true. I read it in a Sunday supplement or on the back of a napkin. Ordering cappuccino after the a.m. deadline is considered dead common on the Continent. Remember that for your Club 18–30 Tuscan break.

Cold Soup

Chilled soups are an unpleasant experience. I always order them by mistake and live to regret it – spitting cold asparagus and leek into a serviette less than three seconds after the first frosty slurp. Spanish gazpacho is off the menu for me; its name alone sounds like a mobile-disco DJ cashing in on the late-nineties Latin-dance craze.

Ordering a soup starter and being served a bowl of icy shrimp or cold pumpkin is like finding an orange wrapped in tinfoil or an educational annual in your Christmas stocking.

At a restaurant recently, as a starter I ordered a light soup. It came chilled and *sans* crusty bread. I'm sure I could hear them laughing at me in the kitchen as I struggled with the icy liquid slush.

I called the waiter over and complained: 'I haven't tasted anything quite like this chilled asparagus-and-lemon soup since I sucked on an AA battery for a bet.'

Coleslaw

Coleslaw: coach-trip caviar; the wattle and daub of British convenience cuisine. Why do we love the shredded-cabbage salad so much? Why does it turn yellow when exposed to room temperature? Who buys those huge economy ice-cream-style tubs of the stuff – what can anyone want that much coleslaw for?

Thatching? Building a shredded-cabbage nest?

You can buy three core varieties of coleslaw in British supermarkets: coleslaw from a 'savers' range (shredded carrot, cabbage, onion and white water); 'Traditional' coleslaw (with a thicker mayonnaise); and 'Luxury' coleslaw (with longer carrot shreds, slightly thicker mayo and a few chive flecks on top).

It's meant as a side dish – a reliable supporting act – though for the three-year duration of my degree I used it as a main course, a recurring co-star in my Mon-to-Sun dinner-plate soap opera: coleslaw on toast for that mid-morning snack; coleslaw with cheese between crusty sliced bread for a crunchy sandwich supper; a layer of the coleslaw on top of a breaded chicken escalope; and even coleslaw as a cold topping to pad out a cheap pizza base with a thin tomato-and-Cheddar topping.

Not long ago I went to a wedding with a vegetarian friend. In lieu of the king-prawn cocktail in thousand-island sauce she was served luxury coleslaw on iceberg lettuce in an oversized wineglass.

In the aftermath of the stingy cabbage starter, she removed exactly half of the John Lewis vouchers she'd bought the happy couple and, using a fingertip smudge of sticky apple-pie filling, re-sealed the wedding card.

Complaints

I'm not a big reader. I generally stick to war comics from the seventies (*Sgt. Rock and His All-Star Hun Patrol*), 'novelisations' of blockbuster movies (with six pages of out-of-focus official film photos in the middle), boxing magazines (purely for the sleazy glamour) and flimsy, unauthorised, quick-to-cash-in hagiographies of fading First-Division footballers and flash-in-the-pan pop performers (bought in charity shops and written by people called Rick Sky or Danny Diamond who use contemptuous, thirty-words-per-page, seventy-two-page formats: '"*Living the D:REAM – the D:REAM Story* is a great read; a must for the discerning fan of Irish dance pop" – ME'.)

I inherit this literary laziness from my parents. Save for half a dozen unread books about naval battles and a sun-faded cache of Catherine Cooksons, their bookshelf is pretty much bare.

The only other books my parents possess came free with a subscription to *Which?* magazine in the late eighties: *The Which? Guide to Understanding Back Pain* and the awkwardly titled *The Which? Book of 120 Letters that Get Results*.

There's a whole chapter dedicated to restaurant-complaint letters in the latter – template missives to fire off when unhappy about bad food, sour wine or iffy service.

These templates have come in handy to me over the years. In response to my letters of complaint I've received cheque refunds, tokens from major supermarket chains, snack-bar credit vouchers and even a grovelling phone call from a Frenchman. Hurrah!

For copyright reasons I can't reprint a *Which?* template here, though I have thoughtfully created my own version for you to cut out and file on *your* bookshelves, nestled next to your *Bravo Two Zero*s and Barbara Taylor Bradfords.

Dear [Insert name of restaurant. It's probably a side-street steakhouse with a large wooden wheel affixed to the fascia.],

On the [Insert date] I booked a table for [Insert number] people at [Insert name of restaurant]. Our meal was unsatisfactory for the following reasons:

[Pick one or more of the following reasons]

Brightly coloured sauce made from tinned tomatos and red dye-40 was spilt on my shirt. It was a polo shirt – £28.00 from a fashion designer best known for his pungent midprice aftershaves. I'd had it for just six weeks and now it's fit only for mixing paint thinner, gardening and sponging down the cabriolet.

Your waiter seemed somewhat over-familiar, especially when spreading the paper napkin over my wife's leggings.

The waiter served us the wrong wine and he didn't show me the label or allow me to taste the wine before he let us pour it out ourselves. That was the first time in all my years of eating out that I'd ever been deprived of these meaningless rituals. The wine was an undrinkable red from a former Soviet state – five whole pounds wasted.

We were seated next to the [**toilet/loo/bog/lavvy/john/ restroom – insert correct term according to your nationality or social class**]. Other diners had to walk past our table on the way to the [insert **toilet/loo/bog etc.**], staring at my lobster bisque and the wife's chest as they did so. There was also the smell . . .

The toilet had no towels and a faulty dryer so diners would shake their hands dry as they passed our table. As a consequence, my wife [**Helen/Jean/Cheryl/whatever**] was unable to finish her chowder.

The bread rolls were cheap sesame-seed hamburger buns. They were pre-cut straight in the middle, thus depriving us of [**a/another**] meaningless dinner ritual: breaking open the crusty white roll while pondering the overpriced entrée options.

I asked to pay the bill with a credit card. Your restaurant didn't have a chip-and-pin system, only one of those huge sliding carbon-copy machines with the Access credit-card logo on the front.

Two weeks later, several mysterious transactions appeared on my end-of-month credit-card bill: £60.00 spent in an Inverness off-licence, £30.00 spent in the Battersea Total garage and £12,500.00 spent in an Estonian strip club.

Since I was unable to derive any pleasure from the meal, I therefore claim [insert sum] compensation and look forward to receiving your cheque for the amount within fourteen days. If you fail to reimburse me I shall have no alternative but to issue a summons against you in the [insert name of your local county court] County Court for recovery of the money without further reference to you.

Yours sincerely,
[Insert your name. Let's face it – it's probably Steve.]

Continental Breakfast

A self-loathing breakfast, with 'ruby' grapefruit juice, small packets of All-Bran, soft-boiled eggs, rubbery middle-European cheeses, dusty, sticky pastries and seventeen different types of limp, watery luncheon meats.

Continental Europe is a big old place, and I have great difficulty in buying into the concept (the one peddled by Thistle-hotel menus and Holiday Inn bills of fare) that the one thing that unites all Continental Europeans – from the Hague to Naples, Madrid to Berlin, Paris to Lisbon – is an early-morning craving for stewed prunes, black-cherry yogurts and waxy 'all-butter' croissants. The only Continental Europeans I know are Italian women, and the only cravings they have before 11.00 a.m. are for cups of stong coffee, high-tar cigarettes, large dark sunglasses and four-inch-thick layers of bronze-tinted hypoallergenic foundation make-up.

Most chain hotels in Britain offer the choice between

a full English breakfast and the healthier Continental equivalent.

Will you be having the full English breakfast or Continental, sir? It's a tricky choice when you're recovering from a minibar hangover and running late for the conference registration (8.00–9.00) with only morning coffee break (10.30–10.45; huge flasks filled with instant coffee and twin-packs of custard creams and stale oat cookies in tartan packaging from the clan McVitie's) and lunch (12.30–1.30; shared with perspiring, ingratiating men called Andy who call you 'mate' when you've only just met and say 'game on, chaps' when it's time to break off into smaller discussion groups and have one eye on the next big sale and the other on the last battered chicken strip with garlic mayonnaise) to look forward to.

The day finishes with questions from the floor (4.00–4.30); by this time Andy Conrad from Fiscal Dynamics has a sweat patch on his back in the shape of Africa.

Continental Larder

I can't help it. I'm drawn to it; I'm drawn to the 'special selection'. I'm drawn to the aspirational aisle of the supermarket that I – and no one else – call the 'Continental Larder'.

It's situated between the multipack cartons of concentrated fruit juice ('Libby's Walkway', as I and no one else call it) and the fizzy-drinks ('Sunkist Alley' – ditto); it's the only section of shelving in the supermarket that's veneered with thin strips of varnished pine. It sells jars of rich chocolate sauce from Belgium; artichoke hearts in oils; chipotle chillis in adobo sauce; mint balls in prewar reproduction packaging; selections of dried shitake mushrooms in sackcloth sachets; sesame-seed oil in earthenware jars; natural-nut nougat squares in brown-paper bags tied with pink-and-white candy-striped strands of ribbon.

And the olive oils . . . Just look at them all – it's like a weathered wood-coated altar to extra-virgin essences.

I can't help it. I have to buy at least three overpriced items from the Continental Larder each week. Seychelles cinnamon sticks; Anglesey sea salt; natural honey made by holy monastery bees; pickled walnuts in jars sealed with wax; garlic-stuffed olives; Costa Rican coffee beans coated with fair-trade organic chocolate; coconut ice candies. There are seven shelves loaded with balsamic vinegar – delicious when drizzled.

I don't know what draws me to the Continental Larder. I think it's the same compulsive urge that gets me spending at least £50.00 a month on pricey products from male skincare ranges.

I've never used that algae-based facial cleanser with azulene, lavender and rosehip oil. The deep pore-cleansing clay with apricot kernels, calendula and nourishing vitamins A, C and E sits unused in my medicine cabinet next to that tube of toothpaste for sensitive teeth I bought after experiencing some brief, sorbet-induced molar pain back in 2001.

I'll never eat anything I've bought from the Continental Larder. If I can't spread it on sliced and toasted white loaf or sprinkle it on my morning Shreddies, it's completely useless to me.

I suspect that I buy this inedible junk in the belief that it'll lead me to a better life. The Continental Larder will make women fall at my feet. Organic foods grown in chemical-free sod and sold in brown, recycled-paper packaging will make me at one with Mother Earth. The Continental Larder will make me appear worldly and sophisticated. The men's logistics skincare range will smooth fine facial lines and reward me with a healthy, glowing complexion.

Cook-Your-Own Steak

Last year I went to a media-industry conference in Tampa, Florida. An American client took a load of us hungry, pale Englishmen out for dinner at the best steakhouse in the state. (I can't remember the name, but you can't miss it. Seven items on the menu are named after Willie Nelson.) I'd picked up a bug while travelling so I stuck to a green salad (is there any other kind?) and a bowl of sweetcorn and chicken chowder. My English colleagues, however, all chose the thirty-four-ounce steak.

Imagine their delight when they were told that the restaurant etiquette demanded that they pick out their own cut of meat and cook it themselves on an eighteen-foot griddle along with slices of Texas toast (French toast, renamed for obvious geo-political reasons).

I've never witnessed such giddy, communal male joy. Even our American dining companions were embarrassed. (Do you know how difficult it is to embarrass an American in a situation which involves large portions of fried food?) Sizes of steak were compared, Texas-toast technique was judged and sweaty backs were slapped. Giggling could be heard above the sizzle of the 100 per cent prime beef.

At one point in the meat-induced mania I had the horrible thought that they were going to start playing with each other's privates.

Corkage

Corkage is the fee that restaurants charge to open that bottle of Zinfadel. That bottle of Zinfadel that you've brought with you in a plastic bag: a thin, plain blue plastic bag with no child-suffocation warning. You cheap bastard.

Corkage in British restaurants is generally between three and four pounds and payable to a waiter who's forty-five, paunchy, seriously lacking in career goals and a fully paid-up member of the Bono Hair Club for Men.

That's if he can squeeze it in between stroking his thinning ponytail and telling your date in an indeterminate accent assembled from aftershave adverts and Van Damme videos that she 'looks just like a Spice Girl'.

Coronation Chicken

A combination of chicken breasts, curry powder and mayonnaise, Coronation chicken was created by flower-decorator and author Constance Spry (the Nigella Lawson of powdered egg, nylon chaffing, sexual repression, back-street abortions and locking women in the attic for thyroid problems and 'hysterics') in 1953 to celebrate the coronation of

Queen Elizabeth II, and kick-started the trend of covering everything in mayonnaise.

Cheap chicken in a sickly yellow curry gunk with six sultanas. God save the Queen.

In recent years mayonnaise has become the glue that holds Britain's crappy convenience food together. It joins the spring onion to the chicken breast, bonds the mashed hard-boiled egg with the cubed ham chunks.

Mayonnaise is generally believed to have been created by the personal chef of Louis François Armand du Plessis, Duc de Richelieu, presumably when le Duke needed to combine his sliced avocado with his peppered crayfish prior to filling his Royale rustic seeded bloomer.

Like a butterfly flickering its wings in the tropics, a French nobleman's chef dicking around with gloopy egg-white-based sauces inadvertently created the entire barely edible oeuvre of Pret A Manger. Merci, monsieur.

Coulis

Runny jam or fruit sauce for trendy-topping types and deluded five-a-day fascists.

Or is that compote?

Cream Cakes

You can't beat a fresh-cream cake. They're such fun. Try peeling the chocolate icing off your choccy éclair, squeezing the oily essence of alcohol from a rum baba by applying spoon pressure, chomping a fresh-cream meringue into a white dust, capsizing a layered vanilla slice; or miming along to New Orleans jazz using a flaky-pastry cream horn speckled with sugar.

I tried the trumpet/cream-horn thing recently. I was tapped on the shoulder and asked to leave the tearoom.

Back in the eighties, cream cakes were the subject of a TV and magazine advertising campaign. The slogan was 'Fresh-cream cakes – naughty but nice' and the campaign was sponsored by the National Dairy Council.

Everyone I know reckons that cream cakes were advertised on TV in the seventies, but I remember seeing the cream-horn commercials during the ad breaks on *Fresh Fields*.

The National Dairy Council. Just who is involved in this mysterious, shadowy cabal? Why were they paying for cream-cake adverts? Did the British Glacé Cherry Association chip in a few quid? When did they stop sponsoring TV adverts for cream cakes? Was it around about the same time that Findus stopped making the Crispy Pancake, the first Our Price record store opened and Prefab Sprout dropped off the 'chart radar'? What is their relationship to the Milk Marketing Board? Do they have a paramilitary wing?

There's something sinister about trade associations. The British Egg Industry Council, English Butter Marketing, the Pickles and Sauces Association, the Quality British Celery Association, the Biscuit, Cake, Chocolate and Confectionery Alliance. Are they loose confederations of producers and buyers dedicated to promoting the interests of their industries or do they operate as some sort of Hellfire Club, sacrificing unsuspecting victims and summoning six-headed demons in between organising National Dried-Fruit Week and Take Your Radishes to Work Day?

Crinkle-Cut Chips

In the early eighties new sophisticated food-production technology meant that chips could be given decorative edgings. The most popular shape was crinkle-cut. Jagged, grooved and ribbed for your pleasure.

Why?

Maybe the serrated edges absorbed oil and allowed the chips to stay crisper longer. Maybe the crispy dog-tooth look of the crinkle-cut potatoes were intended as a tribute to the crimped hairstyles of Barbra Streisand, Cyndi Lauper and Su Pollard.

Dry, spiky 1980s chips. You could cut your tongue on these fries. Avoid accidents and drown them in malt vinegar and red sauce in order to soften them up and render them digestible.

As the eighties progressed, food-production technology marched on. The pickled beetroot was next for a makeover.

Crisps

I just don't understand the British obsession with crisps. Barbecued beef, cheese-and-onion, prawn-cocktail-and-chive or Smokey Robinson; it doesn't matter what flavour they are – the synthetic savoury dust we sprinkle on greasy sliced and fried potatoes tastes like the stairway floor in a multistorey car park.

Still, I'll take genuine potato crisps any day over the 'corn snacks' of my youth: reconstituted wheat and air 'puffs'; cheese-flavoured, tangerine-coloured and shaped like fangs, paratroopers or pound puppies.

Avoid crisps altogether. They gave you a faint, white, dusty maize stubble – like Compo, the rural tramp from *Summer Wine* – and yellow, greasy, dusty fingers that smell like piss.

Croûtons

Don't mention them. I haven't been able to look at one since I ate a whole packet during that power cut.

Curry Pimps

Curry pimps and tandoori touts: those slick salesmen who stand outside city-centre Indian restaurants attempting to steer strolling punters inside with a whiff of generic curry powder, a glimpse of gaudy, burgundy-and-gold décor, cut-price Carlsberg and a three-course dinner for £6.99.

'I only went out for a packet of mints and a paper. I came back with a belly full of lamb pasanda and a made-to-measure suit.'

The Decline of the English Sunday Roast

I love the traditional Sunday roast. I love the sage-and-onion stuffing, the chipped gravy-boat, the steamed-up kitchen windows, the smell of boiling cabbage when it's time to call Father in from the garden. I love the unfathomable little rituals and the curious, classless etiquette. Why, for instance, is it forbidden to serve apple sauce with anything but pork; bread sauce with anything but game; mint sauce with anything but lamb; Yorkshire puddings and horseradish with anything but topside of beef? Does the home-cooked roast dinner still live on as a ritual in the age of sea bass, fusion food and all-day Sunday retailing?

Yes, I know that every urban gastropub and ring-road carvery offers a Sunday menu, but does anyone actually cook a Sunday lunch at home any more? I haven't had one in years and even my parents, who, during my childhood, were stalwart practitioners of the art of the meat, two veg, gravy and gooey sponge 'n' syrup duff, don't bother these days. They're too busy taking my niece and nephew to the Little Ducklings swimming club or popping into 'town' to check whether anything has been reduced in TK Maxx.

Does anyone still mop up their gravy with a slice of white bread? Can you still buy those feeble five-volt electric carving knives? My dad had one. It would take him fifteen minutes to cut through the greasy string on the beef brisket and it seemed to generate less friction than that wind-up toy mouse I bought in the National Trust gift shop. At the end of the meal, while Mum washes and Dad dries (by far the hardest job, as any man will tell you), is it still acceptable to disappear to the living room with a cup of mahogany-brown tea, catch the beginning of *Paint Your Wagon* and read that Sunday-newspaper article about the struck-off gynaecologist with the beady eyes and unorthodox examination technique?

Twenty years ago twenty-five million grimy plastic extractor fans would spend the Sabbath expelling sprout smells from Britain's kitchens – urban and suburban – and there was nothing for me to do apart from recover from a huge Sunday dinner, read the papers and count the hours until a cold-cut salad and *Lovejoy* in the evening.

Today, I can watch *Paint Your Wagon* any day of the week on my multidisc special-edition DVD (with restored scenes featuring a computer-generated Lee Marvin) and I've completely lost interest in the Sunday tabloids. They're full of oversexed soap 'stars', philandering sportsmen who speak in monotone, and faceless politicians on the fiddle (naturally, it'll be a dull kind of fiddle; a dull fiddle relating to a proxy mortgage or a interest-free home loan rather than to a high-class, ex-convent-school call girl, an Eastern-Bloc attaché and a shadowy, syphilitic interme-diary called Dieter).

Whatever happened to the English Sunday rituals? The meat, the veg, the gravy, the suet pudding, the *Great Expectations* on BBC Two and the Technicolor musical Western with the Clint Eastwood-singing 'I Talk to the Trees' interlude? Whatever happened to the Right Honor-able Member of Parliament's pied à terre ménage à trois with Diana Dors?

Whatever happened to the groping vicar of English tabloid lore?

Deep-Fat Fryers

Deep-fat fryers – they were the iPods of the seventies and eighties. Every household had at least one.

Unlike iPods, they played only one song: the frying-chip tune – a bubbling Bo Diddley beat played not on a rectangular six-string but on heated slime extracted from sunflowers. There was no iTunes in my youth, though I snapped my fingers daily to the boiling-oil jangle as I buttered the bread.

No one uses deep-fat fryers these days. Fritters and homemade, hand-cut chips died out at the same time as jokes about Englishmen, Irishmen and Scotsmen and the bubblegum soul of Billy Ocean. Everyone uses oven chips now – fluffy, unsubstantial reconstituted potato cooked in a hard, crunchy casing. Or those flimsy, flaccid three-minute versions served straight from microwaves in soggy cardboard boxes.

My mum was a dab hand at the deep-fat fryer. All those years working the six-form kitchen of Eggbuckland Vale Comprehensive School had given her asbestos fingers. She could pick a stray chip out of the napalm-hot sunflower oil with her bare hands without wincing or taking her eyes off the barbecue baked beans bubbling away on the hob.

We had a huge, round electric fryer made by Morphy Richards (the Apple computers of the hand-cooked-chip era). Oil would last up to eight months. It had hot-grease blisters down the side. Dribbling fruit juice from those pineapple fritters had combined with the hot Mazola oil and corroded the metal cage.

I'd lower the battered pineapple rings into the oil, as if

sacrificing a goat to the gods – cruel, vengeful gods who'd spit their displeasure back over Mum's treasured Autumn Leaves-themed tablecloth and matching cork-bottomed coasters.

Dessert

A couple of years ago I was making an easy living as a freelance design consultant. The job involved spending three or four nights a week in provincial hotels. Since there was never anything on TV and, more often than not, a disturbing water stain on the carpet, I'd spend the whole evening in the hotel's restaurant: a steakhouse or carvery called Sophie's, the Boston Grill, Billy Joe's Saloon, the Texas Road House Buffet, Tastes, Tasters or Charlie's.

I'd eat three full courses and quaff a half bottle of syrupy Merlot. All on expenses, thank you very much.

To end the meal, the waitress would always ask me whether I wanted to see the dessert menu. I'd always reply by saying, 'Go on . . . It'd be rude not to.'

Every time I said it, a part of me died inside.

'Go on . . . It'd be rude not to.'

Diets and Dieting

The general public will buy into any tatty convenience concept: rosé wine, pricey pre-prepared tubs of egg, bacon and mayonnaise sandwich spread; dumb-ass books about Bible codes and the secret life of Jesus Christ. They'll buy into premium-rate horoscopes, chat lines, crystals, dicking around with healing pyramids, feng shui and tarot cards.

Those audio cassettes: 'Speak Spanish in Seven Days'.

Rice cakes, Sunday lunch served in smoky pubs and diets. Especially diets.

Dr Atkins' low-carbohydrate diet; Dr Arthur Agatston's South Beach diet; Dr Hook's Sylvia's Mother diet. Good fats, bad fats. Good carbs, bad carbs.

I can read your palm, help you reveal your true psychic destiny through the stars, and drop six jean sizes in two weeks.

Beware those who swear by the star sign, the miracle diet. Beware the voodoo jinx, the juju hex, the whammy and the fake *Record Breakers* chain-letter.

Diets: programmes, pills, charts, limits, lists, appetite suppressants and body-fat percentages. Weight Busters schemes and slimmer's milkshakes as per those adverts – those adverts in which the actors' accents have been dubbed over and stripped of Californian inflections by established Anglo voiceover artistes.

Personally, I hate points-based diet plans: 'For fuck's sake, I've only had a mini-Twix. I haven't felt this guilty since I stole that pound from my mum's purse.'

Diets: meal plans and celebrity-diet tattle in magazines for women and those big vibrating massage-belt things as advertised on page eighty of the Argos catalogue by Elkie Brooks lookalikes in turquoise leotards.

Actually, I'm not sure if the vibrating belts or pressure pads *are* sold on page eighty of the Argos catalogue any more. If you're trying to find them, start at the gold identity chains and cigarette-lighter wristwatches and stop just before you get to the electronic hand-held bridge games and that small plastic vending machine that dispenses tiny bars of Dairy Milk.

It doesn't matter which one you choose, all diet plans are quackery, snake oil and film-flam; pseudoscience and confidence trickery in a 200-page paperback and a fridge-magnet flash-card gift-pack edition for that extra-special, extra-fat relative.

Thankfully, I've never needed to embark on drastic diets. But if I did I'd use pills, as the diet pill is responsible for rock 'n' roll.

Legend has it that, when a nineteen-year-old Memphis truck-driver Elvis Aaron Presley started hanging out at the Sun recording studios in downtown Memphis, he attempted to ingratiate himself with the record company's session musicians by selling them his mother's diet pills.

Mrs Presley's diet pills were amphetamine-based: pure speed.

The side-men popped the pills, curled their lips in imitation of that weird punk-kid dealer with the pink shirt, black eyeliner and greasy duck-ass 'do and they created rockabilly; that marvellous speed-fuelled hybrid of shit-kicker Southern hillbilly swing, white country and western, and black rhythm and blues.

So, don't diet. Eat hearty. Eat carbs in double doses. Eat more sugar and twice the amount of tempting transfatty acids.

Wolf down glazed, cream-filled doughnuts in honour of Gladys Presley. If it wasn't for her, her love of Cup Cakes, Twinkies, chocolate Ding-Dongs, fudge Ho-Hos, mallow Sno-Balls and mini-muffins bought at the West Memphis

Piggly Wiggly, and her subsequent chemical crash-diet solution, we'd still be listening to the Billy Cotton Band play 'Friends and Neighbours' on *Two-Way Family Favourites*.

Digestives

The name of these coarse wholemeal biscuits suggests that they possess medicinal properties. They don't.

They do, however make a nice base for homemade cheesecake when wrapped in a tea-towel and crushed with a rolling pin.

They also provide conversation points for people who've christened their car with a girl's name or save the Sunday supplements to read during the week.

Dinner Parties

'Have you seen the latest Almodóvar?' 'They'd run out of bergamot and we had to make do.' 'Have you tried their vine-ripened red-peach Trinquelinette jams?' 'More vine leaves, Harriet?' 'Stephen Poliakoff? His work is so middle class. Like Richard Curtis without the jokes. Yadda yadda.' 'We've just come back from skiing.' 'Pass the Simon and Garfunkel.'

Apparently, every week millions of British women dress up in Zara while their husbands make a beeline for their summer-sale, charcoal-grey Hugo Boss suits, select a midprice bottle of red, lock the dog in the gazebo and gather round each other's houses for four courses of rich

food and servings of provocative chatter about the property
ladder, French new-wave cinema and how they like the
old stuff like Public Enemy and Heavy D & the Boyz but
find most modern rap a 'wee bit sexist . . . Another glass
of the black-fruit Provençal, Toby?'

I've never actually been to a dinner party. I've never
been to a black-tie ball, either. Christ Almighty, I'm a
freak. Why not?

Maybe it's because I'm the son of a dinnerlady and not
nearly posh enough; or it could have something to do with
the fact that I've never been part of a proper couple. I
don't even have a workable opinion on Iraq ('That Saddam
chap? Bit of a bad egg . . . No?').

Then again, I don't even know anyone who's ever been
to a dinner party.

I don't think anyone ever *has* been to a dinner party,
apart from characters in seventies sitcoms. (Dinner parties
are just one in a long list of incidents that only ever feature
in seventies sitcoms – a lengthy list that includes cars
backfiring, best suits being eaten by moths and men who've
run up three flights of stairs to answer the phone being
mistaken for heavy-breathing 'sex maniacs'.)

The idea that the British middle classes spend their weekends chasing beef Wellington round someone else's best
crockery, while talking about occupied forces in Afghanistan,
Tracey Emin's embroidered peg bag and catchment areas,
is a myth – lazy journalistic shorthand for describing how
hot topics are discussed by the middle bourgeoisie, and tired
plot devices for stodgy British plays. Stop it now.

The same goes for the casual use of the phrase
'water-cooler television' when describing the social currency

of popular programming. I don't know about you, but I can barely bring myself even to look at any of the sweaty-faced, coffee-breathed dullards I work with, let along converse with them on the subject of last night's *Celebrity Death Camp* or that police-chase-footage programme on Channel Five narrated by Samantha Fox. Especially not while sipping irradiated well water from a leaky paper cone.

Dos and Don'ts

Do: keep all kitchen surfaces clean.
  Don't: eat food after the best-before date.
  Do: store food in clean, sealed containers.
  Don't: store food on the floor.
  Do: store raw and cooked food separately.
  Don't: refer to a job of work as a 'gig' unless you are a professional musician.
  Do: wash your hands before and after handling food.
  Don't: call anyone 'boss' unless they actually are your boss.

Drizzled

Rainbow trout drizzled with dill butter and honey. A selection of wild berries drizzled with white chocolate.
  Is that the same as 'covered in' or 'with a bit of something poured on top', perchance?
  How about 'dribbled'? I tend to dribble my oils.

Enjoy *Fast* Food

A cartoon cod grins from the grease-sodden takeaway paper bag that's pasted to the pavement in a provincial precinct. Feature-wise, he's pure Hanna Barbera. He's holding a Union Jack flag in a mitten-like fin and blowing tiny bubbles from the corner of his mouth. Above him are the words 'Eat Fried Fish: Great British Food'.

The box from a non-franchise fried-chicken vendor lies, crushed and dirty, in the gutter. 'Chicken to Go!' is the snappy motto. The cartoon fowl on the front has Yogi Bear eyes and a beak that breaks into a Quickdraw McGraw-style smile around the edges.

There's another example: lodged in a slimy gutter grill in the city centre, the word 'Takeaway' in a blocky, faux-3D typeface, like the welcome sign on the Civic Centre across the way.

Look: more litter. A French-fry 'pocket' stamped with '*Fast Food*' – swoosh lines around the Fs and funny goggle eyes in the Os.

Beware any food that arrives in generic packaging. Avoid containers and cartons marked with cartoon critters.

Keep Britain tidy and enjoy the great taste of fish 'n' chips.

Entertainment Venues (Formerly Pubs)

I give up on British pubs. I'm just not interested any more. You can keep them. I throw in the towel – the fraying, faded, ale-soaked Bass-branded terry-towel that's draped over the squeaky pump handle every night after closing time.

You can keep the Crown and Greyhound, the King's Arms, the Mason's Arms, the Illuminati Inn, the Ram, the Ship, the Farmers, the Bat and Ball and the Cap and Coil. None of them has anything to offer me.

On future Saturday nights, you'll find me at home with six cans of supermarket shandy and a selection of honey-roasted finger snacks. Don't worry about the time, I'll set my own opening hours – if you call in at 3.00 a.m. I'll still be there, knocking back carbonated drinks, reclining with my bare feet on what I call the 'footstool' and my parents refer to as a 'pouffe', dozing off to a plinky-plonky 'Pages from Ceefax' soundtrack.

It's not that I don't like going to pubs. It's just that I can't seem to find a proper British pub; a pub minus the pan-fried blackboard specials and the prize-winning floral displays that attract day-trippers and local-TV camera crews. I can't seem to find an authentic bar that doesn't flog goat's-cheese-topped baked cod from a chalk-scrawled menu, doesn't hire posey Saturday-night DJs who play choice 'choons' on white labels from Chicago or play host to spotty promotional girls in sponsored Lycra jumpsuits who hand out cigarette samples and scratch cards that promise – as prizes – inflatable beer bottles and bum-bags branded with brewery logos.

I've searched long and hard for a bona fide boozer that doesn't sell itself as an all-inclusive 'entertainment venue'; one that doesn't hold a noisy trivia quiz for dullards and pedants in polo shirts on Tuesday or a weekly karaoke night.

I actively avoid pub karaoke nights. I take taxis, trains and steal push-bikes from members of the clergy in order to escape from their immediate earshot.

Not that I have anything against drunken squaddies stamping their feet while shouting the vocals to 'Careless Whisper' on twenty-second time lags from the video version. I just hate those karaoke-for-cash nights that attract desperate session singers angling for a £100.00 prize, a wild-card spot in the regional final, and another shot at either the 'big time' or the hazy concept that idiots – would-be rock stars and aspiring actors – refer to as the 'dream' . . .

There's this one couple who turn up at every venue and belt out 'Dead Ringer for Love'. She once sang back-up vox for Johnny Hates Jazz and, for one week, he was in the West End chorus of *The Lion King*. They're far too polished. She wears a lace scarf. He sucks his stomach in and sweats through black plastic trousers. They preen, primp and pump their chests out; shake their shaggy, streaked, tangled hair and wag their fingers at each other in time to the soft-rock backing beat. They strut and swagger in the snug space of the Fruiterer's Arms like it was Wembley fucking Arena. I swear to God – they appear in every pub I go to. I think they're following me around.

Last month I thought I'd found a decent pub only to discover that the perky Bible-study group from the Alpha Course use the function room five nights a week. I couldn't concentrate on my Martini and lemonade and the felt-tip kept slipping on my book of puzzles. That smiley, springy born-again girl in the sarong kept rattling up and down the creaky stairs with bottles of lemon squash, jugs of mineral water and glossy pamphlets about the Resurrection.

Last week they were talking in tongues – I could hear them over the Satellite Sports feed and the King Kong

Cash poker machine. It's true. I'll swear it's so on a big fat King James Bible – no word of a lie.

But I'd rather contend with the fresh-faced, slightly scary but ultimately friendly New Testament devotees than the grumpy, ashen-skinned goth-and-psychobilly-night punters with their clingy black denim, painful piercings and stringy dyed-black hair who fill up the function room in the Pack Horse on the final Friday of each month. Contrary to their tight-trousered outsider stance and affected rebellion, they're marked with the same tattoos as the squaddies singing Slade songs and the UK-garage-night regulars who still think it's 1998 (bless them).

The goth club is called the Crypt. The function room is two flights up. Scary stuff.

Find me a pub that doesn't have two burly bouncers on the door, pizza ovens that smell like burnt Cheddar cheese and cremation smoke, or creepy, ingratiating land-lords, like Jeff at the Greyhound, who employ their screechy moon-faced Thai brides behind burnished, antique-walnut wood bars.

Help me search for a pub without loyalty cards – stamped once for a pint, twice for a pitcher of orangey-blue cocktail and three times for a filled baguette; a pub without weekly curry clubs that fill the entire entertainment complex – even the children's adventure playground outside – with an acidic chicken-jalfrezi smell; a pub without notices above the video jukebox that read: 'Please excuse the mess and bear with us. We're expanding our car park to cope with increased coach-trip custom.'

I can't seem to find a pub that doesn't sell tickets for blokey stage hypnotists who turn media-sales students into barking dogs or mesmerise them into mincing around like Mick Jagger while pout-miming to 'Not Fade Away'. Last week I caught five minutes of a stage hypnotist's act in the Bird in the Hand's back room. He was far too socially introverted and awkward to make his crude comments about the 'ladies' seem credible. A drunken fresher flung a spicy potato skin at his head. He unwisely chose to ignore it and a blizzard of scampi fries and battered crab bites followed.

And I could do without the all-female comedy troupe using the room upstairs for their tired sub-French and Saunders shtick every Tuesday at 8.00 pm.

I once went out with a Welsh woman who performed in pub function rooms as part of an all-girl comedy company. I went to one of their shows.

There were three other people in the audience, all of them connected with the ensemble: a bored younger brother who spent the entire night checking the football scores on his fancy phone; a fed-up flat-mate, there under duress and the threat of withheld rent; and one of the troupe's liquored-up live-in lady lover, a friendly, plain-speaking girl from Leeds, as embarrassed as I was by the sketch comedy, who wore a leather biker's jacket indoors in the summer and told me she wasn't into revue comedy anyway – just hard rock, British motorcycles and the films of Jodie Foster.

There were crisps on paper plates, dips in bowls and cold sausage rolls on a tiny table in front of the microscopic stage. One of the cast – the girl with the comic repertoire of two 'posh' voices and some serious hair-flicking – had covered the back seat of her hatchback with clingfilm-wrapped catering nibbles in anticipation of the arrival of the TV-production company and artist-management bigwigs she'd emailed and faxed invitations to. They didn't turn up and she had to sneak the snacks up the pub's stairs under a beach-towel and a showy copy of the *Stage* – a necessary stealth considering the Castle and Cutlass's strict 'no outside catering' policy.

One of the comedy sketches was set in the Garden of Eden. It featured hen-night issue clip-on devil horns from the Claire's Accessories collection, two saggy flesh-coloured body suits, a knitted draught-excluder serpent, felt fig leaves and the punchline: 'I can't wait until the autumn.'

I stayed right till the end. My face blushed ruby red and my jaw ached from suppressed yawning.

I need to find a pub that's never heard of couscous, scallops or sticky cherry beers from Belgium that taste like Benylin; a pub that doesn't display paintings for sale by primitive artists – poppies painted in raised paints on rough canvasses or faint watercolours of long-since-demolished local landmarks.

The notice outside my dream hostelry would read: 'No walkers, no evening entertainment, no chillout "grooves", "indie" music or any kind of weedy student guitar rock on the jukebox – only Merle Haggard and my own personal *Twenty Country Golden Greats* compilation.'

No teams of touring cyclists and no stand-up comedians cracking wise in the certainty that by using the word 'shag' every thirty seconds they're channelling the twin spirits of Lenny Bruce and Bill Hicks. (I would rather be in a pub with 400 pissed-up, belching, Burberry-baseball-cap-wearing snake-eyed teenagers than one single stand-up comic braying on about George W. Bush or the difference between men and women in a monotonous counterfeit-Cockney accent.)

No men wearing blue work shirts with cheap yellow ties, or those crap rugby shirts that are a multicoloured patchwork of different rugby shirts. No students huddled in the corner with their tie-dye T-shirts and dirty roll-up cigarettes. No Scandinavian seafood platters or locally sourced saffron soups. No annual entry in the East Midlands heats of 'Battle of the Flowers'. No local-news camera crews covering the hanging-basket competition or using the pub as a backdrop for interviews with motorcycling vicars or would-be MPs slumming with local drinkers in the week before the by-election.

I don't want the pine-nut brioche, the game pie with the puff-pastry lid or the sticky toffee pudding. I just want a pub with sticky floors, a landlady called Val or – at a push – Lesley, a black Labrador dozing by the door, a flickering fire and a creeper-covered façade. I want a cosy local pub where the only game is one played by lobbing rusty arrows at a dented dartboard.

Ethical Food

I do try but when it comes to being socially conscious I'm always at least a decade behind the rest of the Western world; a dozen years behind the South African apple curve. Is that new breakfast-cereal formula tested on chimps? Don't ask me.

Fair trade? Is that something to do with buying shares?

No? How about 'Maggie' Thatcher or the poorly trees in South America?

When asked by a street seller if I'd be interested in a

Big Issue, my stock response is to shrug apologetically, bite my lower lip and stress that 'Sorry. I don't read magazines. There's nothing in them. I'm more of a book man and not interested in exclusive interviews with the Levellers or Anita Roddick.'

I thought Bobby Sands played rhythm guitar on 'Bongo Shutdown' by the New Dimensions.

I'm told that it's now acceptable to eat South African apples. Genetically modified food sounds simply peachy – especially if the end result includes bigger, juicier peaches, riper tomatoes and super-bananas, resistant to disease and mushy black spots in the middle even though there are no black spots on the peel.

Now if they could only apply that sort of food-improvement technology to cream-cake fillings or doughnut glazes.

Fake Allergies

In no way am I suggesting that the majority of sufferers from food-related allergic reactions are faking it. I'm completely willing to accept that most people who claim sensitivity to nuts, seeds, curds, whey, soft cheeses or any kind of emulsifier are, indeed, telling the truth and would swell up like Elephant Man John Merrick if they came within a mile of a muesli bar or an artificially coloured, strawberry-flavoured mousse.

I'm merely suggesting that there are quite a few people out there who use 'I'm allergic to . . .' as a flimsy smokescreen for 'I don't like the taste of . . .'

For example: an ex-colleague claimed to go all giddy, red and puffy at the gills when she ate a packet of Skittles, considering this a legitimate excuse to miss the three days of work prior to a pressing deadline. When I offered another female friend a marzipan fruit at the theatre, she turned it down on the grounds that she was 'allergic to marzipan'.

Desperate for a sugar rush, she caved in during the interval (I called it 'half-time' just to annoy her and play up to my hard-won reputation as a cultural philistine), ate a marzipan banana and whispered, 'I do quite like them after all' as the safety curtain raised for the third act. (Me: 'The last bit is starting. Is it going to go on for long?' She: 'Munch. Munch. Are those marzipan oranges or peaches? Munch.')

I once went out with a woman who claimed to be allergic to every dairy product, nut, seed, artificial colouring, flavouring and gelling agent. She also made lousy arts-and-crafts fruit-bowls out of felt; she used a 'Kermit the Frog' voice whenever she was happy; and once while watching a TV quiz she insisted that Neil Diamond was the 'first man in space'. She dumped me for some bloke named Kyle, cruelly accepting his offer of a lift home to Stratford in the white van he used to deliver sandwiches in while I waited for the last Tube on the District Line back west.

I'd have loved to have seen her face swell up like John Merrick's.

Family Recipes

Family recipes: handed down through generations, just like fine bone china, homemade quilts, ugly costume jewellery brooches in the shape of peacocks and musty wedding dresses made in the fifties that give too much at the hips. Just like mental illness or congenital heart defects.

No. I don't want the recipe for Cousin Kitty's rustic potato-and-leek pie. I'm not in the least bit interested in Mrs Blake's everlasting rhubarb syllabub. Nana Evans' special red snapper sounds especially disturbing – I may require therapy. And, if the family rumours are true, there's no fucking way I'm going anywhere near Auntie Mary's lemon drizzle.

Family recipes are a total sham. They're not Mum's 'special Yorkshire puddings'. They're merely standard Yorkshire puddings made by your mum.

Farmhouse

I was searching for a frozen-dessert dish in the supermarket frozen-foods section the other day. I'd been hankering for frosty refined sugars, artificial-fruit ripples and a stinging sensation in my sometimes sensitive teeth. You can't buy ripples any more, and I'd been suffering from vanilla fatigue and double mint-choc-chip weariness, so I settled on the raspberry-syllabub farmhouse ice cream.

Despite being born and raised in Devon, I've never actually been on a working farm. I've never been on a farm, but I can pretty much guess what kind of activities take place on one.

Everyone up at 4.00 a.m. (country folk roll their Rs and refer to it as the 'the crack of sparrows') to milk the cows and scrub down the scarecrow. Feed a few birds with scattered seeds; check that none of them has been eaten by foxes or wild cats on the run from Paignton Zoo. Arm oneself with a two-barrel shotgun and check the perimeters for gypsies, longhairs, ramblers and hippie travellers in creaky VW campervans. Cram another 100 hens in the battery coup. Receive six-figure EU subsidy for not growing rapeseed oil and for turning the fallow field into a petting zoo, weasel sanctuary and pick-your-own 'experience'.

I'm really not convinced that any part of a British farmer's day is spent mixing up raspberry-syllabub ice cream, farmhouse sorbet or rustic-style tomato-and-chilli plum farmhouse relish. I don't buy into the idea that flush-faced plough hands and plump, earthy farm *Fraus* concern themselves with the production, packaging and distribution of farmhouse pork pâtés flavoured with organic apple ciders, farmhouse damson jam and wild-mushroom crumbles, Dorset farmhouse chutneys or fresh farmhouse cranberry-topped chicken pies.

Sell some pigs at market. Chew on a strand of straw. Feed the sheepdogs. Point out factual inaccuracies in *Emmerdale*. Kiss the ewes goodnight. Take muddy boots off. Go to bed. Count sheep.

Fish and Chips

Save the authentic fish-and-chip shop. Save the conventional chippie and the bona fide local chipper.

Slap some sort of heritage order on Ken's Fryery and Neptune's Fish Bar. Pretty please, preserve the Happy Haddock and Chris's Golden Fry.

Save the traditional chip shop. Save the chip shop where

the vinegar goes on before the salt, acting as adhesive. Save the chip shop that solely sells cod, plaice and haddock pieces, thick, hot chunky chips, bright-pink sausage meat of unidentified origin covered in a nobbly, crunchy golden coating, mushy peas and scraggy batter bits. Make sure that those gritty orange fishcakes are frying tonight.

Revere like royalty the chip-shop vendors who sell weak Corona-brand fizzy orange in returnable glass bottles, jars of gherkins, pickled onions and ghostly pickled eggs swimming in Sarson's. Honour the establishment that punts battered burgers, thickly cut, thinly buttered white-bread slices and tiny bottles of Daddie's sauce stacked on sloping shelves coated with dried beef dripping.

Tear down the chip shop that peddles doner kebabs, Southern-style fried-chicken nuggets and soy-and-shoot spring rolls. Ban the Beijing Fish, Chip and Noodle Express.

Prohibit the Scottish fry – Dunky's Tartan Jock-anese with its battered meat-and-cheese pizzas and frittered Creme Eggs.

Destroy the chip shop that sells Cornish pasties (prepared off-premises); goat-meat patties and deep-fried confectionary. Boycott takeaway menus that include scalloped potatoes or three-cheese curly fries with ranch-style sauce. Reject falafels, vegetable samosas, pre-packed steak-and-kidney pies and multipack cans of Coke imported from Turkey bearing the warning 'not for resale'.

And no rock-salmon option . . . no one ever orders rock salmon. It's not even proper salmon: it's dogfish, damn it.

Do not save the dogfish. Hunt the ugly fucker to extinction and free up our fryers for cod, haddock and plaice.

Save the British fish-and-chip shop as the venue for

teenage first dates, tentative trysts and saucy banter by
the batter between queuing girls and boys out on a downtown Saturday-night fish-fry.

Save the urban chippie as the setting for the drug deal,
the stabbing, the armed robbery, the unmotivated axe-attack,
the shooting and the sadistic, squaddie-verses-civvy
showdown.

(See also Saveloy.)

Flavoured Water

Strawberry and aloe. Elderflower, lemon and foxglove.
Flavoured waters. Part of our 'make yourself feel nauseous
with sugary tap water in a sticky bottle' range.

Last week I drank a bottle of blackberry-and-echinacea-
flavoured spring water. It tasted like Kouros cologne.

Food Diary

Recently, in a last-ditch attempt to lose weight, a friend
of mine has started writing a food diary, listing what she
eats and where she eats it, plus the meal's fat content and
calorie count. It reminds me of the diaries I used to keep
when I was a child. Since my parents never split up, and
I was neither sent to boarding school nor bullied at the
school I did attend nor abducted by a travelling medicine
show when I was seven, all my diary entries were about
food. I'd recall what I'd eaten that day ('quiche' is spelt

in six different ways), what Mum had bought for the following day (usually quiche), and what I'd had in my packed lunch (cold quiche in tinfoil).

The only other diaries I've ever read are the fake Hitler diaries, Bobby Robson's 1986 World Cup diary and a sneaky peak at my sister's private diary from 1988. I get them mixed up.

8 November 1986   Along with Ray 'Butch' Wilkins, I organised a little beer-hall shake-up. The press were hovering vulture-like after our four straight losses. We were sitting ducks. I jumped on to a table and fired one or two shots into the ceiling. Backs were against the wall. Trevor Steven had pulled a ligament. We had chilli-con-carne for tea and Mum let me stay up late to watch *The Thorn Birds*.

The Food of Love

'What are you drinking, love?'

'I'll get us a bottle of champagne – proper, expensive stuff made in France.'

'My card is behind the bar. It's a platinum VISA – a monthly percentage goes to Africa.'

'. . . and fruit-flavoured vodka shots for all your friends.'

'Are you all sisters? Ah-ha ha ha.'

'Back at mine I have a cold bottle of Chateau Lafite-Rothschild and *Cinema Paradiso* on laserdisc.'

'Let's go mad and drink every cocktail on the menu.'

'Barman, make that Dubonnay and fizzy orange a double and don't delay.'

'I'm kind to animals.'

'I'm a cat person.'

'Wow. I love chocolate, too. In particular, Green and Black's Butterscotch Bar.'

'Oh, you prefer the mint chip? Come to think of it, so do I.'

'I'm a qualified pudding chef.'

'Here's my number. I've written it down on a piece of paper for you.'

'On alternate weekends I volunteer for Médecins Sans Frontières or fly my Corvair 640 turbojet to Martinique.'

'I feel like we've known each other for ever.'

'Would you like to come back to my place? I have a bottle of Veuve Clicquot Ponsardin chilling in the fridge and *Dirty Dancing* on DVD.'

'*How to Make an American Quilt*?'

'Please. I beg you.'

Funnily enough, none of the above drink- and confectionery-related come-ons has ever worked for me. Maybe, just maybe, the way to a woman's heart is through her stomach rather than her liver.

Maybe I should try that recipe for rhino-horn risotto with cinnamon – guaranteed to get anyone in the mood for some 'loving'. I could always try mixing up some sexy Spanish fly from ground-up Mexican beetles. Add it to a fig-and-almond paste before making any amorous moves. Don't worry if you don't get lucky – it doubles up as an exfoliating facial scrub.

Maybe I should give up on the whole amorous angle and concentrate on the food-eating aspect: my longest relationship lasted three weeks, only slightly longer than it takes to digest a Melton Mowbray Pork Pie. Love is a lottery; a bit of a raffle. I've never bought the winning ticket in either but I don't care that much – the prize is usually a bottle of Bailey's with crusty liqueur around the lid or a poor-quality stuffed toy.

Food Poisoning

I used to work with this Italian bloke called Paulo. I say Italian, but he was exceptionally Anglicised. He drank milky tea with three sugars from a souvenir mug and kept an organ-donor card and a mini-sewing kit in his velcro wallet.

Every time someone at work suggested eating out for lunch he rattled off the same stock advice in a high-pitched Neapolitan yelp: 'God, don't go there. I went there with Mary. We both got food poisoning.'

To him, everything 'tasted off'. A mid-afternoon Boost bar from the office vending machine was tossed in the waste bin on account of a 'sour smell'.

Paulo's girlfriend, Mary, loomed large in Paulo's restaurant critiques. She was a Scottish nurse with a stomach susceptible to infection. She was heard of but never seen. Explaining why he'd turned three hours up late for a 9.00 a.m. team meeting or left work at lunchtime holding his stomach, Paulo would offer the excuse: 'Mary and I got food poisoning. We were shitting like dogs all night.'

That's where he gave himself away. Paulo had cleverly worked out that talking about toilet matters in a naïve Continental manner avoided any follow-up accusations of excessive absenteeism. Bosses merely shuffled their feet and changed the subject.

Paulo was by no means the most annoying person I've ever worked with. There was the boss's PA who would apply squishy moisturising cream to her hands every sixty seconds and claimed to live a glamorous, 'single woman in the big city' lifestyle even though she lived in a flat-share with eight South Africans in Tooting and drank pitchers of Sex on the Beach in a sports bar called the Wallaby every Friday night.

Not to mention the the irritating business analyst I worked with on the industrial estate near Twickenham, with the big teeth, sweaty plastic flying jacket and the street-vendor aviator shades. He ate a noisy brie-and-bacon baguette at his desk every lunchtime while tracing routes on aviation maps. He wouldn't stop droning on about his light-aircraft flying lessons and scattered French-stick crumbs all over the office.

Food Rotas

It doesn't happen so much any more – eating certain dishes on certain days of the week. Stew on a Monday; corned beef, beans and potato waffles on a Tuesday; pork luncheon meat and chips on a Wednesday; tinned cream and canned peaches after Thursday's *Top of the Pops*; and fish on a Friday for the meat-abstaining Roman Catholic. The week ended with tuna and chips as a Saturday treat and a full roast dinner and sweet tea on a Sunday.

I'm not sure why we did it – cultural necessity, a lack of fresh ingredients or busy mums with limited repertoires?

Not being part of a family unit, I tend to vary my meals these days. I haven't had corned beef in more than twenty years. I'll happily eat meat on a Friday without fear of Papal reproach – though a pork pie on Ash Wednesday is out of the question, just in case there is a God and he takes exception to meat-eating on Holy Days or turns his divine nose up at pig-mulch-and-jelly pie in greasy pastry.

Foodie

Can you possibly imagine the sort of people who'd want to self-apply the term 'foodie'?

I can: people who buy large-format recipe books for the close-up photography of creamy potato gnocchi. People who use the terms 'Sav Blanc' and 'resto', but never 'spag bol' or 'Sunny-D'. People who own the original London-cast recording of *We Will Rock You*, are really into Formula One racing, other shit televised sports and thumbing through the Next Directory of an evening . . .

People who collect little bottles of liqueurs. People who are seriously considering getting out of the miniature war-gaming scene.

Formal Service in Restaurants

Formal service in restaurants, like that antiques-evaluation event in the civic centre or the country-style wax jacket, is just so tacky. It's an embarrassing, overcooked stab at aristocratic living as envisaged by Dorset Daewoo dealers or retired couples from Cirencester celebrating the fat annual dividend on their petrochemical investments.

Maybe that's part of its appeal, but, even so, I struggle to keep a straight face and hide my blushes when a waiter with an accent, in deference to my Diner's Club card and Dior Homme suit, drapes a freshly laundered linen napkin over my lap and congratulates me for choosing the smoked salmon and roast grouse.

Frappuccino

Don't get me wrong: I have no problem in displaying my feminine side. In my time I've enjoyed many nights out at plays and musical theatre* and, on visits to curry houses, I always order a lager shandy and a mild, yogurt-based lamb dish.

I'd rather read *OK* magazine than books about covert military missions or black-ops commandos with embossed gold-foil daggers on the front and praise from conveniently anonymous military experts on the back.

I own a small tub of cherry-flavoured lip salve from the Body Shop. In summer I even chuckle, giggle, gurn and roll my eyes dramatically at the prospect of biting into a luxury choc-ice.

So, yes, I'm fully in tune with my softer side. But I do not think it's acceptable for a grown man to order a

---

Annie Get Your Gun, starring Suzi Quatro, Plymouth Theatre Royal, 1983.

whipped-cream frappuccino with fresh banana chunks, caramel drizzle and brûlée sprinkles.

Free the Marzipan Animals

Food exposed to the open air in shop windows makes me come over all queasy. Ban it and paste some sort of environmental-health chitty on the windows of the shops that practise it. Let's picket patisseries and the tearooms that flaunt their macaroons, choux pastries and cream-filled vol-au-vents *dans la fenêtre*. Let's leaflet seaside snack shops that expose their blocks of fudge and pink-and-white coconut-ice candies to harmful ultraviolet rays.

Boycott bakeries that display, behind steamed-up glass, long buttercream doughnuts with a single stripe of raspberry sauce down the middle, ham-and-cheese baguettes with the Cheddar slices poking out the sides, egg-custard tarts whose nutmeg has melted, meringue halves glued together with fresh cream, ugly, oversized éclairs with pink icing instead of chocolate glaze . . . And rows of sugary menagerie: marzipan ladybirds, marzipan elephants and marzipan chicks. Marzipan animals – made with ground-almond paste, table sugar and red dyes nos. two and forty – sweating in the sun.

Bring back glossy fake food made from wax for representational purposes. Bring back glossy, garish, misleading food photography. Free the marzipan animals!

French-Bread Pizzas

Findus French-Bread pizzas were individual servings of an Italian favourite: a tough, stale-baguette base, a thin layer of tomato paste dotted with minute cubes of ham, pepper squares, pineapple chunks and grated Cheddar cheese.

Shrink-wrapped and then frozen, they were generally eaten on canal holidays or in Humberside caravan sites and devoured in their millions by latch-key kids on half-term holidays.

My sister and I weren't allowed them, just like we weren't allowed to chew bubblegum, blow whistles or watch ITV.

French-Bread Pizzas looked so good in 1985 – but then again so did West Midlands pop dandies Duran Duran.

Times change and in 2007 Duran Duran look like old men wearing young men's hair. Simon Le Bon, in particular, looks like Richard Nixon in a Lady Diana Spencer wig.

French Markets

These days, every semi-affluent town in Great Britain (and Bromley High Street) has its own French market.

Recently I went to a French market in Lewisham. Bloody Lewisham. Do you think it's some sort of exchange scheme? I wonder what they thought of Lewisham produce in the Dordogne. In lieu of regional wine and cheese choices, do the French go ga-ga and wax '*Ooo la la beaucoup*' over stalls selling disposable lighters, XBox games with blurry photocopied instructions, replica football shirts with thin, poorly printed club-badge decals that shrivel up on the first wash, ropey SIM cards or pink velour fashion tops at £3.00 a piece?

These high-street celebrations of rural French food, drink and culture used to be annual events; it now seems like they're on every week.

Jammed between an ethnic puppet festival, summer Jazz on the Green and that tatty Tudor re-enactment, French markets come with a crêpe stall, eighty-five different kinds of pricey nougat, large dusty sausages wrapped in fishnet string, natural cosmetics, weird, nutty breads, Provençal Honeys (not 'Honeyz' in a hip-hop sense, mind) with a bit of dirty honeycomb left in the jar, handpainted French ceramics and wooden toys (finished, I'd wager, with dangerous, lead-heavy French paints).

Basically, all the same stuff you can buy in any British supermarket, only sold from a gingham tablecloth in an open-air precinct or on the rain-lashed steps of a provincial cathedral.

Frites

Going by the tried-and-tested blokey non-fiction literary formula, it's at around this point in the book that I'm supposed to recall the disintegration of my parents' marriage (glibly comparing it to that of Torvald and Nora in Ibsen's *A Doll's House* and Tim Brooke-Taylor and Diane Keen in *You Must Be the Husband*), how their acrimonious separation affected my eating habits and fuelled my desire to cook/sing/dance/act/host the National Lottery/play an

English butler on an American sitcom or present my own five-nights-a-week interactive phone-in quiz show about squirrels on the Discovery Channel.

I can't recall any of that, however, as my parents are still happily married (though my mum didn't speak to my dad for a whole hour back in 1986 when he carelessly left a damp tea-towel on a hot radiator). So, in lieu of any genuine personal angst, I'll tell you all about frites.

Don't be fooled. They're power-lunch chips, served in large portions. They're oversalted French-fries just served in large hand-carved locust-wood bowls and complemented by a brown porcelain dish filled with a vinegary, canary-yellow hollandaise sauce.

Fromage Frais

Fromage frais is a fruity, yogurt-cheese hybrid. If you're under eighteen, ask your parents.

It was created in a lab. It was huge in the eighties. My mum used it as an alternative filling for her special Sunday Victoria sponge around the time of the *Challenger* shuttle disaster. Fromage frais reigned supreme when the Berlin Wall still divided Deutschland, the New Power Generation were the Revolution and Jimmy Greaves started reviewing 'last night's TV' on *Good Morning Britain* – thus destroying for ever the misconception that you had to be able to read a script, follow an autocue prompt, hold an interesting opinion, possess an attractive face or string a sensible sentence together in order to appear on British commercial television.

Fromage frais-filled cake always went uneaten. Mum got the message and reintroduced jam. Jam returned just as the men on TV stopped talking about re-entry tiles on the space shuttle and started banging on about something called Glasnost.

Perestroika passed me by. History happened and I ignored it. I was fifteen and really cared only about digital watches and sponge cakes with traditional jam fillings.

Frozen Roast Meal for One

In her 1986 single-person cookery book, Delia Smith proclaimed that *One Is Fun*.

Solo dining is a right old caramel barrel of laughs. So said Smith. In so many words. Way back when.

No it isn't, Delia. It's rubbish. It's a recently bereaved man eating a sad-sack single serving of boil-in-the-bag cod in butter sauce. He's eating it standing up while listening to 'Orinoco Flow'. He's had it on continuous loop since Mary died, singing all the vocal flourishes verbatim and finding solace in the lyrics:

Sail away. Sail away. Sail away.

And so doth flow the great river of life, death and rebirth . . . At least that's what he thinks she's banging on about.

Mary passing over to the great hereafter; the winter migration of the pink flamingo; the salmon leaping upstream. Pink salmon from a can tomorrow; cod in butter sauce tonight.

Solo dining is Carole – she's watching *Cash in the Attic*,

eating dry toast and drinking Just Juice straight from the cardboard carton because it's not worth dirtying a glass. She's added some vodka to the citrus concentrate. Just a splash, mind. It's raining. Her husband's on the oil rigs.

Solo dining is the middle-aged man standing on his own at the bar in a deserted chain pub. He's called Doug. He's a divorcee and doting dad with limited access to his estranged offspring. He's eating a jacket potato with grated cheese and a slimy side salad. The wrinkled snack-spud isn't mashed up in an appealing manner; it's been cut straight down the middle with a blunt, murky, margarine-caked knife. He's drinking a half-pint of misty ale and wearing a rain-soaked brown suede bomber jacket. In happier times Marie said it made him look 'dead dishy; just like that Jacko from *Brush Strokes*.' Now they're divorced and the zip's broken. He's watching the football. It's Tuesday night. It's 0–0. It's Cardiff City versus Queen's Park Rangers.

A war veteran pulls a box from the back of the small freezer compartment in his refrigerator. He wipes frost from the brightly coloured cardboard cover with his frail fingers, revealing the words 'Roast-Beef Dinner for One'.

It's one slice of fatty beef, an oily slick of frozen gravy, two smaller-than-average Yorkshire puddings, three carrot batons, green mush and assorted hydrogenated oils. It's suitable for the late-shift worker, the pining divorcee, the unattached émigré living in lodgings and the pensioner contemplating suicide.

The frozen roast meal for one: is there anything sadder?

And I mean 'sad' in the desolate, watery-eyed, Stephen Sondheim's 'Send in the Clowns' sense rather than in the sense of the un-hip or the corduroy-clad – the meaning ascribed by the cheese-string-eating, happy-slapping kids of today.

The 8" by 8" frozen box roast: sadder than Mozart's *Requiem*; sadder, even, than a doe-eyed kitten holding a dewy rose on a Clinton's card (general occasion; no message inside).

Fruit-and-Nut Stalls

You see them everywhere: the old and young; women and men, nibbling on mixed nuts and seeds, chewing soft-dried apricots and gooey dates, spitting the stones into scrunched-up Scottie tissues. Pecking away and looking round to see if anyone is watching, like bloody garden birds.

Dried fruit and nuts will, apparently, save your life. Eating deep-fried banana chips along with dried blueberries, raisins, cranberries, pumpkin seeds, cashews and walnuts will ensure that you live for ever.

I got that information from a Sunday newspaper. I don't really read national newspapers; I scan them for essential information, add a pinch of salt and accumulate key-words in my short-term memory. In this case, I can only remember the words 'nuts', 'seeds', 'delicious', 'dried fruits', 'cancer', 'prevention', 'experts'.

I don't care how good that bag of dry cashews are for my hair, skin and nails. They taste vile.

Recently, pick 'n' mix-style stalls selling nuts, seeds, dried fruit and other scoop 'n' go health snacks have been springing up in train stations, airports and shopping centres across the country.

It's a good idea in theory, but they could try covering the produce up. I don't want to eat nuts, seeds and dried fruits that tens of thousands of coughing, sneezing, scab-speckled, itching commuters on courses of skin cream have been drifting past all day, even if they are coated in natural yogurt or organic white chocolate.

I've always wanted to work on some kind of fruit stall; to wear an apron and a loose-change pouch; to handle oranges and maybe share the contents of my tartan Thermos and some flirty banter with the fragrant lady on the second-hand jewellery stand. In my head she's called Georgina, this fruity posh girl with the flouncy floral dress, sizeable trust fund and a big red slide in her hair.

Just between you and me, for the purposes of crafty social pretext I do occasionally work on a stall.

If ever I want to get out of drinks on a Friday or Saturday night, to leave early from a dinner date, a round of birthday drinks, a leaving do or any other tedious social occasion, I merely say (pointing to my watch and sharply drawing air through my teeth), 'I really need to get going. I have to help out a friend on a stall tomorrow morning.'

It's an excuse that's worked well for me since 2005 when it replaced the standard, 'I need to make a move; I have to pick my dad up from the airport.'

Don't steal any of my excuses, though. Hands off and read on as I'm about to give you a get-out-of-something card for free: 'I have to make a move. I have to be up at 6.00 tomorrow. I'm helping a friend move house.'

Fruits of the Forest

Despite nearly 200 years of industrial expansion, Britain is still rich with unspoilt countryside, fertile farmlands, moors, lakes, lochs, local beauty spots and forests.

Whereas 'local beauty spots' are synonymous with the discovery of headless corpses, British forests are synonymous with fruits: forest fruits grown and harvested for Britain's individual pie fillings, cheesecake toppings, luxury-yogurt flavourings and any old sloppy, sugary shit that comes in purple packaging.

Just where do these forest fruits come from?

As stated on their Website, the British Forestry Commission's mission is to 'preserve and expand Britain's forests and woodlands and increase their value to society and the environment'. Yes, and to provide the ingredients for fruit corners, three-fruit coulis, Sara Lee mini-meringue fillings and pots of Waitrose fruit compote.

In 2006 the British Forestry Commission announced a series of summer rock concerts in forest settings. The line-up for Forest Tour 2006 included the coma-inducing kings of the unnecessary white-bread reggae cover version UB40, bland Bobby Crush-*manqué* Jamie Cullum and vague guitar band Embrace. This line-up prompted the following questions: if a tree fell on Jamie Cullum in the woods would it make a sound (or would anyone care)? And can you see the wood for the trees – or the back of the stage for the 600 members of UB40 playing on it?

Frankly, you can forget the forest. This summer I'll be at a local beauty spot, even if does mean an eighty per cent chance of tripping over a headless corpse and a forty per cent chance of ending up as a headless corpse.

Full English

I'm English. I'm proud to be English. Kind of. Sort of. Sometimes. But I'm proud in a sensible, reasonable, harmless way. I'm not one of these preachy, self-loathing types who cycle to work, sport synthetic slip-on shoes and feel the need to apologise for their country's imperial past. Nor am I one of those preachy, self-loathing types out to preserve the Commonwealth, *Pomp and Circumstance March No. 1* ('Land of Hope and Glory'), tartan rugs in the back of (estate) cars, '(Knees Up) Mother Brown', the Golly on the side of (Robinson's) jam jars and the little bits in marmalade (Golden Shred).

But I have to say – without a hint of treachery – that the full English breakfast stinks. It stinks both literally and figuratively.

It stinks the house out. The stench permeates your morning attire – the fluffy towelling texture on that dressing-gown with the creeping Cumberland-sausage scent will never be the same once it's washed.

Such a tragedy. It used to smell like talc.

A 6.00 a.m. Sunday full English breakfast once set my smoke alarm off, which woke my neighbours, who kicked up a stink and start stealing my mail. It splattered the hob with fine oily spittle. It left a black, greasy grime on my pans and plates.

Do not use your best china for full English breakfasts.

Instead set aside spare crockery for this sort of thing – kind of like my parents do with those chipped mugs they keep in a cardboard box at the back of the cupboard; the ones they offer to builders and removal men; the mugs they soaked in Dettol for six hours once the conservatory was finished.

The full English breakfast isn't any better when it's eaten outside the home. An average full English breakfast in an eatery in London and the South East costs £18.00. For that you'll be served two slippery fried eggs with solid, blackened yolks, two slushy tinned tomatoes, four charred button mushrooms and an oily, unnaturally pink-coloured banger with a steep spherical curve and a thin, greasy membrane of sausage skin stretching across the arc – from top to bottom – like the wing on a bat.

You'll get two strips of streaky, artery-congesting bacon, a close-to-cancerous crispy fried slice, a milky tea that costs more than a whole shop-bought box of 200 brand-name premium-quality teabags (a handwritten sign reads: 'Do not ask for refills as refusal may offend'), two slices of crumbling, half-cooked black-pudding medallions, and bulk-buy baked beans with a vinegary tang that leaves an unnatural taste on a tongue used to thirty-odd years of thicker, sweeter Heinz-style sauce. Bread and butter costs extra.

Despite the lack of free tea refills and comfortable seating, in the average breakfast caff you'll get the use of a stack of well-thumbed tabloid newspapers date-stamped last Tuesday. Grimy, grubby sex stories accompanied by unctuous actors endorsing bent bingo and high-interest loans with no credit checks for convicted car thieves. Your inky fingers reach for that buttered slice of white bread that was twice the price of a whole loaf. You read the paper's page-six splash about a tragic tot's transplant ticker; the medical details and undemanding instructional diagram make your hands go weak. You glance between the diagram, the congealed sauce round the rim of the ketchup bottle and those two stewed tomatoes on your greasy, dirty plate and your hands go weaker still; they're no longer able to grip the clammy cutlery.

You've had enough. It's time to go home for bran flakes, semi-skimmed and, like Mum and Dad's workman-issue mugs, a six-hour soak in a hot detergent bath.

Funfair Food

There was a May Day steam fair on Chiswick Green in the heart of West London last weekend . . .

The hot-dog van – a repurposed Toyota Picnic – was situated between the Fair Trade rubber dodgems and the Freedom for Palestine organic cotton-candy concession. Somehow the fair, along with the wild-boar chorizo on wholegrain herb roll with caramelised red onions and mandarin chutney, wasn't what I was expecting.

I wanted a proper dirty hot dog; a serious cancer risk in a cheap, dusty roll. I wanted the roar of the tattooed throng. I wanted the clinging stench of burger grease, proper yellow, non-caramelised onions and the sickly perfume of candyfloss. I wanted at least one stabbing.

Fusion Food

Fusion food. Embrace it, throw out the rule book. Forget about any regional boundaries. Squeeze some lime on top. Would you like kumquats with your sautéed potatoes?

With its anything-goes, improvisational nature, fusion cooking has been likened to jazz. In a recent interview, a top fusion chef compared his cooking to Jimi Hendrix's guitar technique.

For the record, Jimi Hendrix died by choking on his own vomit.

Gammon Steak

Even though the word 'gammon' originates from the old French word 'gambe' for hind leg of the pig, gammon steak is a uniquely British institution, having been cured by the traditional Wiltshire method for centuries.

The pig is slaughtered; its hind legs are removed, cured, glazed in honey and sliced into steaks. If this isn't indignity enough, the steaks are then topped with a single wet pineapple ring from a dented tin and a waxy maraschino cherry.

Yes, gammon steak when topped with egg or pineapple is a peculiarly British dish: a bloated, pink slab of fatty meat, topped with a garish, fruity hat. Rather like a 'Nikita'-era Elton John.

Garnish

To garnish is to apply a small edible decoration – usually a herb – to a savoury dish in order to enhance its appearance. Popular garnishes include fennel, basil, mint, lemongrass, almonds and tarragon.

Let's face it, garnish isn't fooling anyone. Garnish is food's comb-over. Garnish is like one coat of whitewash over the subway-wall legend 'Donna is a slag'. It's like Jeremy calling himself 'Jez'. It's like hanging-basket displays on provincial train-station platforms.

Gastropubs

They're so smug, aren't they, gastropubs. Describing themselves as serving 'modern British cuisine with a Fijian influence and a splash of Breton rustic'. All those interchangeable combinations of lamb shanks, wild-boar sausages with fennel mash, caramelised onions, chestnut terrines with tomato chutney and crab spring rolls. It's all as ubiquitous and unimaginative as the cheese-and-pickle ploughman's and choice of hot and cold filled rolls they replaced in around 1996.

Gastropubs have no time for printed menus. No, sir – it's all up there on the blackboard in chalk lettering so faint you'd need the Hubble telescope to choose your starter (though you can bet the moon and all the stars in heaven that it's rocket-based with yellow extra-virgin something or other 'drizzled' on it).

And then there are the locals. It's Sunday and they're

all sitting there. Someone's reading the *Observer Music Monthly* and mumbling about 'Arcade Fire' with a mouthful of sea bass and seared scallops. This used to be a decent boozer; now it's all exposed brickwork, Op Art wallpaper, weathered leather banquettes and hardwood floors varnished matt black.

A woman with braided hair has brought a baby to the table in an Egyptian-cotton papoose. The little mite can't be more than two weeks old. The poor thing should be at home, not dangling over someone's nutmeg cheesecake with rum-and-pineapple compote. And that baby buggy is a fire hazard – it's blocking up the exit. What if the flambéed veal cheeks with cognac went tragically wrong?

The locals are chatting and laughing with the owner/waiter while I'm waiting for service and for someone to tell me what's written on the chalk menu the other side of the pub. You can tell by their interaction with the owner that they go there every Sunday. Are they made of money? This is a rare treat for me, like a trip to the theatre, the 'bloopers' on a special-edition DVD or Blue Cross Day at Debenhams. Why aren't they sitting at home watching *Cocoon: The Return* on Channel Five each week like everyone else?

£10.50 for bangers and mash?

Glacé Cherries

It takes six whole years to digest a single glacé cherry. Some bloke on a bus told me.

Gluttony Maths

Rotisserie prices: £4.99 for a half chicken and £7.99 for a whole bird. A chain-pub pitcher of Malibu, vodka and Lilt is £7.50, whereas it's £2.80 per individual glass of the same ice-cool 'Cockswinger' drink.

. . . except from between 7.00 and 9.00 on the over-thirties' seventies night, when all drinks are £1.00.

That's gluttony maths. The series of simple sums that one carries out when deciding if it's cheaper to get drunk on the lousy acidic house white by the glass or by the bottle. It's the mental arithmetic required to calculate whether it's worth punting a tenner on the three-for-two frozen lemon-meringue pies or any other stickered frozen desserts . . .

To clarify: it's the number of years since you last ate a defrosted family-sized fruit pie; minus the cost of that one pie that you'll never eat (the one that'll lie underneath the empty ice-cube tray, nestled next to the strawberry Vien-netta that's been in the freezer since John Major, 'Ride On Time' and *Robin Hood: Prince of Thieves*).

Goat's Cheese

A sticky, tacky, pungent cheese made from the milk of a dirty, scrawny, shitty-assed, kicking, braying, rock-residing mammal.

Somehow goat's milk isn't 'dairy'. I've no idea why.

'Boo-hiss hack-spit' for dairy.

'Hurrah!' for non-dairy.

Since when did dairies become so reviled? My mental

image, persistent since childhood, has them as sunny, stainless-steel places where ample milkmaids tug the moo-cows' udders.

Forget the dairy/non-dairy split – goat's cheese is Dairylea for the middle classes and ladies who loiter in expensive delicatessens, tasting olives, ordering quarters of quince jelly for no real reason and congesting the floor space in front of the counter with string-handled paper bags from apocatheries, aromatherapy outlets and Sloane Street shoe shops. They bray, snort and whinny like the scrawny, shitty-assed, kicking, braying, rock-residing mammal whose stinky cheese they're so enamoured of.

Good Service/Bad Service

In the first weekend of spring I found myself in a sixteenth-century pub in rural Gloucestershire. The guidebook described it as having a 'cosy inglenook', a 'priest hole', a 'rude room with risqué caricatures' and mixed grill on the bill of fare. That's amazing . . . I haven't seen a mixed grill on a menu since 1997. 'Can I have it without the kidneys, though? Call me fussy, but as a rule I never eat anything that plays a major part in the production of a lamb's urine. I don't care if it is pan fried in white-wine butter and garnished with chopped baby parsley.'

I ordered a pint and mixed grill-*sans*-kidneys from the barmaid who, I guessed, was on summer break from agri-cultural college. She was in her early twenties, friendly, bouncy and with a button nose. I'm a sucker for a button nose. In fact, I'm a sucker for anything involving the word 'button'.

Even button mushrooms, unless they're garlic-brushed, baked in a crispy golden crumb and sold at extortionate side-dish rates.

She took my order with a smile that was breezy, genuine and cute in a mumsy kind of way.

Obviously, I didn't actually tell her that. I once told a female friend over dinner that she was 'cute in a mumsy kind of way'. I meant it as a compliment. She tried to stab me in the face with a steak knife.

I handed over the money and sat down in the inglenook (I've decided that, if I ever get round to forming a band, Inglenook would almost certainly be the title of my folk-rock solo project). I poked my head in the rude room. It was a disappointment. I was expecting some good eighteenth-century filth and all I got were etchings of Mr Gladstone riding a see-saw with a Prussian.

''Scuse,' Miss Button Nose called after me.

'Your change,' she added, handing me two shiny £1.00 coins and flashing a heartwarming, cute-in-a-mumsy-kind-of-way, smile.

'Thank you.' I cleared my throat. 'I can buy two scratch-cards with that.'

She nearly pissed herself laughing. Bless her button nose and cute, mumsy manner. That's what I call good service.

Two weeks later I was in a fashionable, low-lit North London bar waiting for a friend to turn up for an after-work drink. (This was one of those friends who I see once every eighteen months out of politeness and then spend the whole evening talking to about which mutual friends I've seen in the intervening year and a half and looking at my watch, wondering whether I can make it home in time to catch the start of that late-night/early-morning mid-period Chevy Chase film on BBC One – the one where he gets his biggest laugh by calling someone 'dickweed'.)

An Ibiza compilation was making the mirrored walls shake and the chrome chairs chime. There was no inglenook and they must have long since turned their rude room into a 'chill out' area. Bastards – no appreciation of silent public spaces and framed cartoons portraying the Kaiser as a giant fig pudding.

Anticipating my friend's arrival, I paid £8.50 for two bottles of cold lager and a small packet of Cracked Black Pepper and Sel de Mer Kettle Chips. The barmaid looked like she was on summer break from the London School of Evil Looks, avoided all eye contact and never once threatened to break out into a smile – though to be fair her facial piercings possibly made smiling stressful.

The grumpy Islington lass handed me my change on one of those silver saucers that says 'Leave a tip. Leave a tip now, you grubby man, for you've had two bottles of Mexican lager served to you in under eighteen minutes.'

Removing my change from one of those platters adversely affects my self-image; psychosomatically cladding my fingers in the fraying, fingerless gloves of a Victorian miser just before I slip the coins into my pocket, next to the single lump of mental coal I carry around.

I cleared my throat, licked my lips as if I was about to deliver the funniest joke in the history of the world (or at least since Ronnie Corbett sat under a spotlight in a leather chair and told that joke about his dog swallowing the TV remote control), and said, 'Thanks. I can buy myself a scratchcard with that.'

She couldn't possibly have look more appalled. Not even if I'd shown her a Polaroid of Mick Hucknall's genitalia.

Which I did. Placing it face-up on the silver saucer as I removed every single penny of my change.

That's bad service.

Gourmet Sausages

The idea of eating luxury lamb-and-mint bangers makes me want to hurl. Take those duck-, orange- and pesto-filled skins out of my sight before I heave.

I don't want apple-and-venison sausages. They don't stick together properly.

They fall apart at the faintest stab of the fork and the rich deer meat clashes with the brown sauce.

Au Gratin

It's an Italian term. It's a casserole-type dish topped with cheese and a breadcrumb crust.

I'm not sure it's really an Italian concept, though. Cheese *and* breadcrumbs? Sounds British to me.

Greek Night

It was a Friday evening and I'd just finished a half-arsed thirty-minute session in the gym (some fast walking on the treadmill while watching women shaking on MTV Base on an eight-inch LCD screen).

As I breezed out of the health-club reception, I noticed an A3 sign printed with the following words along with a scaled, stretched-and-pixilated Greek flag from the Microsoft PowerPoint Flags of the Nations clip-art library: 'GREEK NIGHT. FRIDAY 5TH MAY. PLATE SMASHING. A BAND. DANCERS. FANTASTIC GREEK CUISINE.'

Brilliant. A British staple: the as-advertised theme night – one night only of foreign food and culture; a one-off bunk-up with that swarthy foreign suitor with the bushy moustache who hangs around the docks. A spicy gastronomic fling, then it's back to the chicken Caesar salad, the gourmet burger with avocado and the beer-battered cod. Count me in.

The food isn't bad. There's a choice of mezze (Greek for 'nibbles'): pittas with hummus and oil, three different kinds of olives, stuffed leaves, fried halloumi cheese, potato salad, deep-fried squid rings (working out at about £6.00 for eight of the rubbery little suckers), kebabs with minty yogurt sauces and seven different kinds of filo parcels.

As is the case with coca-cola and ice-cream, every nationality on earth has embraced the deep-fried filo parcel.

The entertainment isn't so good. It's a Mediterranean minstrel show. Clapping, shouting and dancing from third-generation Greeks in baggy, embroidered pantaloons; plate-throwing follows, plus a wandering accordionist wearing a look that says 'And don't patronise me. I could use my squeeze box as a blunt instrument. Don't mess with the Greeks – we invented philosophy, poetry, astrology and the ten-per-cent fat yogurt, and we crash crockery after dinner for the hell of it.'

The gym staff have Blu-Tacked photos of famous Greeks on the walls: Plato, Zorba and a postwar player for Panathinaikos. Slightly condescending – no wonder the accordionist is scowling.

Amateur ethnic entertainment for the white middle-classes has always embarrassed me. Even as a child when the West Indian steel-drum band appeared on *Blue Peter* I'd turn bright red and run out of the room.

In fact, most mass social occasions embarrass me. I can never bring myself to sing along at gigs – I'd rather nonchalantly nod my head in time to the noise near the back. If I'm sitting near the front at the theatre, I leave early if it looks like there's going to be a standing ovation; I like to keep a distance of at least thirty feet from gushy actors in excessive make-up bending forward for rapture and acclaim.

The company at Greek Night is also pretty mixed, mainly comprising people I've seen in the gym but haven't talked to because they're perched on a Swiss ball or sweating through a souvenir T-shirt from a two-mile fun run. They're prattling on about spinning, boxercise and the Elgin Marbles. They're also clapping. I hit British-man embarrassment def-con one, bypass the blushes and start sweating. I make my excuses and leave: 'I have to help a friend out on a stall tomorrow morning.'

I've always avoided Greek food. I used to work in a small office with a Greek-Cypriot ex-pat. He kept banging on about how hilarious *Only Fools and Horses* was and how much he loved the choreography in Genesis's video for 'I Can't Dance'.

Come to think of it, Genesis are the kind of band who are huge in Greece and regularly drag their light-show east to play the Acropolis – which shows just how far Greek society has fallen since the great philosophers and hummus chefs of old.

Every single bloody morning at around 10.30 my Greek colleague would ring his wife and, in his curt Mediterranean manner, ask the following questions of the woman who stole him away from his loving mother: 'Are there any parcels for me? Is it from Amazon? Did you get my Müllers?'

He meant parcels as in postal packages, not as in deep-fried filo pastries, and Müllers as in the fruity yogurts. They're not even Greek yogurts.

Greengage

I've never heard of greengages. I've never eaten one. I've never seen one in a yogurt, as a limited-edition Tic-Tac taste or as a tinned filling for a flan case, so they're not going in.

And the same goes for quince.

Gristle

There's no graceful way of disposing of gristle or fatty meat chunks. And remember that this is Britain – so there's an awful lot of fatty gristle out there for unsuspecting diners to mistake for meat.

After I bite into gristle while eating out, I spit it out again and push it to the edge of the plate – right by the hard new potatoes and the only partially defrosted carrot sticks. Ten minutes later I'll invariably try to eat it again, having forgotten that I'd previously spat it out.

There's a lot of be said for disposing of a ball of fat or gristle in your napkin or serviette or covering it in wax from the table candle (the table candle provided by the restaurant in lieu of brighter, electric light – electric light that would expose the black spots of damp on the wallpaper).

Once, during a particularly tough beef Bourguignonne in a chintzy French restaurant, I spat a ball of gristle against the gold flocked fleur-de-lis wallpaper.

Perhaps the gristle's adhesive qualities would allow you to attach it to the brass statue of the Hindu goddess Kali or the restaurant's wet bar carved out of wood salvaged from a sunken Spanish galleon.

Try throwing it into the fountain or lobster tank. Maybe rub it against the dirty, damp-speckled wall to create a fatty, smeared frieze, or simply fling it on to a passing sweet trolley while the waiter fetches the bill.

Guacamole

A filthy *Soylent Green*-style dip, guacamole is usually served with stale Doritos, a mountain of melted Cheddar cheese and mayonnaise on a chain-pub's nacho platter. It's made from dead people.

Ham and Cheese

I'm sure that other countries use a combination of ham and cheese in their dishes. If so, they doubtless mix it up a little: use a soft cheese, a tangy blue, a buttery Muenster or a sweet ricotta. Perhaps the ham is thinly sliced Parma; maybe they employ sweet slivers of Trevelez or wedges of smoky Dutch.

Meanwhile, in Britain, the average ham-and-cheese dish is a yellow square of rubbery Cheddar slapped on to a thin slice of watery, wafer-thin pink ham: budget food for the petrol-station meal deal or the Alton Towers car park.

To be fair, sometimes you'll get honey-glazed ham in your ham-and-cheese sandwich, which is normal British pig meat with a faint honey tang . . . like someone has rubbed it with a just-licked Opal Fruit.

Harvest Festival and 'The Price is Right for a Tasty Bite'

Harvest Festivals aren't officially recognised as a holiday in Great Britain, though the gathering of the harvest is still celebrated by Anglican primary schools, pagans, Wiccan wizards with beards, Merlin complexes and King Crimson CD boxed sets, Methodists and followers of other antiquated belief systems.

Most Anglican churches still have an annual Harvest Festival collection. Maybe you can donate. Leave your twenty-first-century metropolitan scepticism and secular Englishness at home and your tinned goods in the vestry (put them on the pew under the knave, right next to the vicar's Lord Anthony ski jacket and the woodworm-ridden collection box for the hungry Kenyans).

For my sins, I went to a Church of England primary school and every year we marked the September Harvest Festival by holding a hymn service – singing 'We Plough the Fields and Scatter', 'All Things Bright and Beautiful', the strangely secular-sounding 'Michael, Row the Boat Ashore' to a plastic-wind-instrument accompaniment (the church-hall floor was soaked with spittle after a recorder recital) and the holy roller gibberish of 'Kum-Bye Ya' – and making corn dollies and collecting tinned goods for the poor of the parish.

Well, it wasn't so much a parish as 300 pebble-dashed dormer bungalows, arranged in a grid, a playing field, a primary school, a church, a mini-mart, a chip shop, two shops that sold wool, a Post Office and pub.

Even the pub had a dormer extension. Maybe even the church too.

Every year I'd ask my parents for tinned goods to take to the Harvest Festival. Every year my dad would give me five or six cans of beans, soups or spaghetti hoops to take – cans without any labels; cans with 'beans', 'tom soup!' or 'hoops' written on them in red marker.

He'd have used the labels as the proof of purchase required for competition entry.

My dad used to enter every caption competition, prize draw and giveaway he could find. He doesn't bother now, but back in the mid-eighties he'd bulk-buy everything from Cornflakes to Ladyshave razors and spend whole evenings picking the labels off cans of spaghetti hoops, soaking the stickers off jam jars and peeling off pickled-beetroot proofs of purchase. He'd do practically anything for the slim possibility of winning Fiat Stradas, Caribbean Cruises, His and Hers Quartz Watches or one of fifty runner-up prizes of branded beach-towels.

In contrast to todays cynical, multiple-choice 'text to win' lotteries ('What are the main ingredients of our freshly squeezed orange juice? Type A: Lemons; B: Oranges; C: Ike and Tina Turner'), entry to most competitions in the eighties and nineties required the applicant to compete in a test of condensed wit and penmanship. This test was in the form of a slogan to be completed in ten words or less.

No matter what the slogan set-up was, no matter what the prize was, Dad would use the same gauche ditty for every competition he entered:

'I eat Shredded Wheat every morning because . . . *The price is right for a tasty bite.*'

'Birdseye Potato Waffles are the waffles for me because . . . *The price is right for a tasty bite.*'

'I favour the refreshing fruit flavour of Five Alive because . . . *The price is right for a tasty bite.*'

'I deserve to win the Grundig remote-control Teletext television and front-loading VHS recorder because . . . *The price is right for a tasty bite.*'

Unsurprisingly, he never won anything, but – like an accidental savant of the cut-out coupon circuit – with his feeble slogan, my dad created *the* nutshell paradigm to summarise 200 years of mass-market food advertising . . . and in less than ten words.

The price is right for a tasty bite. That's it. That's all you need. Now if that doesn't deserve at least one-of-a-hundred Bandit Bar commemorative silver dollars in presentation boxes I don't know what does.

Harvester

'Have you ever been to a Harvester before, sir?'

'No. This must be mean that I'm middle class even though my mum's a school dinnerlady. And you should never finish a sentence with a preposition, you greasy prole. For instance, "Have you ever thought about getting that cold sore treated before, sir?"'

No, I'd never been to a Harvester before, but I had a yearning to eat breaded mushrooms with sticky cutlery at a table near the toilets while 'The King of Wishful Thinking' by Go West was piped into a *faux* rural tavern situated just off a ring road between a PC World, a Wickes Home Improvement megastore and a Land of Lampshades.

After considering the 'Renaissance Chicken' and the toasted 'BLT sandwich with hand-cut potato crisps', I plumped for the ham and eggs, described on the menu as: 'Ham and Egggggs: two slices of home-roasted ham with as *many eggs as you can eat*.' 'Why yes, what a treat. I'll go mad and have fourteen. What kind of eggs are they? I haven't been to Harvester before (not being common) so I'll have three of the Antillean short-eared owl, three of the kingfisher, three of the grebe and five of the little ringed plover.'

My companion, the Countess, who couldn't possibly eat more than twelve eggs in one sitting, settled for the 'Grilled Chicken-Strip Platter: six tender chicken strips, grilled to perfection and served with two sensational sauce boats.'

Sensational sauce boats from the Thousand Islands, all-you-can-eat rare-birds' eggs. Oh, the sensual delights that await at a Harvester. Sensual delights comparable to spending Christmas Eve in a candlelit lodge in Aspen and sharing a hot tub full of Krug champagne and pick 'n' mix fizzy peaches with all of Girls Aloud.

Heartburn

Breathe easy and don't worry: you're not going to die. Heartburn has nothing to do with the heart. It's a digestive problem caused by eating a slice of gala pie or ordering cod, chips, a pickled egg *and* a battered sausage.

Actually, you don't hear much about heartburn any more. The TV ads to promote chalky, chewy instant cures have all but disappeared from our screens.

Funnily enough, their disappearance roughly coincided with the fall in public concern about over-consumption and acute nasal catarrh.

Phlegm is dead. As is heartburn and gala pie with the egg in the middle, their down curves criss-crossing with the rise of the healthy option, the five-per-day vegetable plan and the 'as advertised' trapped-wind cure.

Hoisin-Duck Wrap

London pub-bore lore has it that you're never more than seven feet away from the nearest rat. I can't prove that, but I do know that in West London you're never more than five feet away from the nearest hoisin-duck wrap, frosted fresh-fruit frappuccino and bramble-and-mulberry muffin.

Holiday Food

It's the summer of 1981 and on TV's *Wish You Were Here* Judith Chalmers is cruising the Med, enjoying the *S.S. Contessa*'s amply stocked lunchtime buffet. A retired couple from Derby boast that 'This is our sixth cruise' and add, 'It's like a floating hotel; it has everything you'd need,' as they scoop cottage cheese with mandarin-orange segments on to iceberg lettuce. Chris Kelly has a room in a converted coaching inn in the New Forest and, while on an excursion, enjoys a Red Leicester ploughman's in a city-centre tavern. John Carter is brass-rubbing in the medieval town of York. He's brought a packed lunch. Cliff Michelmore is in a room at the Santiago Ramada, nursing a stab wound and ordering a whole rack of the honey-glazed pork ribs from room service.

Frank and Nesta Bough nervously nibble dim sum while playing high-stakes mah-jong for big Renminbi and full Chongqing province heroin rights with tetchy triads in a Shanghai smack house.

Yes, eating while on a foreign holiday can be a tricky business.

If you take a summer break in the Netherlands remember that, while the Dutch, like us, are fond of starchy sliced white bread, unlike us, they dust their medium-sliced Mighty White with chocolate sprinkles – the carb-loving, pipe-smoking creeps.

The French drink wine for breakfast. The French drink wine with every meal and let their children drink diluted red at dinner. French supermarkets are almost entirely stocked with yogurts. Aisle upon aisle of watery yogurts in miniature tubs. Recent statistics reveal that more than sixty-five per cent of France's working population are involved in the production and distribution of Petit Filous.

Ahhh, abroad: it's so hot you can fry an egg on the floor. Foreign folks go for a full forty winks at lunchtime – the lazy bastards.

They clack maracas, smash plates and chow down on snails and froggy flippers – the freaks. They throw burros out of church towers for fun and goad big black bulls with red cloth.

That was how the British defined foreign travel twenty years ago.

Today, people define their trips abroad by the price of food and drink: a four-course feast is fifty pence in Prague; a pint of lager and an open sandwich is sixty or seventy notes in Stockholm city centre.

If the heat is too 'prickly' or too 'dry', or the thought of eating cheese made from goat's milk turns your stomach or you can't afford to holiday abroad, try taking your break on a British campsite or caravan park.

We spent our 1981 summer holiday self-catering on a Dorset caravan site. Some flashy caravans had a tent attached. Our caravan didn't; it didn't even have wheels – it was grey, brick-shaped and stuck on breeze-block stilts. For two long weeks we lived off orange ice poles, individual fruit pies and corned-beef-and-pickle rolls.

During our break in Dorset, and at the first sign of ice-pole-induced malnutrition, we ate at an 'authentic' Italian restaurant. This was my first experience of foreign cuisine and the first time we'd eaten out as a family since that visit to the North Devon steakhouse with an uncle from Cork the previous year; the one where the chef and his assistant came out to sing 'Hey Big Spender' in drag. This time pizza and pasta were on the menu rather than steak Dianne and two dragged-up Scotsman with balloon breasts and flammable red wigs waving spatulas in time to Shirley Bassey while my outraged Irish uncle choked on his breaded plaice and my aunt thumbed her rosary beads and muttered novenas to the Holy Mother of Our Lord.

We ordered a Four Seasons pizza each. I remember that because Dad made a joke to the waiter about someone called Frankie Valli. The waiter glared at Dad and said his name wasn't Frankie, it was Carlo. We ordered one each thinking that they'd be small, individual pizzas like the ones we'd buy, six to a pack, from the freezer centre.

The pizzas arrived and they were huge: equal in diameter to a wheel on the family Fiat Strada. One of them even had little black fish on top. This was madness. We'd never get through all that pizza, there was no refrigerator in the two-berth shed on concrete blocks and we had only a small Snoopy coolbag. Mum said that if we ate all this pizza we'd end up 'looking like a pizza'. Dad threatened to call the police and after twenty minutes of heated nego- tiations the waiter agreed to take the unwanted Four Seasons back to the kitchen – no charge.

'Thanks, Frankie.'

Back at Madame Wong's, Frank gets mah-jong with 1-2-3 Dragon tiles chow. Twenty minutes later and the warehouse district is ablaze. Frank, Nesta and the production crew crawl from the fiery vice den, ladyfinger firecrackers illuminating their escape route and the scattered mah-jong tiles.

In the spirit of early-eighties TV holiday-show reportage,

Frank monologues to a paper lantern cast as a camera: 'Watch out for hidden extras when eating abroad. In some foreign countries you may be charged extra for a napkin.'

Hors-d'oeuvres

After the mini-pizza/little-pitta-pockets/prawn-parcel/cocktail-quiche explosion of the late nineties, I've noticed that the world of hors-d'oeuvres has gone back to basics. Vegetable crudités and canapé-style bruschetta have replaced mini-fish 'n' chips in a paper cone as the nibble of choice for the British wedding or media launch party.

Falling revenues in the media have also changed the way in which hors-d'oeuvres are presented. They're no longer served by midgets on stilts. Unemployed actresses and Australian backpackers with one British grandparent and the lure of a visa – that's yer lot now I'm afraid.

Vodka luge or girls – from a third-rate modelling agency – serving oysters au gratin and chilled champagne? Three-foot-tall ice sculptures of a leaping swordfish and a diamond on a cushion? Honduran shrimp dangling over the side of a bowl of twelve-spice salsa? You'll be lucky. Here, take a warm bottle of bulk-buy Budweiser and a greasy handful of Bombay mix. We have the shareholders to think of.

Hotel Bars

I love hotel bars. They're magnets for the dispossessed traveller, the transient tourist, the sheet-metal sales-conference refugee, the sunburn sufferer hiding from the ultraviolet glare, the international arms dealer on liaison in Marrakesh, the heat-shrivelled ex-pat pining for brown sauce and pickled eggs, the reluctant holidaymaker on the last-minute bargain break, and the water-damage home-insurance exile.

If you're going to frequent hotel bars you need to know how to dress. All the men in foreign hotel bars – staff and customers – dress like magicians.

I could parachute into a hotel lobby blindfolded and still manage to find my way around. The bar is called Sam's. It incorporates the New York Grill, which smells like burning cow and brushed velvet. Hold my hand as I cross the lobby for the three-star establishment Chez Some Frenchman – I don't want to trip over the party from Austria waiting for the free airport shuttle.

One hotel I stayed in while on a business trip to Kent had a movie-themed bar, called Oscars, with mounted memorabilia, including a clapperboard from *Demolition Man* and Timothy Dalton's jacket from an Anglo-German co-production that no one's ever seen.

Last year I spent a restless night in a hotel in Redhill, Surrey. The complex bar was called Jazz and displayed carved, varnished and painted wooden figures of jazz musicians. The carvings' facial features were nineteenth-century Deep South racial stereotype and the jazz music of choice was middle-of-the-road Dutch saxophonist Candy Dulfer.

These days, everything truly rubbish has some connection to jazz music: the coffee machine at work that's called Freshbrew Jazz; the ugly box-on-wheels that is the Honda Jazz; Jazz for Men's musky sprays, lotions, underarm roll-ons and balms; the entertainment in high-end 'you have to book' supper clubs; comeback albums from Lisa Stansfield or Rod Sodding Stewart; and summer festivals in the grounds of Home Counties stately homes. (Dig the brush-beaten Chick Webb-style drum beat. Dig the syncopation. Dig the blue notes, the polyrhythms and the improvisations. Dig the mellow atmosphere. Dig the 3,000 parking spaces, corporate champagne-and-canapé tent and reserved picnic spots for the ICL shareholders, their wives and their hats.)

With all of the above, modern cultural phenomenon jazz has it's evil clarinet-playing hands in there somewhere.

And I'm not talking about classic American jazz – the cool junkie jazz of Charlie Parker or Chet Baker. I'm talking about British jazz – men in straw hats playing 'Sweet Georgia Brown' while part-time workers from Poland walk round offering breaded shrimp.

Hummus

'How It Works: We serve our hummus as a base, with your choice of topping in the centre. Warm pitta bread comes on the side.'

So reads the somewhat condescending menu at the 'UK's first hummus bar' in London's grubby, tacky, overrated, neon-lit, Scottish-steakhouse-filled and chickpea-starved West End. It's so simple. It's so easy. We've just opened, tell your friend. Please tell your friends.

An amusing afternoon email from a friend who'd heard about my quest for the UK's naff food fads had tipped me off about the UK's first hummus bar. I could reproduce her email here (it was very funny), but I don't want to indulge in the cheesy, overripe contemporary literary device of reproducing emails, Web links or SMS text messages on the page just to (as your grandparents might say – in between mouthfuls of spongy pork luncheon meat and dollops of overly acidic piccalilli) 'appear with-it'.

Anyway, the concept of a hummus bar sounded ripe for ridicule so I dashed round for lunch the next day.

Hummus: chickpea pureé. It's huge in the Middle East – they eat it for breakfast, which might go some way to explaining the siestas and regional strife.

Nonetheless, I thought I'd give it a bash. I'd forego my usual rushed lunch of an ocean-cocktail sandwich and packet of Kit-Kat Cubes and feast instead on mushy chickpeas and pitta bread.

The 'bar' was packed with undernourished-looking ad-agency receptionists and underpaid production-company runners along with a right-on dad – one of those essentially well-meaning yet slightly harsh parents, who consider processed meats, refined sugars and brand-name trainers to be abhorrent – treating a birthday party of kids to a chickpea-and-crudités feast. Woo-hoo!

Prompted by a tall, thin waiter with a mop of brown curly hair and a too-large T-shirt promoting the lame, late-eighties pop group James, I ordered the 'special'. And special it was: one large earthenware bowl full of hummus with shredded duck and a small bowl of pickled peppers, tomatoes and onions.

It wasn't bad. It was thick, filling, spicy and packed with protein. I wasn't something I'd choose to eat regularly, but an honest alternative to chicken in breadcrumbs or mayonnaise-soaked salads and sandwiches.

The only aspect of Hummus Bros that rankled was the shameless angling for franchise status: the red and white corporate colours; the unconvincing creation myth printed on the back of the menu ('Hummus Bros was born on a glorious hot day in May 2003, when, as two college friends, we were searching for something filling and healthy that would taste great, and still leave some change for drinks at the Union Bar'); the obligatory puff piece painted on the wall stressing their commitment to fresh ingredients. They'd obviously read Colonel Sanders' biography, taking notes on his expansion philosophies, branding values and side-dish pricing.

It might just work. Use your imagination and picture the possible scene on future Fridays: late-night drinkers mopping up pureéd chickpeas with wholemeal pitta breads outside pubs; half-cut clubbers dipping crudités and pickles in lemon-topped hummus while standing up on stuffed, steaming night buses; hen-night revellers asking: 'Ooooh, can I nick a carrot baton and dip it in your chickpea mush?'

Then again, the whole Hummus Bros enterprise – the KFC-red décor, the Starbucks-issue pine and the franchise-hungry corporate philosophy, the food faddism, the optimistic entrepreneurial spirit – reminded me of a Mongolian barbecue restaurant I used to frequent.

Kubla Khan's burnt down when trade waned. The insurance company refused to pay out – the owner had sold his stock of vegetable oil to Moby Dick's Fish 'n' Chips three weeks prior to the blaze, and his cousin had an outstanding arson conviction.

Impulse Shopping

These days I can't leave the house without spending fifty quid on barely edible junk I don't need.

There's just so much overpriced, garishly packaged crap to buy . . . Thirty millilitres of banana-and-papaya smoothie for £3.00. Encouraged by TV advertising (I live in fear of digestive disorders) I buy peach-and-pear probiotic yogurts that I'll never eat.

A jar of pickled something from the Continental Larder; a dark-chocolate Bounty just for old time's sake; a resealable 'pochette' of shaved Parmesan; a raisin, dried apricot and oatmeal flapjack for the funny cartoon fruit character on the wrapper; a sugar-flecked lemon-and-blackcurrant jelly lollipop in the shape of a football to tie in with the upcoming UEFA Cup Final; a rubbish 1970s paperback about skinhead boot boys and a scratched vinyl '45 of Burl Ives' 'Ugly Bug Ball' from a charity shop.

Funny-looking chocolate milkshake from a bottle shaped like a cow's udder; mysterious, vein-flecked cheeses from some village in Yorkshire; and weird, knobbly ethnic vegetables that I don't know how to cook.

Marinated artichoke quarters in oil, garlic and parsley – purely for the posh silver label: I'm a packaging magpie with far too much disposable income.

An orange-stickered tub of curried chickpea falafel bites, barely thirty seconds from the midnight chime of the display-by-date clock; the repackaged special-edition soundtrack from the film *Labyrinth*; and this month's *Teen TV Hits* magazine just for the free pencil case.

Bugger. I forgot the milk.

Indian Food

There's not much one can say about Indian food without lapsing into old Jasper Carrot routines. Suffice to say:

A small bottle of Cobra lager – £4.00.

A large, flavourless crisp served with green pickles and red coconut paste. Do you break the crisp with your hand or a knife? I never know.

Starters: a deep-fried artificially coloured yellow ball of onions. (Vile.) Hot prawn triangle made from soggy batter. (Useless.)

More starters: reconstituted red chicken pieces on wooden sticks. I always snap the sticks in order to sabotage their re-use.

A hot main course: four or five lumps of lamb, chicken or biriyani beef swimming in a red, yellow or beige stew.

One 'special' rice. Yes, right.

Flat bread (sometimes fried).

A disappointing dessert selection from the wholesaler – listed alongside lurid photographs on laminated menus. You can keep the container the vanilla ice cream came in – it's plastic and shaped like a penguin.

One slightly patronising hot towel wrapped in plastic and served in a plastic basket.

The waiter scrapes popadom crumbs from the white tablecloth with a knife – also slightly patronising. He doesn't care about the crumbs; he's just drawing your attention to red blotches on the white linen where you dripped your masala. The suggestion is: 'You eat like a pig.'

There's an Indian restaurant on London's Gray's Inn Road called Gandhi's. How marvellous, naming a velvet-draped masala trough after a spiritual leader famed for his rigorous fasts. Look, it's right next to Martin Luther King's Fried Chicken.

'Non-violent protests? He brought me the wrong starter so I threatened to slash his face with one of the larger bottles of Kingfisher beer (serves two).'

In-Flight Food

Air travel scares me. Is that Charlton Heston in the cockpit? George Kennedy is sweating like a hog in the control tower. Why is Jacqueline Bisset waving her skirt on the runway?

The red wire or the yellow wire?

Air travel scares me. The imperceptible physics of flight, 300-plus pages of Wilbur Smith, Billy Crystal films on four-inch screens, the possibility of sitting next to Ernest Borgnine . . .

'The chicken or the beef, sir?'

Intimidating Chefs

During the writing of this book I've eaten out a lot. My quest for tasty, reasonably priced food in pleasant surroundings with unhurried service has meant dining out most evenings, sometimes with friends, sometimes on my own, scribbling furiously on a notepad and trying to think of something faintly amusing to say about fennel.

I'm waiting for my main course of roast magret of duck

in an identikit gastropub in South Kensington. I'm researching herbs and looking at vintage steakhouse menus from the seventies that a friend gave me. I look up from my notepad (doodles, squiggles and notes on fennel – 'used as mouthwash by many Native American tribes' – more doodles) to see the chef standing over me. He's unshaven with long dirty-blond hair, is wearing a sauce-splattered apron and is scowling. This is what Klaus Kinski would look like if he'd been to catering college.

'Good scallops, mate?' he asks me, referring to my starter.

Why is he standing over me? Does he want a fight? Is it the menus and the notebook? Does he think I'm reviewing his food?

'Tricky fuckers, scallops. They fucking burn easier than your average fucking Austrian discothèque.'

Is he trying to shock me? I hate it when strangers call me 'mate'. What does he use to condition his hair? Someone should wash his mouth out with fennel.

Will he try to top the shock factor of the Austrian-discothèque jibe? Maybe he'll write a letter to a daily newspaper suggesting that women should return to petticoat-wearing. Maybe he'll carve a statue of Mussolini out of pork fat and enter it in a new art exhibition sponsored by a Norwegian mobile phone company?

Just when did it become acceptable to act like an obnoxious idiot simply because you know what terrine is or you can rustle up a five-kilo noisette of something with the jus of something else and a drizzle of some oily stuff? It's the whole 'rock star' factor; the idea that it's OK to act like an ill-mannered, foul-mouthed, loathsome oik just because you do something mildly creative.

These days everyone acts like an ill-mannered, self-centred idiot: Saturday-night drunks urinating in shop windows, footballers letting off fire-extinguishers and exposing themselves to chambermaids on mid-season shindigs to Dubai, vile city workers on bonus-day champagne-bar splurges. Grow up and learn some manners, the whole, horrible lot of you.

Learn some manners and don't forget to eat your greens, clean your plate and 'refrigerate after opening'.

'Scallops were lovely, thanks.'

That was a terrible response. I put down my pad. I still can't find anything amusing to write about fennel. He flicks his hair and struts back to the kitchen.

Irish Coffee

My childhood hero was a man called Brian Measures. He was the mellow, whispering, late-shift local-radio DJ who hosted the 'Plymouth Sound of Love'. He was silk-smooth. He had a voice like the man who advertised the Kipling cakes. He was on from ten till midnight; from the wind-down zone to the witching hour. 'Stay with us until the wee hours – go on, be a devil.' He politely thanked the newsreaders after the hourly update, using their first names even though the news bulletin was syndicated and arrived on the hour via a satellite feed from London to every in- dependent local-radio station in the country. Even I, at the age of eight, could see through his deception.

Measures played easy-listening sounds, orchestral versions of Beatles songs, Johnny Ray tracks and novelty records;

no wonder my parents worried. Measures worked up a rapport by letting his audience (the bedridden, the house-bound, the securely accommodated and me) in on the secret of his whispered inflections: the Irish coffee he drank.

Measures drank Irish coffee to loosen the nodes, smooth out the nodules and relax as he cued up the James Last Orchestra, Manuel and His Music of the Mountains or 'Teddy Bear' by Red Sovine (a creepy, spoken, Country song about a compassionate Trucker who was in CB-radio commu-nication with a crippled orphan boy in danger of dying).

Irish coffee still exists as an occasional treat; a cheeky 12.00 a.m. nightcap for couples cashing in their Air Miles at the Heathrow Holiday Lodge after a tiring day at Legoland Windsor with the grandchildren.

The waitress doesn't know how to mix it – she's from Warsaw. She calls the duty manager, who looks it up in a cocktail book with loose pages splattered with Crème de Menthe.

It's:

A measure or two Irish whiskey
     (They only have Jack Daniel's – they keep it for truck-drivers from Durham who are obsessed with Native American culture and call themselves Big Eagle.)
1 tablespoon brown raw cane sugar
     (Pink sachets of sugar substitute from the complimentary-coffee basket.)
1 heaped tablespoon whipped cream
     (Anchor. From a pressurised can.)
Hot strong coffee to fill the glass
     (Granules. Lukewarm tap water.)

'We wouldn't have bothered if we'd known it would be this much trouble. And we can't turn the heating off in the room. It's like a sauna in there.'

Irish Ham

My mum is Irish. She's great. I love her and I love the Irish. But whenever she goes 'home' she brings back a 'lovely Irish ham'.

'Taste that lovely Irish ham.' 'Sure, you wouldn't get ham like that over here.' 'Do you want another slice of lovely Irish ham?'

Mum, it's ham. It tastes the same wherever you buy it. The fact that it's Irish doesn't mean it's any better than any other kind of ham. Did it fight against the Black and Tans? Was the sacred Celtic pig blessed by his Holiness Pope John Paul II and Cardinal Cormac Murphy-O'Connor, leader of Britain's Catholics? Has it won the Eurovision Song Contest fourteen times in a row? Does it have a wistful outlook on life? Can it hold a tune on a penny whistle? Did it sing harmony in all-girl pop group B*Witched?

No. It's ordinary ham.

Italian Food

Until recently Britain had, for decades, been badly served for tasty, authentic Italian food.

The Anglo-Saxon desire to blandly appropriate foreign cooking styles, to top every dish with mountains of grated, melted Cheddar, to cover meats, pastas or vegetables with thin, sugary baked-bean-style tomato sauces, has, over the years, resulted in some truly terrible first-generation Anglo-Italian hybrid dishes; dishes that slandered the reputation of Italian cuisine from Land's End to John O'Groats, from Café Cockatoo to Pepe's Pizzeria and Pasta.

Despite some offputting experiences with Italian food – seaside trattorias and their reheated scampi ragus; gunky Cheddar-cheese carbonara sauces; puffy pizzas with diced ham from a can sprinkled over tinned tomatoes – I always knew that Italy, with its cuisine and culture, was somewhere special.

A school skiing trip to the Dolomites when I was fourteen confirmed this. Dishes were christened 'gnocchi', 'zappa' and 'ziti'. Names that sounded snot-dribblingly amusing when bellowed at bored Italian waiters by fifty-five English schoolkids on an après-ski high. I ate fine spaghetti in clam sauce. I ate all manner of pastas, none of which were shaped like letters of the alphabet, wands or small stars, nor Barbie nor Action Man. Vinegar was sharp, fruity and used for more than just splashing violently over cod, chips and frittered spam.

Fresh Italian ice cream containing juicy chunks of fresh fruit and exotic, strangely shaped nuts came in the colours of the rainbow and was served from chilled steel counters in ice-cream parlours, not just from the type of white plastic tub that weird kids used as school lunchboxes as soon as the last of the vanilla soft-scoop had been eaten.

Incidentally, the kids that used old tubs of vanilla ice cream for lunchboxes were also the kids with the lemon-curd sandwiches for lunch every day, jumper sleeves that overran their hands, and glasses with aviator frames and thick prescription lenses. They were also the kids who'd spent the whole school day picking their noses, talking to themselves and referring to everyone – boy, girl, animal, parent, brother, sister or teacher – as 'Thingy'.

Yes, I fell in love with Italy. The television over there was practically all football – football that was paced, measured and not played by clogging, moustachioed, monosyllabic beer-drinkers wearing silky shirts sponsored by Crown Paints – and manic variety shows featuring curvy topless housewives stripping to their frilly Continental pants for tumble dryers and million-lira cheques, followed by perky mice marionettes dancing and miming to 'Chove Chuva' and 'Love Me Do'. (I witnessed a larger, hippo puppet made from Tuscan wood sing 'O Sole Mio' before, thankfully, it was back to Italian chicks wearing pants and very little else.)

Yes, Italian cooking in Britain has improved since those dark days of bleached-white pastas and thin, metallic tomato sauces. But buyers beware, as bland, ersatz Italian food is still available in establishments (usually named Luigi's La Colosseum Italiano) all over the country.

These bogus bistros and replica ristorantes can be spotted by anyone with a keen cultural eye and love of genuine Roman cuisine. Your waiter is called Mick-o. He's from Brisbane and wears a beaded necklace. Plastic vine leaves cling to PVC stucco walls; and on the counter, next to the bowl of complimentary Fox's Glacier Mints, there's a plaster-of-Paris bust of Caesar Augustus. At least I think it's Caesar Augustus. It could be Neil Kinnock in olive-branch headgear during some sort of loopy European Commission induction ceremony; it's barely visible through the flickering glow of a candle in a wicker-covered bottle.

I propose an EU-initiated, Europe-wide authentication system for genuine Italian eateries: fresh pastas made on the premises, meaty sauces, garden herbs, clams fresh from the shell, homemade Italian sausage, all menu items listed in the mother tongue – no lazy English translations – and lifesize busts, hand-chipped from genuine Carrara marble, of Maria, the half-naked housewife, jiggling for cash and Zanussi white goods, and Topo Gigio, the dancing mouse marionette.

Jellied Eels

Cockneys: working-class Londoners born within the chimes of Bow Bells. Several things unite the men and women of East London:

1) A pasty complexion;
2) A love of 'the Hammers';
3) A mother that worked as a cleaner for fifty-three years;
4) A crippling fear that someday their daughter will marry a black man; and
5) A taste for eels served in jelly with pie and mash.

Jumbo Prawns

Before 1984, no one I know had ever eaten a jumbo prawn. In the salmon-paste and crab-stick world of postwar

Britain, jumbo prawns existed only in the tall tales of ancient mariners. When I was ten I thought jumbo prawns were served out of monkey heads as in the maharaja's banquet in *Indiana Jones and the Temple of Doom*. When presented with fanned melon with jumbo prawns in Marie Rose sauce, served in a tall wineglass at a posh cousin's wedding, it was like being offered Jupiterian floating space squid on a bed of sentient Vulcan lettuce.

In 2003, an Environmental Justice Foundation report highlighted the massive waste and destruction behind prawn-fishing. Apparently, prawn fisheries are responsible for one third of the world's discarded catch, despite producing less than two per cent of global seafood.

Steve Trent, director of the Environmental Justice Foundation, urged consumers to boycott supermarket prawns unless they come from environmentally and socially sustainable sources.

All well and good Steve, but what am I supposed to put in my hollowed-out avocado? Huh? Huh?

As a self-confessed animal-hater my all-time favourite sandwich is prawn mayo, heavy on the prawns. For £1.60 I can eat hundreds of the little fuckers.

Jus

Hmmm. I'll have the chicken breast in the watercress-and-plum jus . . . That'll be gravy, then?

Kebabs

Before last week I'd never eaten a kebab or so much as stepped one foot over the threshold of a doner shop. There were no doner shops in Plymouth when I was growing up so I've always associated 'kebab' with cubed-food selections (meat/green pepper/meat/red pepper/onion/meat) barbecued and served on scary metal skewers. I'm not a sword-swallower, I could never see the point in grilled peppers and I've always harboured a fear of being impaled on a sharp, twisted steel spike.

I've also been deterred by the brown, sweaty tube of lamb in the window, displayed like a rancid, rotating, rotting-from-the-inside mutton mannequin – it always put me in mind of the slowly spinning blood-and-bandages sign over the doors of gentlemen's barbers, the kind of 'no unisex please, we're British' establishments that sell combs from cardboard displays and musky Vitalis hair tonic while offering *Titbits* (a proto lad-mag for men with dandruff shampoo and loose teeth), an 'adult' joke book and non-sequential issues from part-published periodicals about the Third Reich as waiting-room reading material.

So, last week, buoyed by cloudy Dutch-lager courage – and putting aside fevered free-thought associations that linked doner kebabs with bloody bandages, tubs of Brylcreem for slick centre partings (centre partings are long overdue for revival; carry that thought to bed with you tonight and see if you get any sleep), men's hair on checked plastic-tile floors and single gents waiting for the communal clippers while reading about Second Panzer Division or staring at their shoes – I crept inside Kebab King and, after fifteen full minutes of acute menu anxiety and rotating-meat-induced hypnosis, ordered a lamb special: one authentic, spicy kebab; one warm can of fizzy orange to wash it down with; and £1.80 change from the grubbiest £5.00 note I could find.

The man behind the counter with the splattered apron and severed earlobe carved three strips from the thick, slippery pipe of lamb with a huge serrated knife. My stomach turned as the meat dropped into the pitta-bread halves – pitta-bread halves that were both bleached-white and spotted with brown freckles, like Auntie's legs on the first sunny day of the year.

The Kebab King was full of drunks – shouting, swearing and holding back the sick. One was singing 'Save Your Love'; one bartered over a falafel filling; one made a vulgar joke that associated the pale, floppy pitta pockets with the anatomy of the mother of someone he knew called Monkey Dave.

My pitta pockets were filled with raw red onions, shrivelled jalapeño peppers and not-so-choice chunks of iceberg lettuce – all crunchy white stalk and no green leaf – and a squirt of some special 'Persian' sauce from a see-through squeezy bottle.

I was ten minutes from home so I tucked the warm, wrapped kebab into my holdall, dodged the drunks and flagged down the bus.

Back home, I examined my purchase. The special Persian sauce had seeped through the paper bag and stained that gas bill I'd been meaning to pay since March: deep-red spicy glue splashed on scary, red-topped notepaper. Final-demand fear and sticky sauce. The salad and peppers had slipped out of the bread pockets and were sliding around the paper bag.

The whole thing was a mess. The raw, sauce-covered salad and strips of battleship-grey meat swimming around in that warm, wet, sauce-soaked paper package filled my lager-fuzzed head with appalling associated images: meat spinning in the window, carved via a jagged Forty Thieves-style sword, unwashed for centuries; the bloody barbershop sign; being shaved by a cut-throat razor; haircut sweepings; and some bloke called Monkey Dave and his mum.

The kebab went in the bin. I wolfed a bowl of cold milk and Frosties and retired to bed for nightmares about dirty lamb meat turning slowly on a heated spit, the return of the Third Reich and the centre parting.

Kiddie Food

Feed the little ones 'fun' cheese chunks: a child's daily recommended dose of calcium disguised as stodgy gender stereotypes – fairy wands or all-terrain armoured tanks. Dish out a distressing slice of luncheon meat presented as a two-tone teddy-bear face; reconstituted-turkey triangles in soggy breadcrumbs – mass marketed as terrifying T-Rex teeth; or 'fun' dried fruit in a 'fun'-sized sealed sachets.

You have to sympathise with parents today: it's impossible to get children to eat anything that isn't pink, topped with a smooth cheese spread or shaped like space pirates or nunchukas.

Parents: wrap up crunchy carrot batons and label them

as 'fun' space lasers. Serve the sprogs golden beetroot and make-believe they're from Mars.

Kids: I'm not sure where the fun comes into any of these products. Maybe you can flick the rubbery cheese triangles at your little brother. Maybe you can watch your dad's face turn crimson when you refuse to eat such tawdry, condescending fare and say: 'Dad, I'm eight. I'm a little old for that "Open for the choo-choo" shtick, *n'est-ce pas*? I need to be challenged as well as fed.'

When I look after my sister's kids I prepare only healthy snacks; *creative* healthy snacks, like chopped and cubed fresh apples attached, with colourful cocktail sticks, to half a grapefruit, or an organic fruit salad arranged in smiley faces on plastic plates.

I also forbid them to watch their *Sesame Street* educational video tape. Not that I have anything against learning through repetition or fuzzy-felt puppets (in fact I have based my table manners on Cookie Monster's biscuit-scoffing technique). It's just that Big Bird's androgynous passive-zealous demeanour brings back memories of an unpleasant verbal encounter – while at college – with the recruitment representative from the Campus Crusade for Christ.

Kitchen Gadgets

It slices, it dices, it chops and it grates. It's endorsed by a top TV chef. It's manufactured from a space-age alloy liquid-metal. It's designed by the chief engineer for SAAB – he rattled it off in five minutes between dashboards. It's made for thirty pence by Filipino infants working nineteen-hour shifts and sleeping on the factory floor.

Kiwi Fruit

Awww, furry food. Can I keep it as a pet?

Knickerbocker Glory

The knickerbocker glory, a layered dessert served in a tall glass and made with ice cream, tinned peaches, chocolate or fruit sauce and strawberry pureé, was the first postwar dessert to be served in Britain that didn't contain suet.

For a young male aged between eight and fourteen in the 1980s, the knickerbocker glory was the greatest sensual experience one could imagine . . . Greater, even, than being interfered with by Bananarama.

The Krypton Factor

I decree that all cafés, restaurants, bars, bistros and snack shops in Great Britain and Northern Ireland should henceforth trade under proper, descriptive names . . .

Chez Pierre; Fred's Reasonably Good Café; Marco's Quiet Seaside Trattoria that Does a Nice Squashed-Tomato Bruschetta; The Prime Rib and Lemon Sorbet Shack; A Taste of Exeter.

They should not be named after individual ingredients

(Plum, Fennel, Cinnamon, Gravy, Pepper, Cumin) or one-word food-related terms (Feast, Gastro, Mange, Dine, Eat, Drink, Man, Woman).

Kai-Chai? (the question mark comes with the name). Isn't that Superman's Kryptonian birth name? What the fuck does it have to do with pricey noodles? H8: it's a great name for a pencil but I wouldn't want to eat there.

Lasagne and Chips

A not-so-clever British twist on the Italian classic. It's a lasagne but made with a spoilt beef filling and a powdered cheese-sauce; it comes with a side portion of moist chips and half a pound of sweaty Cheddar cheese on top.

We just can't leave well enough alone.

I ordered Stilton lasagna and curly fries in a pub last year. It was hands-down the worst meal I've ever eaten.

It tasted like paint.

Latte

Latte is merely milky coffee masquerading as a perky, quirky, upwardly mobile lifestyle choice. It's Mellow Birds for Pearl Jam fans and families who fret about collecting too few Computers for Schools tokens and took the park-and-ride to a Stop the War march.

Lemon Fresh

I can't bring myself to use lemon on my food any more. I can't drink traditional lemonade. I won't squirt my beer-battered cod with that bitter fruit wedge or squeeze its juice on my Shrove Tuesday supper.

In my eyes, the lemon has been devalued for perpetuity by detergents, lemon-fresh bottled bleaches, washing-up liquids and mosquito sprays.

Lemon-shaped air-fresheners and scented, antibacterial kitchen wipes have conspired to rob me of citrus as an ingredient for desserts and biscuits and a garnish for fish dishes and side salads.

What was wrong with the pine tree as the global standard metaphor for freshness?

Thanks a bunch, Unilever.

And I can't even look at a black cherry after all those flavoured antiseptic sweets I sucked on last winter.

Procter & Gamble, keep your bastard hands off the grapefruit.

LIDL

You have to love LIDL, the chain of German discounters that have opened stores in fifth-string retail parks all over Britain in recent years. You have to love their bargain prices, the spicy smell of their superstores (that turns out to be damp packing cardboard); and the 'Gruess Got, who the hell . . . ?!' obscure brands they sell.

When shopping there, I try to pretend that I'm in some

sort of DC Comics-style mirror universe; on a parallel Earth where the food, beverage, branding and advertising capital of the world is Stuttgart. Some sort of evil Bavarian empire stretches across Europe, from the Minsk to Merthyr. Times are hard, civil liberties have been eroded and the populace are oppressed. It's not all bad, though – Crusty Croc Cream Crackers are thirty-nine pence a pack.

Little Man cornflakes; Sunny Glade baked beans with mini-bratwurst; Air Freeze menthol chewing gum; Vitakrone tomato ketchup; Mondos fruity condoms; Eruption for Men cologne. That's your LIDL shopping list. Here's your change from £10.00, and a packet of Grafschafler chocolate biscuits to go with your Baron Knuffer premium teabags. Just make sure you're home before curfew.

Low-Fat Cheese on Toast

Melt, you bastard, melt!

Luncheon Vouchers

The Luncheon scheme provided a method by which employers could issue employees with tokens to be exchanged for food and drink at participating cafés, restaurants, sandwich shops and convenience stores.

Luncheon Vouchers are redolent of wildcat strikes, race riots, donkey jackets and men in pork-pie hats who smell of Golden Virginia and Old Holborn and sneak out of work at lunchtimes to bet on the 'gee-gees'.

They're as close as Britain ever got to communism.

Luxury Ranges

Enjoy our luxury range of foods: the premium selection; connoisseur range; our *finest*. Try our Special Reserve Chicken Dippers, matured for twenty-one days in a mango marinade in oak casks.

Pre-packaged luxury foods are a shrewd attempt by the major supermarkets to replicate the experience of dining in a top restaurant or recommended bistro, and make you feel a bit special.

You can spot a supermarket's luxury range by the packaging. Luxury ranges are presented in silver, gold and deep purples, the exact same colours as the vestments of High Church traditions and the packaging of high-tar cigarettes.

Macaroons

Coconut cakes served on edible paper. They're delicious; you can even eat the paper. They don't count as one of your five-a-day. I've checked.

Make-Your-Own Sundaes

Buckled, rusting shopping trolleys dumped in muddy canals. Spongy, combustible sofas with rusty metal frames left abandoned at park gates. Ratty flyers for ethical circuses, steam fairs and Ministry of Shite *Maximum Bass* compilation CDs pasted on to abandoned shop windows at irritating asymmetrical angles. Rose beds flattened maliciously by ice-white Reebok Classics and tedious teenage pranksters pouring washing-up liquid into municipal fountains erected in order to mark the millennium.

Yes, you can be sure that if there's a communal space the British will abuse it, misuse it, gob spittle and dental chewing-gum on the pavement beside it and have a cheeky little widdle on it after closing time.

The 'make-your-own ice-cream sundae' sections in high-street pizza restaurants are no exception: the Smarties are scattered all over the sunken tub of chocolate buttons; tacky, melting ice cream is slathered over chopped nuts; troubling smudges and sinister smears lurk on the sneeze-guard.

'There's a man with a beard and a dirty wax jacket hovering near the raspberry sauce. He smells of damp nutmeg. He has his back turned. I can't see what he's doing.'

It's chaos – a chocolate-sprinkled, synthetic vanilla-centric microcosm of urban Britain.

Mango Chutney

I call it 'happy pickle'. It's sweeter than a salsa; thinner and sharper than a preserve. I'm using it as a dip for spiced mini-popadoms as I write this piece. There are raisins and sticky chutney smears on my laptop keyboard.

Until recently, chutney was the only mango-related product available to buy in Britain. Now you can't move for the slimy, slithery fruit in smoothies and fruit salads.

I started serving mango in chunky, blocky hedgehog-type shapes – a throwback to the days when radishes were cut in order to resemble waterlilles, cucumbers were contorted and tucked-in like Romanian gymnasts and tomatoes were served in the shape of dead spiders.

There I was, happily cutting my mango – using, as a guide, that porcupine-shaped pencil-holder designed in Milan that sits on my sideboard – when someone told me that the edible part of the mango was called the 'flesh'. It put me off. It made my hands go all weak. It made my entire body go weak, like when someone's talking about their operation or having their widsom teeth removed, or when I see one of those painfully thin female long-distance runners on the Olympics.

'Don't worry about gold medals and personal bests. For the love of God, eat something.'

The Manor

Every area in Britain has its own special-occasion venue. It could be an out-of-town, ivy-clad manor, a regal, Grade

Two-listed steakhouse or a Jacobean country house nestled in a hillside hamlet. Perhaps it's a French-style shooting lodge that serves buckshot-smoked fresh game and roast fox in hound-sized chunks; a converted riverside mill or restored rectory with a chef from Naples and one of those unsatisfying menu options where you can sample everything in small bites for £80.00 per head including three glasses of English Riesling.

Maybe your nearest special-occasion venue is a cove hotel with multiple Michelin stars and a saucier with an accent, several rosettes, a fistful of blue ribands and a busy sampling spoon.

It could even be a grange – whatever the fuck that is.

A manor, a castle, a mill, a hunting lodge or a grange: it doesn't matter which – they're all special-occasion venues with big local reputations and three-star restaurants that are 'thoroughly recommended' by flimsy free guidebooks with suspicious 'sponsored' reviews.

I was once a guest at a wedding in a Scottish castle. Don't judge me too harshly, though – I'm not posh. I'm still the son of a dinnerlady, I've still never been to a dinner party or a black/white-tie ball and I've been sick in a moat.

As a rule, manor hotels are situated on the outskirts of places described as 'historic', which means they have cobbles (olde English paving that serves no purpose other than to turn the ankles of coach-tripping pensioners), a cathedral that charges a general admission, a shop that just sells teddy bears and several gift boutiques that sell sea-shell dream-catchers, shrink-wrapped chakra stones (repurposed cobbles loosened by falling pensioners), coat-hangers stuffed with dried lavender, perfumed pine balls to rattle around in your underwear drawer and scent your smalls with synthetic apple and cinnamon, old-fashioned peanut brittle and eighteen different varieties of Devon double-cream fudge.

I booked a table at a top manor-house restaurant for my parents' wedding anniversary last month. It was located just a few miles from a motorway. Dad drove while I navigated, following the signs for the local theme park with its single stationary steamroller, pottery marquee (seasonal attraction), pony rides (small charges), educational exhibit (a bunker containing ex-C&A mannequins in gas masks plus rusty tins of tea and Bird's custard from 1941), bouncy castle (patched up with masking tape and Juicy Fruit), and feed-the-foals enclosure (behind rusty railings).

Taking a sharp left after the South Devon Glass-Spider-Blowing Centre and Tin Machine Museum, we drove straight past the thatched inn with the beer garden and three-acre children's play area containing a fibreglass Old Mother Hubbard's Shoe and a seven-foot-high polythermoplastic Cinderella's Pumpkin that made the local news in 1987 when it blew on to the main road during the 'Michael Fish' storm.

We took a sharp right after the lock-keeper's cottage – the one that's currently a herbal teashop and, after turning left at the ancestral hall that's been converted into a commune by the charismatic cult from California (you can't miss it; there's a purple glass pyramid next to the gazebo), we arrived at our destination.

This particular South Devon manor boasted a six-hole golf course, a sweeping croquet lawn and a cattle-grid entrance. The fountain in the stately forecourt was non-functioning because of the water shortage (a notice in the foyer said so, with profuse apologies and an emphasis on the optional, ecological bath-towel re-use policy in the rooms).

The gift shop sold golfing supplies (plush badger five-iron covers and floppy baseball caps with two crossed clubs embroidered on the forehead and a single thread of gold cord across the peak. I thought about buying one, but the caps were far too floppy to be hip and far too golf to be hip-hop).

It also stocked sterling silver souvenir spoons in plastic presentation cases and luxurious dressing-gowns in a fluffy forest green with the hotel's name embroidered in an off-the-shelf serif script.

The manor had first-class fitness facilities, colonial-style verandas, refurbished church pews in a bar called The Bishop's with local ales, quick snacks and daily blackboard specials, and a four-star restaurant with a fixed-price menu.

We were dining in the four-star silver-service restaurant – Chez Some Ex-Pat Belgian or Other.

I was impressed. The restaurant had an almost papal gold and terracotta colour scheme and crisp, white linen tablecloths. It had lovingly restored antiques – bolted down and checked off on a clipboard inventory twice daily after multiple incidents during the Lottery-winner's wedding (that was the same night that the in-house harpist broke a plucking finger). It had a no-under-twelves rule for reasons of decorum and a smart dress code – no sandals, T-shirts, tight glittery tops that spell 'Sexy' in pasted-on rhinestone, or short skirts. The sign outside the restaurant, above the leather-bound Sunday-specials menu, read: 'No jeans, jean-jackets or training shoes'.

I can't remember the last time I saw someone wearing a jean-jacket.

On the table next to us two sets of future in-laws were checking out the hotel as a reception venue and getting to know each other. It was a complete social mismatch: Joe and Rose Kennedy meet Terry and June; one pair picking at diced pork belly and braised guinea fowl while the other ate penne pasta and rump steak with frites.

Next to them sat a married couple who weren't talking. I riffed possible narratives in my head, eventually deciding that they were dining out as part of a last-resort reconciliation meal. The wife ate like a bird and even had a bird's plumage: canary-yellow blonde hair, short, spiked and sticking out at the back. As a rule, women with those haircuts always peck at their food like parakeets.

She also wore a woollen shawl with fraying fringes and a cod-Celtic brooch in the shape of a leaf. The leaf had a plastic emerald in the centre. It defined the word 'trinket'. I'd wager that she hadn't worn that shawl for years – not since that pre-Christmas trip to London in 2001 for the seasonal lights, shopping in Selfridges and stall seats for *Phantom* or that lame dance troupe from somewhere shite like Seattle who bang dustbin lids while shuffling sideways like grungy, poorly choreographed crabs.

When you're at the theatre or dining out in granges or manors you can always spot the women who haven't been taken out in six years – they're wearing shawls or cheap fur coats; woollen shawls like the girls from Clannad on a pub crawl, or tatty fur coats, like Background Hooker #3 on *Hill Street Blues*.

The husband, who wore chinos and a polo shirt, was

staring at the brown, mushy loin of something on his plate, wondering, so I reckoned, whether it would be OK to use his hands.

Most of the diners kept quiet. They were British and it was a special occasion so heads were bowed and conversation kept to whispers. The only significant noise was coming from the family group by the door. They were there for their daughter's eighteenth birthday. They were a breath of fresh air. They all looked smart. They talked and laughed out loud. Unlike the couple-in-trouble or the prospective in-laws, they seemed to like each other. The daughter opened a giant, quilted birthday card with a stuck-on plastic key and a plush teddy bear holding a synthetic satin heart. Then she unwrapped a small die-cast Volkswagen Polo. She squealed and clapped her hands together.

Back to our table and it's Rod and Ronnie Lampen's thirtieth wedding anniversary. We didn't do the 'presents at the table' thing – it's too showy and we'd performed the gift-giving ritual before before we left. Dad got Jeff Wayne's *War of the Worlds* on a remastered double CD. Mum got an amber pendant shaped like a flower. They both agreed on a half-share in a juicer.

Thirty years of marriage. Mum said, 'You'd get less for murder,' and laughed, just like she does every year, before scanning through the bill of fare, eyes peeled for the lasagne – always a safe bet. She couldn't spot anything familiar, just strange cuts of meat with fruit purées; fishy terrines and assorted chunks of half-cooked flesh wrapped in Parma ham.

Dad studied the wine list – £30.00 for a Sauvignon Blanc. 'The wine prices in these manor restaurants, they're a complete swizzle.'

'Dad. It's my money. I'm paying, that's the way of the world when it comes to wine, and there's no such word as "swizzle".'

Dad settled on a £25.00 bottle of white, which we shared between the two of us because Mum was on designated-driver duties. He then geared up to order for the three of us. Whenever my dad orders at a half-decent restaurant he acts like he's never ordered food before in his life. His eyes widen like a neglected fun-park foal caught in dipped fun-park go-kart headlights; he pauses, he hesitates and, showing stress, he strokes his silvery moustache.

I plumped for the whole grouse in vanilla gravy. Mum went for the duck with orange jelly and five-spice mash. The menu didn't reveal what the five surreptitious spices were; she wasn't sure if she'd like it and didn't care to ask the waiter – he'd asked four times during her lengthy deliberations if we were ready to order.

Me: 'Make your mind up, Mum. You're not choosing the new Pope.'

Dad: 'You can always scrape the mash off if you don't fancy any of the five spices, Mum.'

Me: 'Dad. Don't call Mum "Mum". She's not your mum, she's your wife and this is your anniversary treat.'

In the absence of lasagne Mum always goes for the duck dish, regardless of the sauce or side dish. I'm convinced it's just because duck gives her the opportunity to say, 'Duck is lovely – but it's fatty and there's not much meat on it.'

'Mum. You say that every year. It's the nature of the beast that quacks. Order a starter, order something different or learn to temper your once-a-year cooked-mallard expectations.'

My dad goes for the lamb shank. Lamb bloody shanks – our era's sausage in a basket. I'm sick to the back teeth of them, sitting there on beds of herb mash, surrounded by caramelised shallots, red-onion slop, redcurrant jus or gunky butternut-squash mush. And that bloody big bone sticking up in the air at an angle – it's disturbing; like the favoured left leg of a first-team footballer on the receiving end of a career-endangering tackle.

I adjusted my attention – away from Dad's disturbing lamb dish back to the prospective-in-laws table. I could make out some contradictory meeting-of-the-families cross-talk: holidays in Southern France on one side of the table; stand-up tanning booths on the other.

Another cross-table rally: a recent fishing weekend in Iceland verses the groom's little sister and her 'excellent GCSE results'.

When I turned back, Dad was scraping Mum's five-spice mash on to his plate. She didn't like it; it was 'too spicy'. Mum scanned the hall while Dad scraped the mash – she was keeping watch for the maître d' as if sharing food was likely to get us kicked out of the hotel.

Dad had eaten his lamb. All that was left was that freaky bone and a puddle of apricot-and-Stilton jus. I couldn't bear to look at it. It makes my leg ache (an old five-a-side injury). He was eating the mash under duress; just because he doesn't like to see good food wasted.

'Dad, since you've finished your dinner, it might be better to swap plates rather than scrape the mash from Mum's plate on to yours. It's a simple manoeuvre, less likely to attract attention from other diners and disapproving wait staff.'

The waiter collected our plates – Dad had stacked Mum's on top of his; uneaten butternut squash squeezed out the side – and offered the dessert menu. Dad said, 'Go on . . . Why not.' Then he laughed.

Bugger, I'm turning into my dad.

My mum is such a wiz with puddings, cakes and fruit pies that, when dining out, she's loath to pay £5.00 to £8.00 for a single slice of something sticky. Whenever she serves homemade 'duff' at home she repeats the mantra: 'That same slice of cake would cost you £6.00 in Dingle's fifth-floor café – £6.00 for a single serving of ginger sponge and a small jug of cream! It's all a hobble.'

'Mum. They have overheads. Fresh cream isn't free, glacé cherries don't grow on trees, centrepiece flower arrangements cost cold, hard cash, Polish waitresses don't work for peanuts, those chintzy antiques don't clean themselves and there's no such word as "hobble".'

Mum was getting edgy. She was our designated driver and she only ever drives on certain occasions – special-occasion trips to Grade Two-listed steakhouses or manor-house restaurants; occasions that call for shawls, brooches or new handbags; occasions that occur once every six years.

As I dealt with the bill, trying to hide the total from my parents, Mum fretted over the drive home: the roads were dark, the hour was late and the signposting was poor. I must admit, she had a point.

In the car Dad suggested some music for the trip. I rattled around in the glove compartment for a tape. I found Jeff Wayne's *War of the Worlds* on an audio cassette from the Britannia Music Club. I bought him that for

Father's Day when I was ten. Come to think of it, I've bought him at least half a dozen versions – on vinyl, cassette, CD, remastered CD with dance mix – over the years. I'm not even sure he likes Jeff Wayne's *War of the Worlds*.

Dad gripped the seat. I leant forward from the back seat – in between the two front seats – to help navigate.

As it turned out, Mum's fear of driving in the dark was unfounded. The moors were well lit by a full moon and we were able to follow the curves of the narrow road by the glow radiating from the candlelit procession outside the ex-ancestral home that now housed the secretive sect from San Diego. We turned off just as our full-glare headlights bounced off Old Mother L. Ron Hubbard's fibreglass shoe in the playground of the Plough Inn and rolled on to the motorway at a careful thirty miles per hour as soon as we could hear the echoed braying of the fenced-in fun-park ponies.

Margarine

Margarine is an artificial butter made from oils and used by slimmers, baking fans and single men called Ray who spend Saturday afternoons in betting shops and keep brown, tortoiseshell-textured combs in the back pocket of their grey slacks.

Marks & Spencer Food Hall

It's a measure of the affection in which the Marks & Spencer Food Hall is held by the British public (or at least by the cross-section of the British public who own a minimum of one breathable-fleece jacket) that Marks & Spencer is referred to by multiple nicknames.

'Marks', 'Marks & Sparks', 'M & S' or 'Muffin & Snookums'. No other retailer or brand is held in such high regard as St Michael. No other retailer or brand has been clutched so tightly to the breathable-fleece-clad bosom of Mr and Mrs Discerning High Street Shopper.

My parents have always called it 'Marksie's'. They've never given me or my sister affectionate nicknames; only Marks & Spencer.

I once worked with someone – we'll call him Jez – who referred to Sainsbury's and Tesco as 'Sasbos' and 'Tezzas'. Then again, he also insisted on referring to every type of food, snack, meal or repast as 'tuck'.

'I'm off to the shops now – anyone want any tuck?' 'I made some great tuck last night.' 'Is anyone else working late? I was going to order some tuck and I need the marketing-department cost code.'

He also wore a black fisherman's cap indoors, along with oversized Michael Caine-type specs, called his holidays his 'holibobs' and spent every single minute of the working day on the phone, talking to someone called Becca.

Marmalade

I'm not eating that. It's got bits in it.

Meal Deal

A sandwich, a packet of crisps and a 500ml bottle of brand-name fizzy soda. Mix and match any three stickered items. Buy two and get the third free. That's your meal deal, Jack. Now scuttle back to your office and finish fiddling last week's timesheets, book the big meeting room, write that strategy document that no one will ever read, or do whatever it is you do.

Boots the Chemist offer a £3.30 meal deal – one of the most competitive on the high street. But (apart from the most promiscuous of reward-card sluts) who in the flaming fuck would want to buy their lunch from Boots?

I couldn't find the shower gel in Boots last week. It was hidden behind the low-fat cheese-and-chive Snack-a-Jacks and the Father's Day Silverstone Racing 'Experience' gift packs.

It's all a far cry from twenty years ago, when Boots made most of their money from selling home-brew kits, Polaroid cameras and high-strength Night Nurse liquid cough medicine . . . Thus being the only British high-street store to cater entirely for deviants.

Meals on Wheels

One of my earliest memories of eating out is during a family trip to London in 1982. The purpose of the trip was to see the Pope at Wembley Stadium, but we also did a lot of shopping. I shopped for pens, a polyester T-shirt, a die-cast London bus and a fake camera keyring that presented six views of the city in slide-show form when held up to the light. It snapped outside the London Dungeon.

We wore matching anoraks that folded up, saw Michael Crawford in *Barnum* and ate at an American-style diner with plastic *Happy Days*-style décor where the waitresses wore rollerskates.

Rollerskates had been huge in the seventies. Everything was on skates.

The 1975 movie *Rollerball*, starring James Caan, depicted a dystopian society of 2018 where a brutal full-contact ball game played on skates was used as a substitute for war.

All well and good, but the film-makers overlooked the fact that anything performed on rollerskates, even an apocalyptic movie murder mystery, is 'a bit gay'.

Medallions

I recommend the medallions of venison with nectarine jus. Feast on our medallions of pork with a cognac-and-pepper sauce.

Here's a replica of a rare Roman coin – from 54 AD, with the head of Claudia Octavia – carved out of fucking veal.

Mediterranean-Style

Let's visit the Mediterranean. Let's go in a group. Let's take a charter flight from the West Midlands and sing rude songs about drinking, bra straps and Spanish women as we descend.

Let's wearily reprise the same songs on the eighty-kilometre bus ride from the out-of-town airport to the beach resort.

'There are no seats left on the bus. We can either stand up or wait four hours for it to return. 'Can I have a show of hands . . . ?'

Anyway, we're here now, soaking up the sun and reflecting on how the Med is a bloody big place; it's a vast geographical region that takes us from Tangier to Lebanon; it includes Southern Spain, France, Cyprus, Malta, the Balearic Islands, Turkey, Syria, Bosnia-Herzegovina and Israel. Its peoples include Jews, Muslims, Roman Catholics, goat-herders with crooks and missing teeth, and worshippers of orthodox Christian faiths with gold-leaf church interiors, bearded priests, chanting and funny mitres.

Marvels of the Mediterranean include stone ruins, sandy beaches, hillside villages and fire-trap nightclubs with faulty foam machines.

You get the idea: it's a big, diverse place.

Why, then, does anything sold in Britain under the banner 'Mediterranean-style' consist of peppers and tomatoes? Maybe there's an olive in there somewhere, but basically its peppers and sundried tomatoes slicked in cheap, yellow oil.

Supermarket buyers and restaurateurs: if you described your dips, marinades or sauces for chicken as coming from Narnia it would be only slightly less nebulous a fucking culinary concept.

(See also Mezze Platter.)

Mélange and Medley

Why not try the *mélange* of mango, pineapple and melon in a citrus-and-chyme dressing?

Or the medley of baby corn, carrot sticks, mange tout and sugar snaps . . . ?

'*Mélange*' means 'mixture'. That's all: mixture. Chyme is the semisolid substance found in the stomach during digestion. I include 'chyme' in order to throw you; to shake you from your complacency over grandiose menu taxonomies.

The suggestion that ingredients have been grouped together to form a 'medley' is just as upsetting. Medley: it's a blanket term that I tend to associate with middle-aged bar bands performing their tributes to the Blues Brothers.

Four bloated white men called Steve in shiny black suits from the Great Universal Catalogue segue into to a hideous cover of 'Mustang Sally', as chyme passes through my pyloric valve into my duodenum.

Menus

Before choosing where to dine I always ask to see the menu. I never bother with the menu outside – the menu that's glass-framed and mounted next to a favourable review in yellow, sun-scorched newsprint, clipped from the local paper in 1994, thirteen years and eight head chefs ago. The newspaper review is still attached to an unrelated article about a fourteen-year-old boy; he's been sent home from secondary school – suspended on account of his severely shaved hair. The article is more interesting than the menu.

I say: 'Just think: he probably has children of his own now with their own severely shaven hair.'

Other potential diners browsing the mounted menu move away from me.

Yes, I bypass the mounted menu and ask inside for the bill of fare proper. I check the paper it's printed on, rubbing it between my thumb and forefinger to inspect its grain, awarding extra points for tempting desserts and raised prints in glossy inks.

I check for lurid sausage or scampi snapshots; for poor-quality printing on flimsy A4 from fifth-grade desktop-publishing packages. I check for labels stuck over text – cheapskate bistros often overlay price changes on adhesive labels rather than ask the printer for a quote.

And I check for brand-name tie-ins – a sure sign of defrosted desserts.

Beware the Grand Marnier gateau with the liqueur's brand logo printed alongside. The same goes for the scallops in Cointreau, the Rémy Martin pot au chocolat and the Nescafé-subsidised after-dinner drinks.

Meringue Nests

I always keep a box of meringue nests in my cupboard in case of emergencies. They're right at the back, next to that Michael Caine movie on DVD that came free with the *Sunday Times*, the half-bottle of Rose's lime cordial and the box of condoms I over-optimistically bought in 1997.

Meringue nests are made from egg white and sugar and always remind me of the Artex ceiling on my parents' first bungalow. Fill them with whipped cream, fresh raspberries, tinned peach halves, deep-fried Brie wedges. Whatever you like – it's a free country.

Mexican Food

It's impossible to find decent Mexican food in Britain. That's not counting supermarket chilli con carne for two and bastard-snack hybrids like the chilled three-cheese-and-Mexican-bean wrap in a sweet chilli salsa in a cracked-black-pepper tortilla.

The only Mexican foods you can buy in Britain are those Old El Presidente kits that contain four buttercup-yellow taco shells, a small packet of powdered chilli that looks like something a corrupt cop would plant on a suspect in an American movie starring Kurt Russell, and tiny, dribbling sachets of hot sauce.

Just add supermarket minced beef, fried in oil until mud brown, and cue up that scratched Tijuana Brass LP from the sixties with the sexy señorita on the sleeve.

Yes, Mexican food available in the UK comes in kit form for the middle-brow hobbyist, South American food dilettante, and Home Counties couples who wish to cook up a spicy treat – a night off from a stir-in sauce – after returning home late from a parent-teacher bowling night or stall seats at a regional tour of *Starlight Express*.

British Mexican food is an imposter, an insulting stereotype. It's a kidney-bean, green-pepper and mild-salsa-sauce swindle.

It's wearing a white suit with huge gold epaulettes, and a rack of tin medals; it's sporting a furry, stick-on Charles Bronson moustache and sucking on a plastic, water-squirting cigar.

Mezze Platter

Usually served as gastropub nibbles for lunching sales and planning types, mezze platters are a selection of Mediterranean-style starters served on unhygienic wooden boards. Hummus from a bulk-buy vat, defrosted pitta pockets, runny pink taramasalata, fatty chorizo sausage and stuffed vine leaves.

The rule of thumb for the discerning diner is: go hungry rather than eat anything that comes on a platter. If dishes come as part of a 'platter', either you're about to be ripped off (mezze platters are generally complimentary on the Continent) or you're staying at the Holiday Inn Winnipeg, thinking about taking the easy way out.

Michelin Stars

Michelin Stars. They're like POGs, antioxidants and those large-eyed Lladro angels that my parents collect. Everyone wants them; no one knows what the buggers are for or what you do with them once you get them.

The star-ratings system awarded by the Michelin Guides is one of the most coveted and influential gastronomic ratings systems in the world. Just like POGs and Pokémon,* kids love Michelin stars: they kick the ass of AA Guide Rosettes.

Michelin Star restaurants are run by top chefs. You can easily spot a top chef. They're talented (a new twist on the bread-and-butter pudding), iconoclastic (collect and keep the recipe cards in this week's *Sunday Express*), entrepreneurial (menu consultant for South West Trains, Beefeater Steakhouses and the English Rose hotel chain) and controversial (they've banned breastfeeding in their flagship restaurant) yet compassionate (twelve pence from the sale of every summer pudding is donated to the Muscular Dystrophy Association).

I remember my dad railing against Pokémon; describing it as a 'con' and a 'swizzle'.

'Dad, I've told you before: there's no such word as "swizzle" and Pokémon is a craze eerily reminiscent of yours and mum's early-eighties collection of small, shiny Swarovski crystal animals. Celebi, the rarest Pokémon

*Pokémon was a late-nineties phenomenon: trading-cards featuring cute stylised creatures were collected, swapped, stolen and laundered by under-twelves.

(who looked like a spring onion) even resembled the coveted Swarovski eighteen-carat goldfish.'

Microwave Ovens

When I was growing up, Lampen-family day trips always involved a disappointing, substandard, below-par or undercooked food experience.

Spilt ice creams and shattered cider lollies – cool, tempting treats that ended up attracting ants on cobbled Cornish footpaths. That one black chip at the bottom of the vinegar-soaked cone; iffy shellfish, followed by violent vomiting, nausea and severe stomach cramps.

On one occasion my big toe was bitten by a crab that wouldn't let go. Then again, I could have seen that on a Looney Tunes show or in a comic Summer Special.

Sensory memory takes me back to a queasy drive home after a day out at the seaside. Six hours of unexpected summer sun, salty air and sand in my sweaty leather sandals while gnawing sickly multicoloured rock candy and picking cockles from a polystyrene cup with a cocktail stick had taken their toll on my tummy. I had cocktail-stick and wooden-'spork' splinters embedded in my tiny hands and we were stuck behind a caravan on the slow crawl home.

As a child, I'd fantasise about travelling from the seaside in the back of a caravan – being able to lie down on the journey home. In those days, travelling in the back of a caravan was illegal and ill-advised and a public-information advert aired in the afternoon warned against doing so. Now it's almost certainly practised as some sort of extreme sport by Canadians with piercings, puffy jackets, Sanskrit tattoos, pointless triangular patches of beard and spiky bleached-blond hair.

Back in the car: the winding country roads with no hard shoulder and the slow, single-file, stuck-behind-a-caravan convoy back to Plymouth made vomit stops impossible. All Mum could do was tell Dad to drive even slower while she readied the wet-wipes and spread napkins on the car floor.

My mum was crazy for napkins. She still is. She carries a huge bundle of paper serviettes around in her handbag, next to her tub of lip salve and emergency cotton-buds. Whenever she eats at a fast-food chain or snack bar she spreads napkins all over the marble-effect Formica table.

Another popular day trip was to Fairway Furniture – Devon's largest out-of-town furnishings superstore. Pleasures available on that particular trip included riding on the rocking chairs and turning on and off the non-functioning display taps in the shiny, heavily veneered woodchip show kitchens. Checking out the fake cardboard books in the sideboard-unit showroom (*The Great Gatsby* and *The Complete Works of William Shakespeare*: the same length!). Pulling the stuffing from the promotional plush Slumberland hippo and the smaller, even plusher duck; playing hide-and-seek with my sister in the double-divan department – wondering why duvets, and nothing else, were measured using the tog-rating system – and pestering Dad for ten pence for a brown plastic cup of powdered, hotter-than-lava chicken soup from the drinks machine.

But the one family trip that stands out above all others was a microwave demonstration at Bejam, the frozen-foods and electrical-appliance retailer, who, to promote their own brand of compact ovens, had advertised an evening of microwave-cookery advice at their Plymouth branch.

It was a school night in winter. The audience was buzzing. My dad had soaked himself in Aramis and wore that tweed jacket he usually reserved for speech days and parent-teacher evenings. Mum wore a soft musk from a Revlon range and a flowery frock.

Tangerine-coloured plastic chairs were arranged, school-assembly-style, in a space the store had cleared by moving choc-ice chillers and shifting potato-waffle-filled chest freezers.

Dad's wafting Aramis aroma and twice-a-year tweed attire gave me parent-teacher evening flashbacks. The standard feedback of 'Martin is a dreamer' echoed in my head.

I was thinking: 'Why am I here?' 'My parents are insane, dragging me to Bejam on a Tuesday night.' 'What are these new micro-waves, anyway?' 'Surely an oven is an oven is a blinkin' oven?' 'There must be better ways to spend a Tuesday evening. I should be out scrumping apples or sniffing solvents like normal kids my age.' And, 'Did Dad set the video for *Boon*?'

This was the worst night out since than the PTA cheese-and-wine barn dance. It was even worse than that beetle drive in St Peter's church hall, where teams of four had to draw an insect on a scrap of paper after throwing a dice. The none-too-thrilling beetle-doodling was followed by 'refreshments': orange squash in plastic cups and stale garibaldi biscuits. At first I thought the whole exercise might have been some sort of obscure high-Catholic ritual: representing Christ crucified by drawing an insect in Biro with its six legs splayed wide. But, no, it was supposed to be good, clean, wholesome Catholic fun in synch with the rhythm method and several encyclicals.

Bejam's demo dolly arrived. She wore cerise-pink lipstick and her tiny head was topped with fluffy, crimped blonde Dusty Springfield-comeback-era hair. She proceeded to make a Battenberg cake using standard cake ingredients and two of these new microwave ovens.

The ovens looked like televisions. I hatched a plan right there and then: if we ever got a microwave, I'd execute ten years' worth of chirpy 'Mum, there's a chicken on television'-type jokes. I sniggered at the gag and picked my nose as the cake-making commenced.

She hand-whipped the cake mix, never once getting any on the too-tight fluffy angora sweater with the owl-in-flight motif that she'd stretched over her pointy chest.

Look at that rising cake mix. Round and round it went. Round and round. 'It's better than most of that rubbish on TV anyway.' If we ever got a microwave I'd have a ready-made repertoire of oven jokes.

An hour later, and after a half a dozen thirty-second heating sessions on a high setting, there it stood: a real Battenberg cake – pink and yellow sponge glued together with apricot jam – all baked from the inside by these revolutionary microwave rays.

The demo dolly's chirpy chatter had rendered her hoarse. A round of applause followed. There was no sign of any stray cake mix on that knitted owl emblem: bravo! Maybe that's why everyone was clapping. Thankfully my parents didn't join in. They were never that insane.

They did, however, put their names down for a

microwave oven. Dad wrote the cheque as I plotted more precocious shtick. 'Mum, it's the *Rotating Battenberg Cake* show on TV . . .'

The tog-rating system *hasn't* ever been used to rank anything other than duvets, no one else *has* ever made a cake in a microwave and, to this day, no one else knows which heating category their microwave is.

For the next ten years our Bejam microwave was used every day, though never for making cakes. I never got round to making the 'microwave as television' joke; Mum wouldn't go near the microwave while it was on 'because of the radiation.' When I eventually left home I lived on microwave food for years, using that same Bejam microwave – a leaving gift from my parents.

It served me well, heating soups, milk for cereal, instant oats and baked beans during my first two years in London.

I sold it in 1999. I'd broken the frosted-glass turntable and was using a dinner plate instead – one that didn't quite fit the oven's groove and rattled when rotating and reheating ravioli. At the time I was striving for a healthy diet of salads and raw vegetables; I wanted to get away from ready-meals and tins of beans and hoops in tomato sauce. Also, the light had started to flicker and I was going through my own thoroughly unfounded fear-of-radiation phase: it was better to be safe than sorry.

I sold the oven for £6.00 in *Loot*. When sealing the sale, I jabbered and explained to the buyer my fear of the microwave rays. He said he'd take it with the caveat that his wife was six months pregnant and if 'anything went wrong' he'd 'be back'.

With the microwave money I bought an exercise bike.

I used the bike once. It rocked from side to side and it squeaked. It annoyed the couple downstairs – they slipped a letter of complaint through my letterbox and blanked me on the stairs.

I listed the cycle in *Loot* six months later and received a phone call from an interested buyer. 'Do you use the bike?' he asked, Then, 'Are you in good shape? Has it toned your thighs?' I put the phone down – really slowly.

I eventually sold the cycle and bought another microwave: back to beans and ready-in-two-minutes mush in disposable plastic trays.

Round and round it goes. Round and round.

Montelimar Nougat

The Montelimar Nougat is the jewel in the crown of the Cadbury's Roses range. It's also the name under which I check into hotels.

Funnily enough, all my noms de plume are food-related. I once wrote an erotic novel for women under the pen-name 'Monroe Peach'.

Moreish

A word used by your mum to describe chocolate biscuits. No one else ever uses this word in any other context. Ever.

Moroccan Food

It's a sunny Saturday night in early May and I'm stuck at home; solitaire is the only game in town and I'm faced with drinking a £5.00 bottle of clammy Merlot and falling asleep in front of the World Championship snooker.

OK, solitaire *and* tournament snooker. There are only two games in town. Though the snooker is in Sheffield, which is a different town.

I switch over from the snooker. On the television hospital drama an elderly man has fallen through a plate-glass window. Maybe his injuries will precipitate reconciliation with his heroin-addict daughter. Maybe I'll eat that microwave Cajun-chicken fettuccine that's in the fridge and cry myself to sleep.

I take the ready-meal-for-one out of the fridge. Four and a half minutes in a 750-watt oven. I have no idea what wattage my oven is. The fettuccine goes back.

Bugger this, I decide, as plate-glass man, currently being dabbed with cotton wool by the regular cast member with the improbable Northern accent, chokes back tears and exposits huge dollops of lonely-old-man backstory. I decide to play this week's 'table for one' card and eat out.

I've spent the last three weeks eating in gastropubs, brasseries and riverfront cafés offering Modern European menus. If I eat another kind of organically farmed fish grilled and covered in a rich port, almond and Stilton sauce I'll stab myself in the eye with an oyster fork.

I've heard good things about the Moroccan place round the corner and, dammit, my all-time number-one grain is couscous. Perhaps North African food will prove to be the perfect dining experience I've been searching for. Maybe I can write about it without using the word 'Moorish'.

'Table for one, please,' I mumble at the waitress; deciding not to justify my solitary dining with the usual lies about visiting London on last-minute weekend business, being an orphan or having been recently released from jail.

She shows me to a seat by the window and, on recommendation, I order a bottle of traditional Moroccan white wine, waive any bourgeois tasting privileges and gulp down a glass. A selection of starters follow . . . Fried cheese that makes my teeth squeak, shallow-fried sardines (suspiciously metallic in taste) and a selection of deep-fried minced-beef, cheese and potato filo-pastry parcels.

It's indicative of British urban food snobbery, and testimony to the level of sadly acceptable anti-Americanism within the chattering classes, that ethnic restaurants – from North African and Chinese to Thai and Argentinean – are permitted to serve fatty, deep-fried meat- and cheese-filled starter dishes without anyone accusing them of creating a nation of waddling, thick-thighed chubsters or furring up the arteries of our children as part of an evil neo-conservative plan for world domination.

If McDonald's or Burger King served deep-fried minced-beef filo parcels and battered cheese chunks as part of their value menus, they'd cop a six-page cover story in the *Guardian*'s soporific Society section, fifty-five minutes of primetime *Panorama* and a damning dossier on a desk at the Crown Prosecution Service.

But, no, it's perfectly acceptable for ethnic establishments to served deep-fried pork or battered Brie because families on limited incomes can't afford to eat there on a daily basis.

I down my third glass of wine while waiting for my main. Slightly giddy, I jot down a plot suggestion for a Saturday-night drama: elderly man badly burnt by contents of artery-clogging filo parcel.

My main arrives at last. It's lamb with couscous. I'm full from the complimentary hummus and bread (at least, I *thought* it was complimentary – until I saw the bill) and the stodgy deep-fried meat, fish and cheese parcels. It's nice. It's basically a lamb stew. You can't go wrong with a lamb stew. I order my second bottle of the house white. I don't really want to, but the waitress suggests it and I'm too polite to refuse.

I'm regretting the white-wine encore. More than one glass of traditional Moroccan white wine makes me hallucinate.

Saturday-night drunks swear and sway past the window. One of them shows his backside to a gaggle of girls. One of the girls has a tattoo of Tigger on the pink flesh that covers her tibia. She shouts back at the bottom-exposer, calling him a word that I've only ever seen used in health-information leaflets. The waitress tuts: 'Drunken idiots.' I wish she'd displayed the same sort of predilection for temperance when she spotted the empty bottle on my table. One of the drunks sways and falls just outside the window. For a split second I think he's going to fall through it. That's how accidents happen.

Mouthwatering

I used to temp for a local newspaper. My job description: advertising tasks, selling double-spread space for furniture-warehouse blow-out weekends and two-for-one coupon bonanzas for the all-but-bankrupt bowling alley and inserting glossy pullout leaflets promoting weekly supermarket food deals (usually a bottled-cola scam or a family-sized apple-pie loss-leader deal). I'd spend all day on the phone to car dealerships or proofreading lawnmower listings and sweetly optimistic small ads for overpriced bean-bag animals.

I had a desk opposite the restaurant critic. He was also the editor. His food feature was at the back of the paper, in the inky no man's land between the TV and radio listings, the 'Looking Back' feature – which included every week the same photograph of the High Street in 1928 – and the regional rugby results.

His reviews were a scream. He wrote them in the syco-phantic afterglow of a free dinner. They were all positive. They all gushed. They all glowed. They all contained the term 'mouthwatering'. They all mentioned the owner by name: 'Accomplished and mouthwatering dining in elegant Regency venue from owner Malcolm Yates . . .' 'Good hearty fare in Terry Yeo's renovated coaching inn . . .' 'Top Marks for Simon Marks' modern bistro with a mouthwatering menu.'

And for gland-slam hyperbole you couldn't beat 'Sadie and Ron Felloes and their classic mouthwatering menu in sumptuous surroundings.'

I didn't trust any of his reviews. He was on first-name

terms with the owner or head chef everywhere he ate. He also wrote the paper's leaders and opinion pieces. He wholeheartedly recommended the Persian Grill. He recommended its veal (it was 'mouthwatering') and the setting (which was 'magnificent'). He recommended, in print, banning the Gay and Lesbian Festival at the Arts Centre and the return of public lashing – by steel-tipped cat-o'nine-tails – for drug addicts, Benefit cheats and litter-louts.

Mozzarella

Mozzarella cheese comes in Silly Putty-shaped shiny balls and is made from pasteurised cow's milk or the unpasteurised milk of water buffaloes. It tastes of nothing.

Mozzarella is stored in those unsettling little water-filled tubs – displayed like some sort of soft-cheese Petri-dish specimen. I bought some the other day with the intention of using it in a salad (as a kind of self-punishment) and left it in the fridge for three hours.

I swear to God it had doubled in size by the time I came to use it. I threw it away and went with the mature Cheddar.

Mr Kipling

'Sunday, wrote Mr Kipling . . . and the allure of my almond slice.'

It's the eighties. We're halfway through the second series of *Howard's Way*. Jack Rolfe has yet again threatened to 'close the boatyard, Avril'. Over on ITV, smug cake magnate Mr Kipling peddles his sugary individual pies and cakes during the ad breaks on Harry Secombe's *Highway*.'

Choose from slices, swirls, treats, pies, tarts, rolls and fancies. All 'exceedingly good', all promoted on TV by Mr K's plummy male friend.

No, it wasn't Kipling himself who voiced the ads; it was his friend, reading aloud in a mellow timbre from Kipling's cake-obsessed diary.

Yes, he let another man – a man with a fruity tone, an interest in baking and individual Battenbergs – read aloud from his personal journal. They probably called each other 'Dear Heart' and cat-fought over the final pink Fancy.

During my youth Mr Kipling's cakes and the weekly fight with my sister over the last Cherry Bakewell were as much a part of Sunday nights as laugh-shy sitcom *Hi-De-Hi*, short-arsed radio playboy Bruno Brookes and his weekly Top Forty countdown and acute, aching melancholy.

Muffins

Since when did it become acceptable to eat fairy cakes for breakfast? What happened to the old-style savoury muffin; the type of flour-dusted muffin that you'd smear with salty full-fat butter and dunk in your country-vegetable soup for lunch?

You can keep the modern breakfast muffin. I'll take the fairy cake any day. Not one of those chi-chi chain coffee shop cupcakes; a proper fairy cake, one with icing and those edible rice-paper cake-toppers in the shape of Mickey

Mouse's face, that crab thing from *The Little Mermaid*, the Wuzzles or the Popples.

According to the blokey non-fiction writers' template, it's about time I detailed my chemical excesses; my lost decade spent dancing in fields and the colossal (and highly improbable) amount of illegal substances that I smoked, toked, freebased and mainlined in my twenties. It should read like Thomas De Quincey's *Confessions of an English Opium Eater*, as written for a men's magazine by some nitwit called Giles.

But I don't actually know what any of those terms means (I read about them in an American novel set in 1920s Kansas City) and I've never taken any drugs. None. Never. Not even once.

Those edible rice-paper cake decorations remind me of the reason why I've never taken any drugs. Never. Not even once. One night, my dad returned home late from a Navy course that taught officers how to spot recruits with drug problems: how to tell when Jolly Jack Tar is a little bit too jolly; when 'heaving up and lashing out' means more than rising from your hammock in the morning.

After the lecture Dad confiscated my Airfix glue and divulged another piece of drug-related scuttlebutt that he'd learnt on the course. It was the old chestnut about how LSD was being distributed around the mess hall on cartoon-character-branded temporary tattoos. Apparently, one recruit had slapped a decal of, say, the Lone Ranger or a sad clown on his arm, then, off his rudder on acid, chopped his wife's head off with an axe because he thought that she'd turned into a dragon.

Lovely. 'Thanks, Dad. I'll sleep well tonight.'

Though I was only ten at the time that story scared the Holy Jesus out of me and, to this very day, I've never taken any drug of any kind. Not grass, cocaine, heroin, E, whiz, wuzzles or popples.

I have, however, spent the last twenty years licking the edible rice-paper tops of Smurf cupcakes and rubbing the grinning faces of marzipan animals in brightly lit high-street bakeries on the lookout for a cheap, sugary 'trip'.

Whatever 'trip' means.

Music in Restaurants

I love the unpredictable nature of restaurant music; the bizarre songs that clang over tinny sound systems and provide muffled accompaniment to the clatter of cutlery and the breaking of defrosted bread rolls.

One minute you're waiting for your starter while listening to the type of authentic ethnic folk music used to invoke spirits during ancient tribal ceremonies. Five minutes later you're dipping your fingers in the lemon-scented finger bowl while baby-faced, power-suited Hi-NRG crooner Rick Astley pledges to never 'give you up'.

Mutton Pie

I once went to a Dunfermline home game in the McEwan's Special Strength Lager and Shortbread Scottish Football League Second Division.

A poor performance by Dunfermline resulted in the

home fans throwing their mutton pies on the pitch after the match.

I've always had a soft spot for the eccentricities and generally rubbish nature of Scottish football – for the way in which the passion of the fans is offset against the shoddy quality of the play and administrative structure.

Scandal overshadowed Scotland's 1978 World Cup campaign when, after the defeat by Peru, Glasgow Rangers winger 'Wee' Willie Johnston was sent home in shame for failing a drugs test (given the Scottish diet, maybe it was a cholesterol test?). No matter, speculation suggested that he'd taken two paracetamol with his Irn-Bru or that someone had laced his Tunnock's Tea Cakes with beta-blockers).

Natural Yogurt

Virtually fat free and very much vile. I refuse to eat any yogurt that isn't bright pink, flavoured with cheap, mushy summer-fruits compote or bursting with allergy-inducing refined sugars.

I refuse to eat any yogurt that isn't, in some small way, affiliated with the Munch Bunch.

Navy Food

My dad was in the Submarine Service. HMS *Sceptre*, 1976–1982. Maybe it was 600 years of British naval slang, maybe it was four months at sea, two to a bunk and no female company, but they had some 'rum' culinary terms in the senior service.

Spithead pheasants Kippers (which are always served at breakfast), Spithead being the name for the entrance to Portsmouth Harbour.

Yellow peril Smoked haddock (my mum calls it 'foxy fish'; but then again she's also scared of balloons).

Shit on a raft Devilled kidneys on toast.

Adam and Eve on a raft Two fried eggs on toast. There's a pattern developing here.

Yellow peas and trees Sweetcorn and broccoli. Obviously.

Tonsil varnish Strong tea.

Tits Tomatoes in tomato sauce. (Bits are beans in tomato sauce. Hits are herrings in tomato sauce.) Yes, like I said, sometimes they wouldn't see a woman in six months.

Slush The fat skimmed off a pot of boiling meat, which was sold to the purser for making candles – hence slush fund.

Nelson's blood Rum.

Hammy cheesy eggy topside As it suggests.

Gobbling rods Knife, fork and spoon.

Elephant's footprints Battered spam fritters, served at breakfast.

Dockyard tortoise Cornish pasty.

Custard bosun The chief cook.

Chicken Chernobyl A very hot curry.

Cackleberries Hen's eggs.

Babies' heads Steak-and-kidney puddings. Charming.

Arrigones Tinned italian tomatoes. Signor A. Riggoni was the main supplier to the Royal Navy – his name was on the tin.

Kye A hot cocoa made by scraping flakes from huge blocks of unsweetened industrial chocolate into a fanny (naval slang for a large cooking pot, among other things). This would then be heated up with milk and water, to provide a winter warmer for those on duty during the middle watch.

These days, Kye is the name that couples called Ben and Natasha give their firstborn son.

Yes, all very well, Dad. But you left the Navy sixteen years ago, you smell of rum and you're making Mum cry.

Nestlé

Nestlé was once the target of a boycott in twenty countries for its aggressive marketing of baby foods.

This may be true, but they also make Kit-Kats, Kit-Kat Cubes, Chunky Kit-Kats, Aeros, Mint Aeros and Orange Aeros. Confectionery treats so delicious that I wouldn't boycott them even if it were proven that Nestlé made baby milk from the ground-up spines of kitten foeteses.

'New Flavour'

'Butterscotch, is that you? Butterscotch, as I live and breathe. How long has it been? I haven't seen you since that party at Vanilla's place. You know the one – the one where Raspberry Ripple wound up in the fruity four-way tryst with the Neapolitan triplets.'

Whatever happened to the old food flavours – the wild strawberries and the black forests, the bitter lemons and the tropical pineapples? Where did they go once the new, improved, limited-edition mandarin- and mango-flavoured treats rose in their place?

Whither rum-and-raisin? Stabbed in the back by dulce de leche.

Newsagent's

If you're in a hurry and in the market for a quick sugary treat 'to go', then forget the peach-and-raspberry muffins at Café Franchise – you could do much worse than visiting a traditional British newsagent's.

Choose from a wide range of chocolate confections and salty snacks, browse through dog-eared back issues of the *People's Friend*. Purchase playing-cards, cap guns and boxes of pastel chalks on sale since the Queen's Silver Jubilee.

Let's celebrate the fact that, excluding WH Smith (who are now more interested in selling Wiltshire hot-air ballooning weekend experiences than newspapers and chocolate bars), no global conglomerate has taken over Britain's newsagents, market-tested and brand-positioned their point-of-sale products and installed wi-fi booths where customers can download the day's news to their Bluetooth PDAs.

Breathe a sigh of relief that no corporate monster has monopolised Britain's news and magazine vendors; purveyors of such retail delights as the four-year-old *Puzzle* magazine with the free felt-tip pen three-pack, the Premier League sticker book from 2002, the broken Cornetto, the dusty Caramac and the dirty magazine.

Noodle-Bar Bench Seating

Noodle bars of Britain: when I eat out, I want a table. I want a whole table or a booth to myself or for my dining party. I wouldn't mind a velvet curtain on goldplated curtain rings covering the booth so that I don't have to watch anyone else eat and no one can watch me. I do not want to share a narrow, arse-numbing wooden bench with shifty, ramen-noodle-slurping strangers. I want reasonable leg room; I don't want to knock knees with sweaty businessmen on their midday breaks or far-too-young, far-too-fashionable Swedish tourists on snack stops from sneaker-shopping.

I don't want to listen to people mispronounce 'yasai cha han'. I don't want the wait staff to nudge me out of the way in order to scrawl my order in spider-walk short-hand on a paper placemat. It's impersonal, it's rude and I always end up with a black Biro smudge on the inside of my wrist.

No, I don't want to leave my business card in the giant fishbowl in reception – I don't give a ring-tailed lemur that you are giving away a jeroboam of cheap fizzy wine and free yaki udon for a year; you're not getting hold of my personal details for your irksome viral marketing campaigns quite that easily.

The last time I sat at a communal bench in a restaurant was last December in a Soho noodle bar. I was between jobs and killing time and keeping warm before an interview. I didn't even have a business card to drop into the draw – hence the anti-raffle hostility.

I was guided to the end of a wooden bench and told to sit. In my tiny corner I was opposite a lunching academic. He had hoisin sauce in his beard and was reading a musty, dog-eared Penguin paperback from the sixties about feminist theory with a scratchy charcoal cover drawing of a vagina.

Thinking about it now, It could have been a scratchy charcoal drawing of an apple.

The table was sticky with sweet chilli sauce and the fusty odour of the vintage tome's browning pages and the clotted Chinese plum juice dripping down his red whiskers put me off my sesame prawn toast.

I pushed my plate aside, left a tenner on the table (no tip) and dumped a greasy toasted prawn triangle in the business-card bowl on the way out.

Nouvelle Cuisine

Nouvelle cuisine was huge in the 1980s. It was minimal, colourful and didn't come with a 'combo' option. It never caught on.

It was a style of cooking that was all about visual pres-entation: setting vividly coloured ingredients against white-plate space – bringing to mind the Optical Art of Bridget Riley, Athena posters of airbrushed hot-fudge sundaes and men in cream linen jackets who looked like Daryl Hall or John Oates and who click-finger danced with themselves to Classix Noveau club mixes in LA discothèques named after Weimar Republic youth movements and that smelt like sweet-and-sour pork before checking the hour on their wafer-thin Swiss timepieces, rolling their jacket sleeves up and returning to their warehouse apartments to snort six lines of coke and brew Ethiopian sidamo in their stainless-steel cafetieres.

Nutrition

It used to be that you couldn't move 100 metres down the street without meeting a man who claimed to 'DJ on weekends' (playing a 'set' at his friend's stag-do; searching for that Shakatak 12" while nursing paintball wounds and turning the collar up on his best Fred Perry shirt) or a woman who did 'a little bit of modelling' (page eighteen of *PC Format* magazine in March 2002, holding a hard drive), or young folks of both sexes involved in hairdressing apprenticeships, forensic-science training, lengthy legal degrees or nail-technician diplomas.

Everyone has a dream.

These days, everyone aspires to having a career in nutrition. I've lost count of the number of people, male and female, who've bored me to tears recently by droning on about their upcoming disordered-physiology module or complex-pathology course.

My parents have some of my niece and nephew's artwork stuck to the refrigerator in their 'utility room'. Three-year-old Louis scrawled a red Power Ranger. For a school careers project my eight-year-old niece

Crayola-sketched a stick-woman with yellow Jackie O-style bangs, scarlet circles on her cheeks and a triangle frock coloured pea green. Underneath the stick-figure she's written: 'Accredited Practising Dietitian'.

Everyone I meet rabbits on about how good cashews are for skin, hair, nails and dodgy guts. Down the pub, colleagues swirl white wine in foggy glasses and tut-tut about bad-food Britain. They debate how many gallons of water one should drink per hour, and the iron content of broccoli. Friends push vitamin supplements, trying to get me hooked on wheatgrass granules or spirulina capsules; they're also fixing a hex on the doughnut industry and planning a petition to tax the Twix.

Observer Food Monthly

Also known as the *Smug Food Guide*, the Food Monthly is the *Observer*'s guide to food culture and dining.

Here's a Frenchman you've never heard of reviewing chocolate puddings in a blind-taste test. Page six: Emma Freud in a twenty-question vox pop about her favourite root vegetables. Flick forward: architect Richard Rogers says he couldn't live without his local brasserie.

Leaf past the fair-trade Aga-buyers' guide and some self-satisfied finger-wagging about under-twelves and saturated fats.

The crescendo: Brian Eno and Anthony Minghella rate the top-ten tea infusers.

Open Your Own Restaurant

I've always dreamt about opening my own restaurant.

In the dream I'm wearing a tuxedo-print T-shirt, chewing on a stick of Wrigley's Big Red and sipping from a tall, frosty glass of Pernod and orange. Doberman-pinscher-faced piano man Billy Joel is heard through the stereo system as I stand at the bar – owner and host of Chez Martin, my self-run restaurant – musing on what Noel Coward called the 'potency of cheap music'.

At least, I think it was Noel Coward. It could have been Chris de Burgh.

VHS copies of *Arthur 2: On the Rocks* are playing silently and on a loop on fish bowl-shaped television screens set into chocolate-coloured textured walls.

Welcome to my retro-chic restaurant chain, serving up long-forgotten dishes. Soup of the day is Brown Windsor. The main course is your choice of chicken chasseur or something in a can from Crosse and Blackwell. There's a ninety-nine-cent special shrimp cocktail, and the house rosé with the long Italian name is bottled in Chanadaigua, NY. Spirits are served solely from cut-glass decanters.

Laugh, if you will, at my antediluvian carte du jour, but ten years ago you'd probably have laughed at the idea of the UK's first hummus bar (oh right, you still do? Fair enough) or inner-city spit, sawdust and cider pubs serving braised lamb shanks with shallots and blackcurrant jus (still has you in hysterics, you say? I can't argue with that).

If I'm honest, I know my nostalgic nosh would never sell. British dining culture is now completely aspirational. Unlike fashion, pop music or product design, dishes from previous eras that were subsequently regarded as naff will never make a comeback. That's not including mashed potato – although this came back only once people were sick to the stomach of scalloped spuds; the reinvention involved herbs, spring onions, savoy cabbage or herbed cheese.

Mashed spuds aside, naff foods and beverages will never enjoy a renaissance. I just know that, in my lifetime, I will never see another man walk on the moon, a third *Arthur* film to form an *Arthur* trilogy and the return of the rissole.

Here lies macaroni cheese. Rest in peace. Do not disturb. Save a space in the family plot for Pinot Grigio, paprika, beef Stroganoff and onion bread.

Besides, I've never had much luck with my entrepreneurial schemes.

In 1999 I attended a six-hour seminar given in a Thistle hotel by a man from Miami wearing an electric-blue suit and with Terry Wogan hair. It concerned bulk-selling opportunities in health supplements.

As I write, eighteen cases of liquid aloe-vera extract moulder under the stairs and I still haven't met my optimum fifty-grand monthly income target like the sales rep of the month who spoke at the seminar – Pam from Tamworth with the big hairdo, bright-red lipstick and sing-songy speaking voice.

In 2001 I invested six months and several thousand pounds of my own money in printing and producing a glossy photographic coffee-table book about 'Weepuls' – those little furry promotional bugs that idiots stick on their work PCs. The ones with the googly eyes, oversized peel-and-stick felt feet and ribbons that read: 'GKL

Consultants Bradford'; 'I Heart Xerox Reproduction Products'; or 'I've Been to the Snape Maltings Steam Museum'.

I have yet to make my first million.

Oriental Buffet

Recently, during a period when I hadn't been paid for three months, I ate at one of those cheap Chinatown 'all you can eat for £5.00' Mandarin buffets; one with a strict 'two prawn crackers per person' limit, curt, frosty service from the grumpy wait staff and an extortionate alcohol surcharge.

After eating the syrupy, bloating, orange-tinted meal, I took the long walk down a narrow stairway to the toilet in order to pass the grudgingly complimentary tap water; as I went past the kitchen I saw three small Chinese guys sleeping on shelves next to huge drums of yellow vegetable oil.

Either they were illegal immigrants, working for buffet scraps and shelf-space shelter, or they'd passed out after inhaling excess soy fumes.

Overeating

Last year, during a three-month period of working from home, I started overeating. I've always had a bit of an appetite but last winter I started eating enormous quantities of food every day.

I'd happily polish off half a box of Frosties with

full-fat milk, a double pack of pork-and-pickle pies, six freshly baked white-chocolate-chip cookies from a super-market bakery and a large plastic tub of cold Chinese-style chicken wings.

It was no big deal. It was a passing phase. It wasn't a cry for help; I didn't have to buy bigger clothes and my health didn't suffer.

I always regarded my gluttony as a cheery, British kind of gluttony – the kind of jolly greed as practised by a smudge-nosed, flat-cap-wearing scamp in the *Beano* who, for a wheeze, charges £1.00 each to wash the neighbour-hood dogs and spends the proceeds on either a slap-up fish supper or a plateful of sausage and mash (proper sausage and mash, without the Maris Piper/grain-mustard mash and £10.00 price tag).

I ate so much slap-up fish supper that my stomach expanded. I groaned and gurned, my tongue sticking out the side of my mouth and hash symbols replacing my eyes.

The episode ended with me being chased down the road by irate, slipper-brandishing local dads and an angry horde of drenched dogs. I'd washed the dogs all at once with a hosepipe, which I'd left on and which subsequently flooded the whole of Acacia Avenue or Gas Works Lane.

None of that actually happened. I read it in a comic. But you get the idea. I was a happy glutton. And, while I'm on the subject, why are all American comics about muscled superheros and power fantasies while the four-colour, six-panel narratives of their British equivalents concern themselves only with greedy schoolboys, cheeky mongrel dogs and talking footballs? I could delve into the diverging semiotics of Anglo verses America comic-book narratives, quoting, among others, Umberto Eco, Jean Baudrillard and in all probability Arthur Mullard, though I'd rather talk about biscuits and individual fruit pies . . .

During my brush with overeating, I'd spend all day running to and from the fridge, picking at food and getting no work done at all. No big deal. I put on a little bit of weight, though I never topped thirteen and a half stone and I stand at over six feet, so the weight gain wasn't noticeable.

During my gluttony days I wasn't a 'compulsive overeater' or a 'comfort eater', merely a 'greedy-guts' or a 'gutsy-chops' with 'eyes bigger than my belly'. Old-fashioned terms for overeaters in the pre-therapy, pre-antioxidant era.

After I made myself sick on pork pies one lunchtime I didn't write an article on the British food industry for a national newspaper or an angry missive to the Mayor of Melton Mowbray. I had a lie-down and half a glass of mineral water and made myself a light lunch the following day.

I didn't need intensive therapy, hypnosis or intervention; all I needed was a kick up the arse, a backside tanned by a tartan slipper or a regular office job.

Once I was working from a client's premises again, I started walking a good mile a day, to and from Tube stations and up flights of stairs, and the weight just fell off me.

So, if you have the tendency to eat every biscuit in the assortment tin in one go, even the stale, beige wafer sand-wiches with the sickly vanilla paste in the middle, then get yourself out of the house. Go for a walk, go for a run . . . get yourself chased down Gas Works Lane by woof-woofing dogs and angry dads.

Own Brand

I love the cheap copy. I love the cash-in, the watered-down imitation and the flimsy facsimile that appears just before a fad fades.

I love the anaemic Atomic Kitten cover version. I rate Judge Reinhold's performance as a child trapped in a man's body in *Vice Versa* above Tom Hanks' Oscar-nominated turn in *Big*.

I choose Chubby Checker. Fats Domino can get fucked.

I rank Michael over Kirk in the Douglas-dynasty, father-versus-son wooden act-off sweepstakes. You're more likely to find me licking a King Kone than a Cornetto. I relish the two-dimensional challenge of Rubik's magic; I have no time for that damned Cube.

Feed me a chunk of milk-chocolate Coconut Grove, a bite of Walnut-topped Mallow Swirl, a Swiss Mountain segment, a Honeycomb Crackle-Crunch or a Choc-O-Bubbles Bar.

Hand me a Turkish De-Lovely.

Pacific-Rim Cooking

More fucking mangoes.

Packed Lunches

Despite my mum being a dinnerlady (a proper dinnerlady, mind; one who worked in the kitchen, manning the big fryer, frittering the spam and burying the offal in the shepherd's pie. Not one of the rain-lashed women who patrolled the playground, clad in taupe duffle coats, armed only with a plastic whistle on an old shoelace, a righteous sense of justice and a crippling fear of being hit in the ankles with a mini-leather), my sister and I weren't allowed school dinners. Maybe Mum knew that school dinners, even then, utilised inferior ingredients while cutting corners on hygiene and preparation standards. Maybe she knew we'd spend our lunch money on burgers, chips, chocolate bars or cheap chews while falsely claiming, squeaky voices straining under the youthful deceit, that we'd had the 'meal of the day: full roast with six veg and a wholemeal apple turnover'.

Since canteen dinners were frowned upon in our family, nine days out of ten a Tupperware box would rattle around in my satchel ready for the twelve o'clock bell.

The centrepiece of my lunchbox was usually a tuna sandwich. It could either be eaten or chucked in a hedge on the way to school (to this day the bird population in South Devon hasn't fully recovered from the mysterious clingfilm cull of '84–'89).

Typically, I'd also always have a chocolate Club biscuit or a mint Viscount (pronounced *vi-count*) in my packed lunch. At my school, having a mint Viscount in your lunchbox meant that you were 'posh'. You were also posh if you had a Parker pen or a brand-name sports holdall.

I don't have too many phobias or irrational fears.

Obviously, I'm not too fond of Mexican bird-eating spiders, Glenda Jackson's teeth or avant-garde theatre. And someone else's packed lunches. The thought of eating someone else's packed lunch, prepared by someone else's mum, makes we want to retch.

Paint-Your-Own Crockery Café

A confession: several years ago I went into one of those paint-your-own crockery studio cum cafés.

I know. I know. It was a moment of madness during my own personal summer of near-contentment, and I was in an almost cheerful mood. It was a Friday and I had the day off; my inner soundtrack was birdsong, baby bunnies bounding in green grass, the *Pastoral Symphony* and some sunny solo song by Stephen Stills (*sans* sidemen Crosby and Nash).

I craved a large soya-milk latte, a wholemeal carrot-and-raisin muffin, and the prospect of daubing a mug-and-plate set with floral patterns and left-wing slogans in ethical watercolours seemed a fine one.

I dipped a brush in pastel paint and applied it to the cup and plate. I drew lemon-coloured daisies, dew-drops and bright buttercups; I styled saffron-shaded sunbeams and even rendered those bouncing bunnies in broad brushstrokes.

I drained the bottom of my milky coffee and, with a true artist's flourish, swept my brush over the unglazed mug for those final personal touches. I glanced down at the cup I'd drunk the coffee from moments earlier to see whether it was all gone or any soggy muffin dregs remained.

There was a long hair in there. A long, brown curly hair – it certainly wasn't one of mine. The man who served me was an Australian, a gaunt surfer in his early forties with long, curly brown hair, a small, tatty beard and a shark's-tooth necklace. He'd been out in the sun too long. He'd shrunk, he'd shrivelled and he'd nearly drowned, yet he'd retained a curly mop of hair. He looked like the corpse of Michael Hutchence; back from the grave to spook me with his weedy Australian funk-rock.

A dozen or more final touches and I was done . . . Painted on the mug in bold, blue strokes: 'Shedding Son of a Bitch!'

I left under a cloud, without paying.

Pan-Fried

'Pan-fried?' Funny, I'd automatically assumed that these garlic mushrooms had been prepared in the bowler hat of a city gent.

Or maybe in a rusty bucket.

Passionate about Fresh Ingredients

I'll use any excuse to eat out of an evening. Maybe I can pretend it was a business meeting and claim back the VAT. I have nothing in the fridge. My dining table wobbles . . . I've run out of tinfoil. Help!

Researching this book saw me eating out every night for two months. As a result, I added half an inch to my waistline and spent my days scouring through restaurant guides and 'where to eat' newspaper columns. I'm sick of reading about how 'passionate' every single chef is about 'fresh ingredients'.

Top chefs apparently flutter their eyelashes, blush and start adjusting their trousers at the sight of a twitching, fresh lobster or a dirty, earth-caked carrot.

A dirty, dirty, dirty carrot.

A few weeks ago I went to a West London restaurant for lunch and drank a smoothie that was, according to the self-satisfied ethical menu, squeezed to order from untreated fresh fruits and cleansing organic algae. I rinsed my palate with mineral water whose profits supported water projects in Africa and Indian irrigation initiatives. I scoffed potatoes from an urban garden maintained by former drug dependents and their ex-addict mentors – six years and five months off the methadone. I ate fish that was caught wild from non-depleted stocks; pasta prepared with herbs that were grown locally and hand-cut twenty-four hours prior to preparation; bread freshly made on the premises without added trans-fats or extra enzymes; and organic meat with traceable numbers and organic certifications.

I paid £28.00 for lasagne and chips with a soggy sardine-and-sunflower-seed side salad. I waited thirty-five minutes for service and copped frosty looks and a plateful of stroppy attitude from an Eastern European waitress with an ashen, malnourished look, holes in her ragged restaurant-issue blouse and third-degree welts on her wrists from serving Suffolk shellfish skillet on heated plates and the bubbling beef fondue.

Pastry

Pastry-making is a fine art. Its secrets and techniques can take years to learn. Whether you need some flaky sharpish for a cream horn or a nice bit of lattice work for a ham, cheese, asparagus and leek pie, here's a guide to the movers, the shakers, the kneaders and the platters of the pastry world.

Filo A paper-thin Greek pastry used for baklavas, strudels, savoury-meat and cheese parcels, samosas and spring rolls. Cooking with filo pastry is an unnecessarily time-consuming hobby.

I'm proud to say that I don't have any hobbies. I was looking at CVs the other day with a view to recruiting an office assistant. One applicant had listed her hobbies as 'kite-flying and html'. Her CV went straight in the bin.

Hobbies are to be avoided at all costs. Time spent on hobbies has destroyed many a budding relationship: her Wednesday-night ceroc dance classes; holidays in the snow rather than the sun; obsessive-compulsive hours spent distressing new jeans with the pumice stone intended for my sore feet; whole weekends spent trawling boutiques for 'unusual tops'. Cooking filo at the correct temperature . . .

Shortcrust The backbone of such pantry favourites as the mince pie, the quiche, the jam tart and beef Wellington. Beef Wellington is named after Arthur Wellesley, the Iron Duke and first Duke of Wellington, who, when not defeating robber chieftains in India, serving as British Prime Minister and naming weatherproof boots, liked nothing better than a fillet-of-beef and foie-gras pie. Wellington died in 1852 after losing his greatest battle: the battle with indigestion.

Choux Ooooh laaaa laaaa! Choux is used for cream puffs, éclairs and profiteroles. It's my favourite of all the pastries, just for the chocolate-éclair factor.

I wrote 'Ooooh laaaa laaaa' there as I once heard an American tourist from one of the Southern States shriek 'Oooooh laaaa laaaa!' as he was presented with a chocolate éclair in a London coffee-shop.

He then laughed at his own joke and ordered another one.

Puff A thin pastry that rises when cooked. Switch on the oven light, crouch down and watch it inflate like some sort of schlocky H.P. Lovecraft monster – an even scarier prospect than a Fray Bentos pie. Steak and kidney with fangs.

Puff pastry is used for a wide range of dishes, both sweet and savoury, including cream horns, pie toppings and vol-au-vents.

The vol-au-vent, like Sting, New Labour, the Royal Family or the *Daily Express*, is way beyond parody.

'Vol-au-vent' translates literally from the French as 'flight in the wind' – which, funnily enough, is also the title of a Sting album.

Pâté

Pâté is a spreadable paste – a meat butter, if you will – served as a starter with two grapes and not nearly enough bread in pubs run by couples called Shirley and Terry, who recommend a walk to the causeway after the cheese plate with Bath Olivers.

Compelling evidence that I am, indeed, working class comes attached to the method I use for preparing my pâté. I'll lightly toast a slice of white bread, spread a thick layer of margarine on it then spread an even thicker layer of pâté on top of that.

Yes, I actually spread pâté on top of margarine. I then etch the words 'Hard Bastard' in the thick farmhouse paste with the prong of a fork.

Patronising One-Minute Porridge

Oat-so crappy.

Pease Pudding

It's a Northeastern hummus: a split-pea paste eaten by Geordies and other people who wear replica football shirts to work and keep budgies.

Pesto

It's 2007 and pesto, that green pasta paste, sits alongside tomato sauce, spicy salsa, curry powder, mustard mayonnaise, olive oil and sweet-and-sour gunk as a lazy garnish for sandwiches, chicken strips and starchy pasta squiggles;

a ready-in-ten-minutes dinner for homesick first-year students who take their washing home at weekends, spotty postgraduates in faded *Red Dwarf* T-shirts, far too timid to face the working world, and other people who live in 'digs' that smell like cabbage, pets and aromatherapy oils.

In the face of economic revival in the North – docks being developed into studio flats, galleries, antique-teddy-bear shops and branches of the Cheesecake Factory – it won't be long before Lancastrians and Geordies are spreading pesto – that nasty, nutty substance that tastes like the forest floor – on their snack-bar curry and chips.

Pick 'n' Mix

I've led a blameless life. I've never taken any drugs. I always pay my taxes on time. I've never been involved in the unauthorised hiring, lending or public performance (in schools or hospitals or on oil rigs) of a VHS home video.

I hardly ever swear in public. After belching in public I reel off the rhyme: 'Pardon me for being so rude; it was not me, it was my food'. If I ever drop a chip or a chunk of chocolate I run it under the cold tap before eating it. I once tried binge drinking in Southend city centre on a Friday night, but I got bored and hurried home to watch the *Late Review* and get a good eight hours' sleep in. The only items I've ever stolen are: a novelty scented eraser shaped like a lightbulb and a small felt clip-on koala from a newsagent's when I was eight and, while on a pub crawl in 2005, six coloured plastic game pieces from a giant Connect 4 set from the basement bar of a gastropub that described its food as 'urban farmhouse' – I pinched them as revenge for the poor-quality (honey-roasted) ham-and-Brie croque Madame I'd eaten there.

Oh, and, over the years, I've stolen more than ten kilos of pick 'n' mix sweets.

Chewy strawberries, white-chocolate mice, juicy lips, foam bananas, wiggly worms, giant jelly spiders and vaguely amusing candy teeth . . . In my time I've stolen them all.

Try it – they're easy to pinch. Fill your pockets with pineapple cubes and strawberry shrimps; though don't bother stealing anything that appears to be covered in milk chocolate – raisins, Brazil nuts or honeycomb hearts – as it's actually just a cocoa-based coating of inferior quality.

Pick 'n' mix has been around for decades. It was one of the first formats based entirely around customer choice; the precursor to the shopper-comes-first consumer culture of variable phone plans, salad bars, Chinese dinner buffets, personalised saving schemes, secondary-school selection systems and flexible mortgage strategies. They're all pre-packaged, substandard and, metaphorically speaking, covered in shit chocolate – there are just more of them to choose from.

The idea that we now have greater consumer choice is an illusion. I tried to buy a carton of apple juice last week. I couldn't find any apple juice that didn't also have mango in it. I couldn't find a pork chop that didn't come smothered in a gloopy honey-and-mustard sauce.

Well, I reject such joyless consumerism. My money is staying in my pocket – nestled next to 350 grams of stolen sour apple rings.

Pick-Your-Own

When I was growing up, every summer we'd go to a local farm to pick our own fruit. We'd don our wellies, get knee-deep in mud and fill flimsy wooden baskets, and our stomachs, with mangy-looking berries. We'd emerge three hours later with our Wranglers muddy and sticky fruit smeared around our mouths. I never liked it – it was too much like being in the country for my tastes.

I prefer the 'semi-country', the feeling of getting out of town without actually coming into contact with any mud or locals. You can keep Britain's farms, woods and fields. Give me a picnic park with life-size fibreglass dinosaurs. Give me a traction-engine rally or an out-of-town retail park where I can buy nearly-out-of-date fudge from the Thornton's outlet; a petting zoo where I can flick Lyons Maid lolly sticks at rabbits, ducks and miserable-looking South American goat things (it's a long way from the slopes of the Andes to the Tiverton Small Mammal Petting Park and Family Camping Ground, so cut them some slack and feed them some of your crisps).

I'd even rather pay £3.00 to park in a field and spend half an hour gawping at vintage cars (then four hours trying to get back on the A361) than nibble Kendal Mint Cake in the wilderness.

Pickled Onions

I love pickled onions and pickled eggs, but most people can't stomach them. Ask seven out of ten people if they'd like a pickled onion and they'll wrinkle their noses and maybe stick their tongues out as an act of displeasure.

It's the exact same reaction I have when I'm watching a film on television with my parents and there are 'rude bits' in it, or when someone discusses their body piercing or going to the cinema to watch a romantic comedy starring one of the actors who used to be in *Friends*.

Pips

Avoid any foods containing hard pips. Avoid fresh fruit, gritty fruit compotes and natural fillings in yogurts, crumbles, preserves and pies – they're hazardous to your health and long-term job prospects.

One morning last year I was running twenty minutes late for work so I replaced my usual slurped Shreddies-and-creamy-milk breakfast with a luxury loganberry, raspberry, apple and pear yogurt from a supermarket's six-pack 'Orchard Selection'.

I wolfed the contents of the pot with a plastic spoon while fast-walking for the bus. I didn't even have time to lick the foil lid.

As I rode to work I could feel a raspberry pip wedged between two of my upper teeth. It rose steadily towards my gums. It was stuck. It wouldn't dislodge. It made my eyes water, my gums tingle and my teeth itch.

I tried chewing gum en route and a cold-water rinse when I arrived at work. I ran to the chemist at twelve-noon sharp and spent my lunch hour rooting around in my mouth with taut toothbrush bristles, dental floss and a fingernail.

The situation got worse: a splinter joined the pip when a wooden cocktail stick snapped.

Nothing would dislodge it. The pain didn't ease. I tried gargling, rubbing the area with my tongue and even inserting the edge of a supermarket loyalty card. I broke my fingernail, a Tesco Club Card and three wooden toothpicks. Nothing worked. The pip remained there for more than forty-eight hours.

One sleepless night and two bloodshot, watery eyes later I took extreme action at work the next morning: I jammed the pointed pocket clip from a Bic Biro cap right between my upper teeth in the direction of the pain – straight past the pip and a good centimetre and a half into soft, raw gum. The pip loosened and slipped on to my tongue, along with saliva and what looked like half a pint of blood.

I was spitting out blood for four days, all because of a luxury orchard-fruits yogurt sold in a silver label.

In the corridor at work the human-resources manager caught me drooling bloody spittle into a soggy paper tissue. One week later and the head of human resources sent a company-wide email about a confidential drug advice service for employees. I couldn't be certain but I suspect the corporate narcotics policy and 'employee wellbeing' strategy was introduced on account of my pallor and fruity-yogurt-induced bloody dribble.

So, maintain healthy gums and the respect of your colleagues. Avoid fruit pips, natural yogurts and orchard-themed dairy desserts. Stick with smooth processed purées, artificially flavoured whipped mousses and layered yogurts with the fruit at the bottom – in plain view and easy to avoid.

Piri-Piri

I was working late last week so I phoned one of those office food-delivery services – the kind of services that charge £15.00 for a damp club sandwich.

On this occasion I fancied the half rotisserie chicken with piri-piri chips (£12.00).

'. . . I'm in W6. On the Goldhawk Road. I'll have the half chicken with the . . .'

I hung up. I couldn't bring myself to say it. I'm from Plymouth and the son of a dinnerlady: I'm not genetically programmed to order things like piri-piri chips without feeling like an affected bourgeois fool, a lisping dandy or a hungry shift-worker with no self-awareness.

They rang me back. I didn't answer. The phone rang three times. I sat there blushing for ten minutes, until I got up and fixed a bowl of breakfast flakes with semi-skimmed milk.

Piri-piri is yet another off-the-shelf sauce; a spicy mayonnaise marinade for coating chicken breasts and selling them at inflated prices with a side slice of mango, seasoned potato wedges and additional Portuguese paprika pizazz.

I like chicken-based recipes. I like chicken. I just don't want to see it on the same plate as a fucking mango.

Pizza

I'm very picky when it comes to pizza – it's a form of inverted snobbery. I like something meaty, doughy and synthetic. I like to order from the garish leaflets of gimmicky local delivery services (Space Pizza, Hippo Pizza, and the Leaning Tower of said dish). I want a mound of sweaty, waxy topping on top of a huge, puffy, decidedly Anglo-Saxon base; something to make the thin-crust purist hyperventilate and the Parma-ham zealot spasm, shake and spray spittle. I want to sit at home and eat it with half a roll of kitchen towel rather than a lightly laundered linen serviette on the table.

I'm also partial to pizza purchased for less than £2.00 from a supermarket's own-brand range; something to munch on while I'm crashed out on the sofa, half-asleep, half-watching a straight-to-DVD thriller starring Frank Stallone and opening with the memorable credit: 'Special Guest Star – Cameron Mitchell as Eddie'.

I hate dining out for pizza. It feels wrong, like going to the theatre in your pyjamas or meeting UK-based Americans in the workplace. I like Americans. I like their country and I like their culture (even though when you go there everyone you talk to seems to be involved in 'real estate') but working with UK-based Americans is bizarre – they appear to me to have wandered in from one of those TV adverts for PC microchips or communications consultancies; one of those ads that imply, 'We can't be bothered to produce a new advert for the UK market as we only make microchips and sell communications consultancy and if you're watching *Coronation Street* or that *Rising Damp* repeat you really don't care about such things – so here's the original American advert with men in chinos, glass buildings, balloons and some vague nonsense about changing the way you live.'

Whenever I talk to an American in the workplace I want

to change the social channel; to flick over and talk to someone about the Football League or chocolate biscuits, before the American tries to instigate a 'team cheer' or a daily 9.00 a.m. progress meeting.

But say what you will about Americans – they do at least know how to eat pizza: from a cardboard box and topped with non-biodegradable plastic cheese while watching rigged pay-per-view boxing or the back-to-back Chuck Norris marathon on Turner Classic Movies.

How are you supposed to eat pizza when you eat out? Are you supposed to use a knife and fork, or pick it up with your fingers like you do at home? Where's the ketchup? There's no ketchup. I always have ketchup on my pizza. And the starters – £6.00 for five tiny dough balls and a thimbleful of salty yellow hollandaise-style sauce?

No, I don't want to join the Pizza Express club. I don't want a free medium pizza of my choice, a pocket diary, a complimentary dessert on an annual basis where terms and conditions apply, a paper membership card and discounted tickets to the Pizza Express Jazz Club in Soho.

And the pizzas: thin crusts, ricotta cheeses, Parma ham, stringy strands of spinach. There's even one with a fried egg in the middle. A bloody fried egg.

I don't want an extensive wine list with my pizza. I want two litres of Pepsi – gratis – and some sort of seasonal deal on soggy garlic loaf and hickory-slicked chicken wings.

Where are the flakes of grated Cheddar cheese, the withered, sliced, non-shitaki mushrooms and the not-quite-defrosted pineapple chunks?

I should be at home eating pizza. It's where pizza belongs. I'm missing a documentary on Channel Five about tornado damage in the Midwest followed by the big movie – Chuck Norris starring as Lone Wolf McQuade. Even money has Cameron Mitchell costarring with Karate Chuck.

I'm sitting in a tiny, black stainless-steel chair – a chair that's at least half the size of my smaller-than-average male backside – in a middle-brow pizza restaurant that's jam-packed with women wearing shawls and embarrassed-looking first-daters.

Every one of them is talking up the décor; stuttering, stalling and staring at their medium Margherita Reginas.

I can't think of anything worse than a night out sitting on a tiny black metal chair, eating a thin-crust spinach pizza with a fried egg in the middle . . .

Apart from having to listen to live fucking jazz.

Plants

Nettles, dandelions and thistles can all be used as ingredients in salads, risottos and pasta dishes.

Even though people have been cooking with plants for centuries, the idea of making wine and preparing food with wild ingredients underwent a popular revival in the seventies as people rejected the starchy, bland, processed foods of the postwar generation.

Environmental concern and the interest in natural ingredients as a cultural fad reached its apotheosis in 1979 when Stevie Wonder released *The Secret Life of Plants*, a synth-heavy, largely instrumental concept album that explored the spiritual connection between people and plants . . .

Stevie's love of plants continued unabated until he unwrapped the cactus I gave him last Christmas.

Ploughman's Lunch

Tarnished horse brasses hung on white textured walls in Tudor-type taverns. Pre-Industrial Revolution milk pails used for convenient crisp-bag disposal and cheeky three-point practice for the occasional dry-roasted-peanut Michael Jordan manqué. Ceramic shire-horses gathering dust on crooked shelves. Oak-panelled floors scattered with sawdust and scratching dust. Burnished brass hooks that hang Scampi Fries sales cards in Farnham Fleece & Firkin Free Houses.

These days, most pubs seem to strive for an aesthetic that's half Scandinavian summerhouse and half the bridge of the *Starship Enterprise*, but, for a while, there was no aspect of British pub life that was untouched by the need to invoke an imaginary agrarian past in order to sell pub grub, salted snacks and pale ales from a pump.

The need to apply a bucolic veneer to everyday ingredients reached its apex with the ploughman's lunch – that Cheddar-cheese, crusty-bread and sweet-pickle repast that, while conforming to a generic, mass-produced nationwide standard, conjured up the image of a red-faced, tousle-haired nineteenth-century farmhand perched on a bale of hay, unwrapping a wedge of crusty bread from muslin cloth and slicing through a chunk of cheese with a scrimshaw-handled penknife.

Despite its perceived rural roots, the ploughman's origins

lie in a 1970s promotional campaign by the Milk Marketing Board to popularise cheese-centric lunches in Britain's bars and hostelries. I don't know what mental process or idea pushed them towards the ploughman's – it still seems like a strange concept and something of a dairy *non sequitur*. Maybe they had a lazy month before the big strawberry-milk push.

It's surprising that, even in the face of such competitions as garlic mash, monkfish and pan-fried venison, the ploughman's lives on as a menu stalwart in Britain's pubs; as much a fixture as a Trivial Pursuit machine on the blink, the chewing-gum-clogged urinal, the cellar man (recently paroled for sex offences) and that funny little fella from Singapore who comes in on Thursday nights to sell bootleg Marlboro Lights and DVD copies of *Spider-Man 7*.

Recently I ordered a 'Boatman's Lunch' at a roadside pub in Great Wyrley, near Walsall. It comprised three crabsticks, a leaf of brown iceberg lettuce, a green cherry tomato, six prawns, a wedge of crusty bread (well, it was either crusty or stale – I just can't tell any more) and one foil-wrapped creamy-cheese triangle – a sneaky refugee from the children's menu. It was appalling. It was contrived. It was a marine version of the ploughman's – a taste of the sea for the landlocked minibus tourist en route to the Ideal Home Exhibition and the *Cutty Sark*.

Plymouth Argyle 1–Luton Town 2
(A Large Traditional Cornish Pasty)

My contract for this alleged work of blokey non-fiction obliges me to mention the sport of Association Football at least once; to parallel my personal struggles with those of my chosen team, even though, between the ages of eight and sixteen, I went to only twelve first-team matches, preferring to spend Saturday afternoons reading fantasy fiction with disturbing, airbrushed covers about lawless desert planets where a talking lizard hegemony ruled over man and where green space cinnamon was twenty times more valuable than gold.

I'll write about my time running with a 'firm' of hooligans, about how I cried when we finally won the 'Cup' and about how, as I sit here in my North London home watching my fragrant wife, on maternity leave from her top public-relations job, cradling Kye, our newborn son, Association Football doesn't seem quite so important any more.

Unfortunately Plymouth Argyle, my chosen team, have never won a trophy of any global significance and I tend to avoid North London like the Ebola plague. I've never had any personal struggles to speak of, I don't have a wife or newborn child and whenever someone mentions 'United' to me I think not of the Reds of Manchester but of United Biscuits, revered manufacturers of the Jaffa Cake and the milk-chocolate Hob Nob.

Whenever I did attend football games as a child, I was never allowed to eat at the ground. Before Argyle home games my mum would contrive to cook me and my dad an iceberg-lettuce, tomato-half and sliced-ham lunch;

healthy (if you cut the inch of white fat from the watery pre-sliced ham) and just filling enough to stave off half-time hunger and the gristly, greasy lure of the terrace meat pie, pasty or sausage roll.

However, it's an Easter Bank Holiday, I'm back in Plymouth, tired of my mum's quiche, determined to feast on some proper football food and maybe shout something at the referee – something about his mother being free with her affections, or whatever is the insult du jour in the Haze Air Wick Crystal Sparkling Citrus Football League Division One.

Maybe a pre-match pastry before an end-of-season, mid-table, essentially meaningless 'clash' between Championship giants Plymouth Argyle and Luton Town will present me with the perfect British dining experience; an experience I was cruelly denied as a scarf-waving youth.

In the most fitting deal in world football, Argyle are sponsored by Ginsters pasties. This means that the only pies and pasties available in the ground are made by Ginsters – no fun at all when you consider that Ginsters snacks are available in every service station, metro supermarket and tuck shop in the country. Plus service-station pasties are all wrong: they're all heavy pastry and excess handle, two minutes in the microwave and sixteen days in the digestive system.

I eschew the lure of the all-day brunch or mass-market ham-and-mozzarella slice and join a queue outside a white transit van some 500 metres from the ground (presumably outside the Ginsters-snack exclusion zone), eventually purchasing two 'large traditional' Cornish pasties for £2.20 each.

I give my dad his pasty and ease mine from its grease-sopped paper bag. It's slightly burnt. A few years ago I'd heard on Radio Four that burnt food can give you cancer. For a split second I consider going back to complain. I think better of it – the queue of hungry football fans, which is snaking all the way back to the public toilets, might take exception to me keeping them from their pre-match snacks; maybe they'd suggest in song that my mother is promiscuous or that I have predilection for self-abuse.

I've eaten half of the pasty by the time we arrive at the Home Park turnstiles. Not bad. The pastry is moist yet flaky, the swede, potato and beef have melted into each other and the spicy seasonings have put me in the mood for a pint of fizzy lager and an easy victory for the South West's premier Association Football team.

The steward at the turnstiles tells me that I can't take the pasty into the ground. It's five minutes to kick-off so I wolf it down. Like a wolf.

We pass through the gates and take our seats. The referee's whistle signals kick-off and also kicks off some serious heartburn.

Maybe I've lived in London for too long, but I start to wonder if they sell mint tea at the snack bar. 'It aids diges-tion and settles the stomach,' I shout to my dad over the dirty chant about the referee's wife.

'Maybe they have some nettle and ginger.'

Yes, I've lived in London for too long. No mint tea. They don't have any stomach-settling yogurt drinks, either. I buy a can of Sprite (the league is now sponsored by Coca-Cola so Panda Pop Shandy, cans of Dandelion & Burdock made from well-water in Peterborough and other flat, sugary regional variations on the carbonated beverage are, regrettably, a thing of the past).

The Sprite has made the indigestion worse. It's 0–0 at half-time, a deadly dull match.

A sweet volley from our Bulgarian midfielder puts us one goal up. I don't care; I still have half a large traditional Cornish pasty stuck somewhere in my chest. Luton respond with two lucky goals. The man in front of me is eating a Ginsters minced-beef-and-onion pie – scooping out the filling with a large salt-and-vinegar crisp. My dad has his head in his hands; my hands are covering my mouth. I must start reading fantasy fiction again.

Porcini Mushrooms

Posh mushrooms, often sold dried and shrivelled – like those bath-towel cubes that expand once immersed in water – and used in sauces, risottos and pasta dishes. They taste like 'the woods'.

Portobello Mushroom

Vegetarians of Britain, I feel for you. Not only are you constantly beaten with the Paul McCartney stick (beware, it's the stick that's beaten in the lame, shuffled meter common to his Wings-era hits rather than the stick shaken in meaty, beat-y early-Beatles mode), but also, when I glance at the vegetarian entrées listed on the average British bill of fare, I feel your pain.

Stuffed peppers; mozzarella-topped beef tomatoes; baked aubergines. Peppers stuffed with baked aubergines; peppers stuffed with mozzarella-topped beef tomatoes and baked aubergines. And the Portobello mushroom: that big, brown, cultivated mushroom that tastes like packing foam and is used as a meat substitute in vegetarian burgers.

Anything with the prefix 'Portobello' is rubbish. Especially London's Portobello Market; a place where neon-bumbag-wearing Germans and dead-eyed neo-hippies throng on Saturday mornings to eat noodles from polystyrene boxes, buy shopping bags made from Japanese washing-powder packets, T-shirts screen-printed with Cannon and Ball covers from *Look-In* magazines and combat trousers made from hemp.

I demand better entrée choices for Britain's vegetarians. I like vegetarians. Most of my friends are vegetarians. Despite what jibes from meat-eaters might suggest, vegetarians are not hippies. They're normal people with genuine and legitimate concerns about the meat-production process. Besides, hippies don't exist any more . . .

Those fuckers you see now with the long hair, the badly trimmed goatee beards, the loose-fitting clothes, the love beads, the Roman sandals and the ratty leather jewellery – those fuckers are Australians.

Hippies were a different breed. Hippies were into 'dropping-out' rather than 'getting a good job in IT then converting pounds to Australian dollars and buying a three-bedroom house in Melbourne'.

Hippies were into free love, making love and not war, and love-ins. The dirty buggers.

I'm not completely sure what a 'love-in' is. Maybe it's a 1960s version of today's tabloid 'sex romp' – only with body-painting and not necessarily described by the words: 'His Sex Shame' and 'Crisis Talks about Their Marriage'.

The hippie generation could teach us a lot. They knew that universal peace can be achieved only by bed-ins and joining hands. They knew how to live with the rhythms of the Earth. They also knew that on a high-amphetamine diet you can eat all the carbohydrates you want.

Heavy use of LSD offsets the weight-gain effects of complex starch sugars and is a non-fattening alternative to omega 3 liposomes.

Potato Longboats

'I heartily recommend the pork medallions in honey-and-lemon sauce with a julienne of vegetables.' 'To start with, I'll have the smoked-salmon pinwheels and meat-pastry crolines with the poached mushroom hats.' 'Try our deep-filled potato longboats with a choice of country-fresh fillings.' 'Can I tempt you with our award-winning summer-berry opera?'

Restaurant owners: do not try to make your anaemic, unimaginative fare sound slightly more appealing by pretending that it looks like another object. They are not scale replicas of Viking longboats made from potato. They're hollowed-out spud skins filled with mayo and tuna chunks from the cash 'n' carry.

Poussin

They're mini whole chickens. They're loads of dinky fun: pretend you're a giant. They're fee-fi-fo-fiddley to eat.

Pre-Moulded Potatoes

Potato waffles, potato bites shaped like letters of the alphabet, and oven-baked potato fritters. They're all pre-moulded, processed potato products. They're all revolting.

I'm half Irish, on my mother's side, but even I yearn for the return of the spud-munching blight bug in the face of such shoddy potato-based convenience foods.

My mum still holds a grudge against the British for the Potato Famine that killed between 500,000 and 1,000,000 people between 1845 and 1848.

During the whole mid-eighties Live Aid and Band Aid era she relentlessly complained that the 'English didn't raise a feckin' finger to help us [the starving Irish]' during the nineteenth-century Potato Famine.

I used to say, 'Mum, the Irish Potato Famine was more than a century and a half ago. Get over it, and, anyway, surely you've read about Music Hall Relief: a thigh-slapping charitable ensemble featuring Sarah Bernhardt, Lottie Collins, several men dressed as tramps – wearing top hats whose lids were hanging off (a bit like a mid-nineteenth-century version of the Boomtown Rats, but significantly less shit) – two toff tenors who sang songs about "fillies", the races and drinking champagne, and even an early incarnation of Pink Floyd. They all got together for larks-a-plenty and to sing "Stop the famine and feed the Papist savage Tar-ra-ra-boom-der-ay".'

Pre-Washed Salad

A wild-wild rocket salad with softly seasoned baby leaf. Six-leaf Italian-style with wildish rocket and lamb's lettuce. Leafy salad with tatsoi. Crunchy summer special with carrot shreds. Herby aromatic salad with chervil and our old friend coriander.

Pre-washed salads: they all taste the same, they all shrivel after five minutes. Just what is chervil anyway? I couldn't even find it on Google.

Provenance

Line-caught sea bass; grilled Danebridge trout with fresh Spanish almonds; roast Barbary duck in a Seville-orange sauce; pan-fried escalope of corn-fed chicken; Lundy cod with forest-fresh mushrooms; Hampshire Downs lamb with wild Basque mushrooms.

Just who is that John Dory bloke anyway and why does he have the monopoly on fresh fish?

Aberdeen Angus beef fillets and roast pavé of Pyrenees lamb: the provenance of the tasteless mass of mush on your plate. You won't finish it. You shouldn't have ordered it. But at least you know where it came from.

Provenance is everywhere; I bought a four-pack of supermarket apples yesterday.

Country of Origin: UK
Farmer: Mr Charles Wilbur, Somerset

There's even a picture of Farmer Wilbur. He looks like an old-fashioned friendly farmer with honest mud on his boots and an ample wife called Rosie who bakes a mean apple pie. Not the type to spray his crops with dangerous chemicals, shoot New Age travellers or feed powdered carcass to his livestock.

Too much information.

Pub Thai

'We're going down the Cock and Lion. Upstairs it's the Palms of Goa. They have wicker placemats, paper lanterns, battered tiger-prawn starters, sticky rice, green curried chicken, Champions League on plasma screens and Bombardier Best Bitter on tap.'

(See also Thai Food.)

Pubs In Summer

I hate drinking outside pubs in the summer. The beer is warm. Either the petrol fumes bake as they rise from the street or the polluted canal broils and simmers a soup of decaying prophylactics, crisp packets and brown mutant perch.

The man in front of you at the bar wears a sweat-soaked

blue office shirt and offensively unfashionable wraparound shades. What is this – 1996?!

Midges and wasps buzz around sticky, uncollected glasses. Bankers with red faces and pints of fizzy European lager clap aggressively and shout 'nice one' and 'well done, mate', fake-Cockney-accented, football-terrace style when someone drops a pint glass on the pavement.

'Whaaay. Nice one, mate!'

'Leave her alone. It's only a glass. It was an accident – no need to be so hostile. Jesus.'

Women with excessive eye make-up and estuary accents shake plastic collection containers for children's charities that no one's ever heard of.

A donation of at least £1.00 will get you a sticker saying 'Sexy', a peck on the cheek or a cola Chupa-Chup lolly. Cola Chupa-Chups are the coffee cream of the lickable confectionary world. And I've never even heard of the Rainbow Kids Foundation.

The business drinker from the City with the late-nineties extreme-sports-style sunglasses barks at her: 'What is this for – the AIDS or the kiddie cancer? Haven't they cleared those landmines yet?' before choking with mirth on his own wisdom and a mouthful of warm, watery lager and parting with any change. Charming.

While drinking by the river on a summer's evening three or four years ago (I can't quite remember – it was either the summer of 'She Bangs, She Bangs' or the year when every woman wore a coin belt and a frilly, low-cut white 'peasant' top) and under the influence of several sour glasses of the house white wine, I confronted the tin-shaking dolly with the caked-on Rimmel mask and the overzealous rouge-application procedure and tried to get her to admit she wasn't a registered charity worker but was a trainee nail technician from Kent and the whole collection was a shady scam, an eyelash-fluttering girly grift; there was no such charity as Music Therapy for Kittens and cola-flavoured Chupa-Chups seriously sucked.

She burst into tears and an entire eight-man rowing team threatened to 'kick my fucking head in'.

Pulled Pork

Pulled Pork, jerked chicken, seared scallops, dicked-about-with duck. Slices of roast beef *rolled* around in watercress and Béarnaise sauce.

Stop messing with your food – you're frittering your life away.

The 'jerk' in jerk chicken actually refers to the method of poking holes in the bird and stuffing them with spices before cooking. Fifth-rate restaurant owners and menu consultants for the chain steakhouse off the bypass: it does not refer to the method of sloppily brushing cash 'n' carry, bulk-buy hickory marinade on to processed chicken strips.

Pumpkin Seeds

You can eat as many of those ubiquitous green seeds as you want – they're not going to make you live for ever.

You can mix them with your cookie dough; sprinkle

them on your Special K; roast them for risottos; and shake them on to salads. You're still going to die like the rest of us.

Quaker Oats

My sister once told me that the genial Quaker on the front of the Quaker Oats cereal box was what God looked like.

Then again, she also told me that Satan looked like the dragon from the Disney movie *Pete's Dragon* so she's not exactly an expert in artistic representations of divinities.

Quiche Lorraine

There are certain statements that you never hear people make any more: 'Your hair looks nice. Is that mousse?' 'I love that tribal tattoo. Most unusual.' 'Make sure she's on the pill.' 'I'll have the quiche Lorraine please, waiter.'

Quiche is dead. It's deader than disco, the dodo and the twelve-part fly-on-the-wall docusoap about Dover dentists. After a covert rebranding exercise, the quiche is now the 'savoury tart'. The holy Cheddar, chopped-onion and cubed-ham trinity has been usurped by the sunblushed-tomato, asparagus and goat's-cheese axis.

My parents still cook quiche as the central dish of their Saturday-evening meal. Quiche Lorraine accompanied by crinkle-cut oven chips with a raisin-and-carrot salad on half-moon-shaped side plates.

My parents are always at least eight years behind the rest of the country in their food choices.

They've pencilled-in crème fraîche for 2012.

Raisins

I'm not too keen on them. I found a little twig in one once.

Real Ale

I've recently decided that I don't actually like beer.

It's OK. I haven't converted to some strict Presbyterian faith. I've just realised that all beer looks and tastes like week-old rainwater.

I don't like bitter, lager, stout or even real ale.

Real ale is flat brown beer for old men with froth in their beards, marmalade in their moustaches, fluff and toast crumbs on their thick woollen sweaters, time on their hands and *Time Team* on their (VHS) timers.

Be careful, they're liable to refer to small change as 'shrapnel' and to their boss as 'the gaffer'.

Reduced Fat/Low in Salt/No Saturated Fats or Added Sugars

'Here at [insert name of manufacturer, supermarket, restaurant, food chain or coffee-shop] we take your health seriously and have taken out all the crunchy, teeth-sizzling sugars, the fun, chewy fats and the exciting neon colours. Now everything we serve is a runny, low-fat beige mush speckled with pumpkin seeds that leaves half a litre of water behind in the packaging.'

Well, good. Bully for you. Award yourself a badge that reads 'chuffed'. They shouldn't have been in there in the first place. What do you want? A sugarlump, my smudged Biro squiggle on a wallet-clogging loyalty card, a strawberry-swirl lollypop in the shape of a dummy?

A reduced-fat rabbit-and-chicken cat-snack with extra antioxidants?

Renowned Hostelries

The 600-year-old coaching inn is where King James II spent a weekend with his mistress, Arabella Churchill. Room thirty-four at the Packhorse Hotel was Meryl Streep's while she was filming *A French Lieutenant's Woman.*

While staying at a Devon coaching inn Sir Arthur Conan Doyle, inspired by the dramatic Exmoor landscape, wrote a short ghost story while making full use of the hairdryer and complimentary tea- and coffee-making facilities.

I love local legends: tall tales about the spirits of murdered maidens with broken hearts and severed heads; restless cavaliers; satanic rites, standing stones, child sacrifice, escaped panthers and other sheep-worrying cryptozoological creatures.

If you're from Devon you'll have grown up hearing many stories about witchcraft: the old oak tree looks like a witch's hand; the standing stones were used for the weekly satanic ritual; a big black cat – possibly a panther – is slaughtering livestock by the model village.

Talk of goat sacrifice, howling man-wolves and frenzied cattle-slayings has been buzzing around the Rotary Club ever since a man with a nose-ring, greasy hair and Saxon T-shirt was spotted busking near the annual farmer's market.

Restrictions

You can't have the seafood linguine after 6.00. The dauphinoise potatoes are off. Gala pie is out of season. If you want the ham hock on a weekend, you're shit out of luck.

The guinea fowl? In March? You are having a laugh.

Lump it or leave it.

Risotto

Risotto isn't yet a British favourite or a snack-bar stalwart; nearly but not quite.

Al dente? Sod that. It won't be long before it's boiled down to a rice-pudding mush – a thin white gruel – and topped with a thick layer of lumpy Cheddar cheese and diced ham from a oval can, sprinkled with coriander, undisclosed herbs from a poly-plastic packet and gelling agents, and served with a sprig of flora and curly chilli cheese fries.

You'll know exactly when the British public wholly embraces this Italian creamy rice dish. You'll know just by looking at laminated menus and chalkboards: 'risotto and chips'.

Romantic Dinner for Two

I hate sitting near young couples when I'm eating out. It turns my stomach and forces me to skip the soup, click my fingers, gauchely yell '*Garçon*' and request the mints, the cheese biscuits and bill – pronto.

It happened last weekend: the loved-up young couple one table over were driving me nuts and the harried head waiter refused to move me to a different table.

The amorous young man was wearing a cheap grey suit in order to impress. His paramour had streaked and curled her hair for the occasion and stuffed herself into a chintzy lace dress.

He billed and she cooed. He whispered: 'You are my world. I'm only half a man without you.' She spoke softly in response: 'I love it when you breathe in. I also love it when you breathe out.' They spoon-fed each other a sickly orange, brandy and fresh-cream gateaux, goo-goo'd, gurgled, made doe eyes, baby voices and spit-bubbles. They held hands, meshed fingers and lip-synched along to Labi Siffre's 'Something Inside So Strong' while sipping honey-scented dessert wine.

Get. A. Room.

I grated my teeth and came close to piercing the skin on my thigh with the prong from a silver-service fork. I just couldn't eat after witnessing such a revolting display.

I swear to Christ, that's the last wedding I'm ever going to.

Salad Bar

I am not obsessive-compulsive. I do not wash my hands
every ten minutes: gummy workplace liquid soap in
bright-pink shades induces in me anxiety attacks and
shallow breathing.

No, I do not have any kind of obsessive-compulsive
disorder, but I do feel this urge to tidy Britain's salad bars.

There's a slice of beetroot in with the cucumber –
consider it contaminated. The cover's missing on those
chicory bacon bits – they're in a 'hole' rather than a silver
tray; maybe that's some sort of metaphor. '18/3/01:
replaced tongs' is scrawled on the clipboard cleaning rota
– the last entry.

The ranch dressing is rancid.

Have you ever been on a ranch? I haven't but I saw
one on the TV version of *Lonesome Dove*. It looked like
it stank.

The tongs are shackled to the bar via weathered
washing-line wire; the scratches, grazes and grooves on
the plastic prongs are an ideal environment for dinky
germs and mini-bacteria monsters with poison-tipped
fangs.

Several of the chickpeas are blackening and the iceberg
is on the turn. Are those cherry tomatoes or kumquats?
Those croûtons have been there since the first Gulf War.
There's a gloopy 'skin' on the Thousand Island, giving it
the shiny, metallic sheen of workplace liquid soap.

He shudders.

Salad Selections

I always talk myself into buying salad selections – those little tubs of side dishes they sell in supermarket chiller cabinets. Tubs of potato salad with spinach, cubed beetroot, plankton-sized prawns with cottage cheese and chives; luxury Mexican coleslaw with peanuts, carrot shreds and sweet chilli mayonnaise.

There's even Thai satay coleslaw and rustic coleslaw with apple chunks and cashews, for Christ's sake.

I buy them and I never eat them. There's a 200-gram tub of three-bean salad at the back of my fridge. I bought it in 2002. I'm scared to touch it. I'm sure it's the cause of the flickering bulb. It's waging a private war with that egg-shaped Fridge Fresh odour-absorber. Removing one of them could set off a chain reaction.

Salsa

Made from tomatoes, peppers and vegetables, salsa is ideal as a dip. Serve it with spicy tortilla chips on a Thursday night while watching Aston Villa play second-string European opposition on Channel Five.

Salsa is also the name of the Latin dance that first gained popularity among the Spanish-speaking population of New York in the 1950s.

I recently went to a salsa night in South London in the hope of meeting a leggy Brazilian woman who'd dance the cha-cha-cha, cook food that sizzled, curse me sexily in Portuguese, then make the sign of the cross after a brief-but-stormy tiff, and walk round the flat in a yellow bikini even thought it was November.

   She wouldn't even stamp her foot and demand that I send £300.00 a month to her mother, grandparents and six brothers in Porto Alegre. What a sweetheart.

   Unfortunately, the only women there were excessively hair-moussed, Tweed-by-Lentheric-wearing, hot-flushing divorcees in cerise silk shirts with diamanté cameo brooches covering their top buttons; every one of them a dead ringer for Elaine Paige or Barbara Dickson in the video for 'I Know Him So Well'.

   Bugger.

Saturday 27 May: My First Dinner Party

I have absolutely no idea what class I am.

   As you know, I am – like the stocky, decidedly blue-collar soccer star Wayne Rooney – the son of a dinnerlady. I spent my childhood in a small, pebble-dashed bungalow in Plymouth. These autobiographical details would suggest that I'm 100 per cent working class. No arguments.

   On the other hand, I've never taken my shirt off in public – not even on a really hot day. I have no tattoos. I never spit in the street unless I have some really severe phlegm that I have to get rid of (even then, I'll turn around to any passing witnesses and rasp apologetically: 'Sorry for spitting. It's winter. I have a bad case of nasal congestion, the need to get rid of some mucus and no handkerchief handy . . .').

   And the evidence stacks up: I have absolutely no

idea how to work a fruit machine. Maybe, then, I'm middle class.

I own three Italian suits which I wear for occasions other than weddings, funerals and visits to the magistrates' court or Tuesday-afternoon Job Club. I buy organic fruit and veg in a health-food supermarket called Back to Nature that offers gluten-free wine gums and wooden abacuses as point-of-sale purchase items rather than lime and orange Tic-Tacs and women's magazines printed on noisy, flimsy paper that tear easily and promise sudoku, slimming and true-life sex stories relating to squalid son-in-law seductions by sixty-something Southport mums.

Despite all this, I still feel intimidated while shopping in the House of Fraser. I do my regular Thursday-night 'essentials' shop in a budget supermarket and I listen to Country and Western music.

I shot a man in Asda just to watch him die.

But, as I've said before, the fact that I've never been to a dinner party means that I can never really be middle class.

So, at the invitation of Bev and Chris, a couple of married ex-colleagues, I cleaned my fingernails, moisturised my coal-smudged working-class face, dusted off my cufflinks, gargled heavily on something mint-flavoured with an advanced fluoride formula and readied myself for some personal history: my first (Saturday-night) dinner party.

I was nervous. My cufflinks had Italian actor Marcello Mastroianni on them. I hadn't worn them since I was a media student, more than ten years ago. Did they make me look like a twat? Isn't fluoride supposed to be bad for you now? (Years ago it was associated with brilliant white teeth and healthy gums. Now it seems to be synonymous with the word 'cancer' and stock footage on the local news of water-treatment plants and bereaved families lobbying for adequate compensation.)

I didn't know Bev and Chris that well – I'd worked with them for only four or five months. What if they were odd? What if their house had a funny smell? What if they lit a cinnamon-and-sandalwood candle to mask the odour and set the mood with a Lighthouse Family compact disc? Would they force me into the cellar and molest me, serve me chicken with cheese or set me up with a girl called Emily with disturbing teeth, a pear-shaped figure, a nose like a mole's and multiple pets?

Bearing in mind that I'm a freelancer, generally working on short-term contracts, it's not often that I see co-workers socially. If I'm honest, it's something I try to avoid. I'm a maverick, a loose cannon. I'm a gun for hire. I go to the bank in my lunch break and stay behind for an hour in the evening to doctor my personal expenses. The last time I socialised with co-workers was in April 2004 on a Friday-night trip to an Hogshead chain pub near Liverpool Street with colleagues from the advertising agency I was contracting for at the time.

It was 6.30 and I was stuck in a one-sided conversation with a junior marketing manager called Tilly. After commenting on how ugly everyone else in the bar was, she ordered a glass of cheap white wine, rolled her eyes, looked straight through me, explained how she'd had been 'reading a lot of books about lucid dreaming' and showed me her mobile-phone 'wallpaper': a pencil sketch in a heavy lead of her ponies, Toffee and Truffle.

I left straight after the mobile pony art exhibition, saying that I usually 'help someone out on a stall' on Saturday mornings and needed my sleep.

So, with butterflies in my rumbling stomach and Marcello pinning my twatty, fraying, coal-dust-caked cuffs together, I left for Bev and Chris's suburban semi.

I was looking forward to it. I thought it should be fun: a few hours of friendly chat and good food on a warm Saturday night in spring. Plus, I hadn't been out in months. Not since a friend's engagement party in February and that night was memorable only because the taxi driver on the way home insisted that I was the spitting image of Neil Sedaka.

I'd bought a pretty decent bottle of red wine with me, too: a £30.00 Merlot from Francis Ford Coppola's Californian vineyard. Not only would this grant me gravitas with Chris – a man who liked his New World wines – but also, if things got really desperate, it'd give me *carte blanche* to weave elaborate booze-and-film puns around the phrases: *'The Godfather'*, *'Apocalypse Now'* and, if the wine had done its job and I was feeling especially orally adventurous, *'Tucker: The Man and His Dream.'*

Just for the record, I don't look anything like Neil Sedaka. I Googled him when I got back home. He's a short, tanned American with a ball-shaped face, much like a sun-withered tangerine; a happy, singing sun-withered tangerine that tours resorts and takes requests.

I have a long face and I don't know the words to 'Oh Carol', so that's all settled.

7.45 I arrive at Bev and Chris's. I'm fifteen minutes early. Chris is still in his jeans and polo shirt. His jeans are sky blue with tapered legs. The type of denim only ever worn by geography teachers on field trips to standing stones and Francis Rossi from Status Quo. Bev is upstairs, reading *The Very Hungry Caterpillar* to Sophie and Jake. Chris doesn't seem pleased: he said to turn up at eight-ish. He takes the Coppola wine. It's still wrapped in the white tissue paper. He doesn't take the paper off to look at the bottle. I hope he looks at it before the other guests arrive with their wines in the £5.00 to £10.00 range, also wrapped in white tissue paper: the old wine mix-up. That's happened to me before. Or did it? I may have seen it on a sitcom when I was half-asleep.

7.46 Yes, the wine mix-up was on a sitcom – I've never even been to a dinner party before.

7.48 Chris ushers me towards the living room and flicks on the plasma-screen TV – I can wait here while everyone gets ready and the other guests arrive. He flicks it on with expert nonchalance, like he's had it for ever, even though the instructions, extra batteries and guarantee certificate are still sealed in plastic envelopes on the sideboard. The Saturday-night hospital drama is on and an old man has fallen down the stairs.

7.50 Yes, the house does indeed have a funny smell. They must have hairy pets and no scented candles.

7.55 The old man's hospitalisation has precipitated reconciliation with his daughter with the unlikely East London accent and solvents addiction. He has a granddaughter he doesn't know about. It touches his frosty heart. Strangely, I'm happy for him, even though he's fictional.

8.00 *National Lottery Live.* It's a rollover and I forgot to buy a ticket. Bugger.

8.05 Chris enters the living room. He's wearing his good slacks and a black roll-neck jumper. Maybe the party is about to start. Woo-hoo!

8.06 No, it isn't. Bev told him to 'put a tape in' for *Rory Bremner*. He can't find a spare one and doesn't want to tape over *Alan Yentob Investigates Art*, or whatever that smug show is called.

8.10 Someone runs up the stairs. Then silence. Ten whole minutes of empty, eerie silence, apart from some poorly scripted rural murder mystery with John Nettles.

8.20 The doorbell rings. The host and hostess yelp greetings – 'Hiiiyaaaa' and such. I never got that warm a welcome. All I got was attitude, the wine-bottle-snatch and an eyeful of Dad-rock denim.

8.21 Bev and Chris usher the other guests into the living room. They seem nice enough. Andrew and Annalise: a smiley couple with an impressive set of complementary names. Pleasant couples always have complementary names – names that scan; names that harmonise like sophisticated drawing-room double acts with Tuesday-night residences in places called the Colonial Club; one of the partnership playing piano and the other one standing up, whistling and singing 'Don't put your daughter on the pill, Mrs Wigginbottom'; names that balance and support each other, like wafer-thin metal bookends made in Scandinavia.

Andrew and Annalise look like they own their own personal set of Swedish bookends.

Graham and Denise, for example, aren't a good set of dinner-party-couple names. They're the names of that childless couple three doors down with the two-berth caravan parked in the drive for fifty-one weeks of the year,

the shelf full of colourful hand-blown glass clowns, the
Viennese whirls served on Sundays from a three-tier cake
stand, the sun bed in the shed at the bottom of the garden,
the daily delivery from Kays Catalogue, the layaway
payments to the Christmas Club, the monthly swingers'
club for couples and the eventual trial separation.

8.23 I'm also introduced to Teri, an American woman –
small, toothsome, shaped like a pear and in her mid-twenties
– who immediately announces that she's from 'Atlanta,
Georgia', even though no one asks her.

Yeah, all right, love. Don't get the map out. She's
another American straight out of a computer-chip
commercial, though she's not wearing chinos, sitting in
front of a flat-screen PC or holding a symbolic balloon.

8.24 'I'm from Plymouth, Devon. Don't go there – it'll
probably be closed.'

8.25 'No, It won't *actually* be closed. That's just an
expression.'

8.26 Chris offers drinks. I ask for a red wine; he produces
a non-Coppola red. Either my Merlot is still in the white
tissue paper or he's keeping it for himself.

8.28 Chris makes a joke about Bev taking the food out
of the packets. Everyone laughs.

8.30 More small talk: Saturday-night traffic, the prices of
property and printer ink.

8.35–8.48 Without anyone asking her, Teri tells us her
personal history, including a rundown of her relationships
and her previous jobs, all without pausing or using any
punctuation. Actually, to be fair, she *does* pause – every
thirty seconds, in order to laugh at her own jokes.

Actually, she doesn't make any jokes. She just laughs

every time she's said something. I hope she's not going to keep that up all night.

She constantly plays with her hair, curling it between her fingers. That's unhygienic. I hope she's not sitting next to me.

8.55 Andrew asks: 'Is that Sacha Distel on your cufflinks?'

8.57 Standing there with a glass of sour red wine, making dumb small talk, I feel like a character in a seventies sitcom. If one of the guests suddenly announced that they 'work in oil' I'd be compelled to counter with, 'What are you – a sardine?' before the canned laughter kicked in.

Outside, in the leafy suburban street, I can hear a car backfiring to a perky Ronnie Hazlehurst soundtrack, canned laughter and the anguished cries of a father whose daughter has brought a new boyfriend home for the first time. He's a 'lout' with long hair, a tartan bomber jacket with a sheepskin collar, a clip-on earring and an overpronounced gum-chewing technique. I can hear sitcom Dad dropping his pipe as the backfiring Vauxhall Viva splutters to a start.

Sitcom daydream over. I snap back to the conversation: Andrew doesn't 'work in oil'. He's a therapist, so I can't make the sardine joke.

9.00 We take our seats at the dining table. Chris mentions that 'Martin's writing a book about the anthropology of dining in the UK'. Everyone 'Oooos', 'Aaaahs' and demands an extract. I tell them no: any extracts I could give them would be out of context and unrepresentative.

9.01 I give in and tell them how my first crush was on the woman on the Quality Street tins. I've always been a sucker for women in bonnets. Nobody says anything. I go bright red and say, 'As I said, it's all about context;

you'll have to read it.' I make a note: edit out the bonnet-fetish revelation – the world isn't ready.

9.05 We sit down. I tell Teri about an American friend of mine who's also from one of the Southern States, a 'fellow Septic'.

9.15 Chris has printed out menu cards in Microsoft Word. The print is smudged: he has a dot-matrix printer rather than laserjet. My surname is wrongly spelt: 'Martin Lampeter'. It's only ever spelt like that on those weekly letters from the *Reader's Digest*. Fuckers. I let it pass.

9.18 I explain to Teri that in Cockney rhyming slang 'Septic Tank' means 'Yank'. She says that she's a first-generation Hispanic-American and asks, 'Is there a term for that in rhyming slang?'

'No, love. You're completely missing the point there.'

I don't actually say that. I just shake my head.

9.26 Starters: seared scallops in a wine-based sauce. Nice. I hope Bev didn't use the Coppola Merlot on the shellfish.

No, she didn't. It's a white-wine sauce.

9.28 A misjudged joke: 'What are scallops anyway? What do they look like? Do they make good pets?'

9.30 'Do Sophie and Jake have any pets?' They don't: confirmation that the house just smells funny.

9.35 Everyone has finished their starter. Annalise gets up to photograph the dinner-party guests with her digital camera. I hate having my photo taken. The Native Americans believed that a photograph could steal a person's soul. I don't believe that, but, while I scrub up reasonably well in the flesh, even the kindest photography makes me look like Lee Harvey Oswald. She takes the picture anyway.

It's one of those social photos that capture a moment for the sake of it; a photo that no one will ever look at again – just like all those blurry snapshots of cake and the Red Arrows in my parents' leatherette-bound albums.

9.38 I explain the Red Arrows to Teri. I don't actually know what the point of the Red Arrows is, so I make it up: they were flown by the Red Baron in the Battle of Britain and soar in formations at provincial air shows for no real reason. The final show on Bank Holiday Monday is usually cancelled on account of the fatal Fokker Wolf fireball from the day before.

She doesn't even laugh at the Fokker Wolf reference. The realisation: Teri doesn't laugh at anyone else's jokes – just her own non-jokes.

9.45 The main course arrives. It's a confit shoulder of lamb with Anna potatoes. It looks nice. Thank God it wasn't another lamb shank. I can't even look at one without my legs cramping something chronic. More jokes about opening packets. More 'ha ha ha's.

9.46 Talk turns to music. Chris puts some background 'tunes' on – some band from Iceland. 'Post-rock', he calls it. I call it bloody fucking rubbish; Tangerine Dream on ice. Andy licks his lips and mentions that he and Annalise recently attended one of Bob Dylan's London concerts. I say that I'd rather drink neat Toilet Duck than pay £45.00-plus to see some wizened, haggard fake gypsy, some mumbler of hollow doggerel who hasn't made a half-decent record since Richard Nixon ran the White House and Richard O'Sullivan ran *Robin's Nest*.

Frankly, I'd rather listen to Richard Marx.

That rubs Andy and his wife up the wrong way. Annalise

doesn't make eye contact when I ask her to pass the creamed spinach.

9.47 The lamb is a bit undercooked. It's pink in the middle. I have to eat it, though. It really *would* be rude not to.

9.49 I explain *Robin's Nest* to Teri.

9.52 Damn. After the 'Dylan-sucks' episode, everyone thinks I'm dogmatic and boorish. I must learn to keep my opinions to myself.

9.54 Annalise is talking about her horse. She rides it at weekends. It's called Dotty. It seems that, as well as being the only person in Britain to have never before been to a dinner party, I'm the only one not to own a horse.

9.56 I quip: 'If I had a racehorse I'd call it Imperial Leather.' No one laughs.

9.58 At last: Chris brings out the Coppola Merlot.

10.05 Even though we get only half a glass each, everyone agrees that the Coppola Merlot is a nice drop of red. Words such as 'spicy', 'sage', 'reedy', 'cherry', 'wood-chippy' and 'black peppery' are bandied about, mainly in self-conscious jest. I suggest that it's rich and thick enough to tempt your average thirsty vampire. Say, the one from *Bram Stoker's Dracula*. Everyone laughs. Even frosty Annalise laughs, though still no significant eye contact.

10.08 Now the fun really begins. Good red wine, sparkling conversation – I could get used to this dinner-party busi-ness. Andy holds his glass up to the candlelight, closes one eye and suggests that it might well be the '*Godfather*' of Californian wines – a pleasant gesture, more laughter. Nice touch there, Andy.

10.13 I announce that anyone who doesn't like this full-bodied red knows '*Jack*' about wine.

10.14 I explain that *Jack* was a 1996 Coppola film starring Robin Williams as a ten-year-old boy who, as the result of a rare ageing disorder, finds himself trapped in the body of a forty-year-old man. It was part of a cycle of mid-eighties boy-man body-swap films that peaked commercially with the Tom Hanks movie *Big*.

10.15 'There was also the film *Like Father, Like Son*, starring Dudley Moore from *Arthur 2: On the Rocks*, but I haven't seen it yet it so I can't comment.'

I'm rambling now. I can't stop myself.

10.16 'Personally, I rate Judge Reinhold's performance in *Vice Versa* as the best of the bunch.'

10.18 I explain to the table that Judge Reinhold is the likeable, jug-eared star of *Fast Times at Ridgemont High* who's best known for his portrayal of Detective William 'Billy' Rosewood in all three *Beverly Hills Cop* films.

And, while we're on the subject of movie judges, how come all the judges in mainstream American cinema are played by black actors? If such portrayals are accurate then it's reassuring to see that there are ample equal opportunities within the American legal system. I laugh. It's a nervous 'ha ha ha'.

Now I'm laughing at my own jokes. It's contagious.

Embarrassed looks from everyone at the table. They all think I'm being facetious, maybe even racist. I just about stop myself from saying 'I wasn't being racist'. I still have a modicum of self-awareness left.

10.25 Chris takes the 'post-rock' CD off, puts on *London Calling* by the Clash and clicks his fingers. I show incredible restraint by not pointing out that the Clash were overrated, stodgy pub rockers with twatty drainpipe jeans and flimsy, lame, shouty agitprop lyrics, with all the genuine rhetorical depth of that Che Guevara poster Blu-Tacked on to Jemima's wall, right above her gymkhana trophies, her plush St Bernard called Diggles and her collection of fluffy Forever Friends bears holding hearts.

10.28 The conversation has ground to a halt . . . '*The Conversation*. That's another Coppola classic. Gene Hackman was in it.'

10.40 The topic of live music comes up again. Neil Young. He's rubbish as well. He looks like a comedy yokel from *The Two Ronnies* and plays unlistenable folk-rock for the scented-candle crowd.

Andy disagrees. I tell him that I hate any music that's serious or worthy. Pop music is all about sex and glamour and should be made by young, sexy, dumb people, not old white men with stubble and checked shirts. Live music is fine, though I generally prefer acts who lip-synch and wear stupid hats. I point out that I'd rather listen to Black Lace than Pink Floyd. I'd rather listen to Taffy's one-off pop hit from the eighties 'I Love My *Radio* (Midnight *Radio*)' than the entire recorded output of *Radio*head.

'I don't want abstract lyrics with hidden meanings or social commentary. I want songs about gettin' *it* on, doing *it* all night or shakin' *it* on down. I want songs about hugging, squeezing, kissing and rocking all night long.'

Frankly, I'd rather jack than Fleetwood Mac.

10.43 I'm forced to sing the Taffy tune – or, rather, to speak it while making 'musical' hand gestures. 'Woah my guy, the deejay after midnight/I love my radio, my midnight radio', etc.

10.52 Homemade Bramley-apple pie with cinnamon ice

cream. The conversation has stalled. 'This pie is amazing, Bev.' Everyone nods. No jokes about packets.

11.05 Bev goes to check on the kids. Chris offers coffee and mini-Turkish Delights – proper ones, without chocolate coating.

'Interesting. I didn't know that they made Turkish delights without the milk-chocolate coating.'

Bloody hell. I really am common. I shouldn't have come. I'm not cut out for dinner parties.

11.15 I should never have eaten that undercooked lamb. I'm sure I felt my stomach turn just then.

11.18 No one has said anything for more than a minute.

11.30 'I really need to get going. I have to help a friend out on a stall first thing tomorrow morning.'

Sauces, Powders and Pastes

My cupboards are full of them.

Full of bottled sauces – traditional ketchups; squeezy BBQ and other varieties of smoky, sticky, hickory-soaked shite; hot chilli pastes and powders (there mainly for reasons of machismo); fruity brown sauces for drowning chips and chops with; sweet chilli from that Thai supermarket that only sell packets of little dried fish and chintzy china cats who salute for good luck (the supermarket makes its money from Oriental superstitions and salty noodle toppings).

There's that packet of dried seaweed I bought in 2004 at the height of the antioxidant explosion. I tried it once, spat it out and decided to stick to blueberries for my vitamin fix.

My cupboards contain countless tubes of tomato-and-onion paste, used once; squeezed from the top of the tube on to lazy pasta dinners and then abandoned next to that half-pack of Lockets that melted during the summer heatwave. There's also some chicken stock cubes and dried stuffing mix from when Paxo were running their 'Rooster Booster' campaign. I should throw them out but they're ripe for use as last-resort lunches during that nuclear winter when I'll be munching mustard powder and licking a jar of tartar sauce from the last millennium.

My fridge is teeming with stale mustards I've used only once. I have a row of grainy, mottled Continental types, two tubs of disturbingly brown Dijon and a jar of traditional strong English mustard from Norfolk. 'Refrigerate after opening and consume within three weeks.' I have spicy sauce from that English county that no one's ever been to. There's a bottle of 'Super Grade Oyster-Flavoured Sauce' with a pagoda on the label. At least, I think it's a pagoda – it's covered in oyster-flavoured sauce. I can't even remember buying that. I may have stolen it from that all-you-can-eat Chinese in Soho.

Sauces, powders and pastes: they've all been in there for years. They were all purchased in order to liven up bland British dinners; to spice breaded plaice and bony, scrawny pork chops; to season and spruce up mushy pork sausages and triangular frozen hash browns.

I propose an amnesty, where Britain hands in half-used bottles of Newman's Own with oily labels (look: Butch Cassidy with a dried chive on his grinning Hollywood mug), festering soy sauce left over from the spring-roll craze twenty years ago, mouldy jars of chutney, sweetcorn relish with dried yellow gunk around the lid, and Spanish tomato paste from the General Franco era.

Sausage in a Basket

Last Tuesday I went to work stark naked. On Wednesday it occurred to me that I hadn't started my maths coursework and, as a consequence, my hands had turned into horse's hooves. The day after, I was in the midst of an intense cocktail-party conversation with American pop singer Cher concerning the secret Benny Hill cameo in *Apocalypse Now*. A few hours later I couldn't find my teeth.

The events chronicled above all occurred in dreams. Dreams so vivid as to make me feel like all that stuff had actually happened, even hours after I'd woken up.

There are other events that have stuck in my mind through the years. The trouble is, I can't quite work out whether I dreamt them or not.

Was there a *Top of the Pops* presenter in the mid-eighties called Dixie Peach? Was there a lad at school called Eon Hare? Was there once a brand of toffee-coated popcorn called Hanky Panky? Did we really eat pub food out of plastic baskets in the seventies and eighties?

Yes, we did. During the wildcat national dishwashers' strike and crockery shortage of 1976, we were all chowing down on chicken in a basket, scampi in a basket and, strangely, sausage in a basket. All served in a plastic 'wicker' bowl, lined with a burgundy serviette, two leaves of brown lettuce and a slice of lemon.

I'm the only person that remembers sausage in a basket?

I swear it was true. It came with half a tomato, which I didn't ever eat because I thought it 'looked like guts'.

And dixie peach for dessert.

The '. . . in a basket' craze lives on in popular etymology as a way of describing low-rent dinner theatre and the current engagements of previously popular recording artistes on the slide: 'With his performance as Fletcher Christian in *Mutiny on Ice*, David Essex is playing the Chicken in a Basket circuit.'

Sausage Rolls

'Pork En Croute'. It's only a matter of time.

Sausages on Sticks

1) Convenient method for serving chipolatas.
2) Alan Bennett fishing for cheap laughs.

Saveloy

A saveloy is a seasoned, scarlet-coloured sausage sold in British fish-and-chip shops.

I've never had one. I never want one. I don't know what's in one. It's so red I'd want to apply Oil of Olay to one rather than eat it. It's so red it doesn't even look edible – it looks like something that should be hanging off the Singing Detective.

(See also Fish 'n' Chips.)

Savoury Croissant

The savoury croissant, also known as the 'croissandwich': that ham-and-cheese-filled mutation that sits, unloved and uneaten, in the snack-bar chilled cabinet. Only, the cabinet isn't chilling anything. You can tell it's not turned on: the Snapples are warm and the Cheddar slice in the savoury croissant is starting to perspire. The sticker says the ham is cured. It doesn't look particularly cured to me – it's got little white spots on it and it's sweating.

There's a notice above the basket of Kettle chips seasoned with Seychelles sea salt: 'All edible, unsold snack items are donated to local homeless shelters.' I wonder if they mean the flapjacks or point-of-sale chewy muesli bars (both of which keep for months). Nevertheless, that's a gracious corporate gesture. Homelessness is a dreadful situation for anyone to find themselves in. I mean, these people have no chance at all of getting on the property ladder.

I don't own my own home – I rent. Most of my home-owning, fifty-five-year-mortgage-slave friends – fake socialists who really care only about equity – regard me with the same degree of pity that I reserve for homeless people. Maybe I could snag myself some free snack-bar food with the plea: 'OK, I'm not quite homeless, but I do only rent . . .'

Then again, at least I have somewhere to live, and I'd much rather have a roof over my head than a free savoury croissant.

Scampi

I haven't seen scampi on sale for years. Why not? I miss it.

I've listed it next to goulash in my monthly Ripe for Revival report. Let's pull it out, pucker up and plant the kiss of life on the scrawny pink proto-prawn. Let's stick it in a risotto or a stuff it in a Mexican-style wrap.

Scampi are actually langoustine. I think they become scampi only when they're coated in breadcrumb, deep-fried and served with chunky chips in a roadside pub with a fake fireplace. It's a Batman/Bruce Wayne thing: langoustines change their identities when they don the crispy-golden-crumb cape and cowl.

Along with Elvis Presley (that other postwar, right-wing, crime-fighting, cape-wearing pop superhero), Batman is the American Zen Riddle: he can be both cool and schlocky.

Scampi is just schlocky. Let's make it cool again. Let's mix it with mango and stick it in a juice-bar smoothie. Let's include it in a mezze platter, nestled next to the stuffed olives.

Scampi is also known as the Dublin Bay Prawn, which is not covered in crumb. It's ruddy of cheek, tousled of hair, blowing a penny whistle and wearing a Manchester United team shirt.

The last time I had scampi was in a pub in Dover. Scampi, crinkle-cut chips, peas and beans on a plastic tray shaped like an artist's palate with separate slots for oily sauces and slippery sides.

Peas *and* baked beans? It was such an incompatible, curiously British combination. It planted the following brief-but-treacherous thought: I hate my country.

The Dover pub's main attraction was a jukebox which,

according to word of mouth, provenance and the local-newspaper clippings framed and mounted above it, had featured in the George Michael's video for 'Faith'.

With a penknife, someone had etched on the side of the jukebox: 'George Michael is gay'.

Deadpan graffiti and downright disrespect: I love my country.

School Curry

It's 1987 and one of the rare days when I eat a cooked lunch in the school canteen. Unluckily for me, it's also curry day. Freaky school curry . . . stewed chicken chunks left over from yesterday's flaky pastry pies, mixed with sultanas, mild curry powder and desiccated coconut.

Apart from coconut, the only thing that comes desiccated is a variety of pig thyroid used to treat certain hormone conditions.

In the canteen at St Boniface's Roman Catholic College for Boys, Plymouth, the chicken curry isn't the only freaky sight. A stray chip floats in the jug of tap water that provides free refreshment.

There's Brother Bailey – the Christian Brother with the hangdog expression who takes our RE classes. He's hanging on in the hope that the meek really will inherit the Earth. He's chosen the shepherd's pie with chips and is always good for some dry laughs in lessons. The week previous I'd asked him during our Old Testament catechism class what 'manna' was – referring of course to the Israelites' chow in that Exodus epic. He said it 'tasted not unlike cornflakes'.

The class erupted and he had to field multiple 'does it taste like Weetabix, Brother?' and 'Did Moses eat Coco Pops, Sir?' questions for the next ten minutes before he turned red, banged a wooden blackboard ruler on his desk and told us to 'simmer down'.

A maths teacher with a fearsome reputation for chalk-throwing, sharpening his pencils with a 'Rambo' knife, organising the annual ski trips to the Dolomites and wearing hand-knitted sweaters strides to the front of the queue. His white plastic tray holds a slippery Cornish pasty, a scoopful of pale, undercooked chips, tinned apricot crumble with strawberry-flavoured pink custard and a box of twenty Rothman's. The freakiest thing about him is his hair. It's snow white on top and jet black on the sides. Reed Richards from the Fantastic Four has grey hair on the sides and black hair with blue highlights on top, but I've never seen the condition reversed. It could be hormonal. If so, maybe he should try that pork thyroid therapy.

My best mate, Duncan Humphrey, observes that this type of rare hair condition occurs once in a blue moon, under a shocking set of circumstances. The follicular trans-formation takes place instantly and without warning when a young man loses his virginity to his mother.

I start choking on chips and greasy tap water dribbles from my nose.

Scotch Egg

The Scotch egg is a snack food of Scottish origin, devel-oped as part of the Caledonian urge to deep-fry the holy fucking shit out every single animal, vegetable and mineral in existence.

The Scottish love Scotch eggs – the Scottish and the Scottish alone. They can't get enough of them. Scotch eggs, heroin and Del Amitri.

It's a bit like a Kinder Egg, only in this case it's the egg that's inside as the surprise rather than a plastic windmill. But, since it's called a Scotch egg, it's not strictly speaking a surprise to find an egg in there.

The Scotch egg also begs the Zen riddle: how did it get there? If the mystery meat that surrounds it is deep-fried with the egg inside, shouldn't the egg go all gunky during the frying process?

Here's a recipe:

6 hard-boiled eggs, well chilled
450g/1 lb breakfast sausage
$^1/_2$ cup flour
2 eggs, beaten
$^3/_4$ cup fine breadcrumbs (small, gritty, baby-sick-yellow British breadcrumbs from a plastic tub)
vegetable oil for frying

Peel eggs and set aside. Peeling eggs is a horrible activity, they look like eyeballs and make your fingers smell.

Divide sausage into 6 portions. Roll each egg in flour then press a portion of the sausage around each egg.

Dip the sausage-wrapped egg into beaten eggs and roll in the breadcrumbs.

Heat the vegetable oil to 180°C/350°F. When was the last time anyone ever used a chip pan? 1983?

Cook each Scotch egg in the hot oil for about 4–5 minutes, or until it is nicely browned.

Can anyone really be bothered to make Scotch eggs? Surely that's why we have twenty-four-hour petrol stations. In 2000, sales of Pork Farms Scotch Eggs and pornographic magazines were the only thing that helped Britain's petrol stations survive the fuel crisis.

Drain on paper towels. Serve warm and enjoy.

Sea Salt

Sea salt – it's a special salt, a salt for the connoisseur and sodium-chloride epicure. It's not normal salt – table salt, salt by Saxo; salt in a cracked cellar with a single hole served in caffs; or salt from small sachets in local-council cafeterias or motorway service stations.

The worst thing about the sea-salt explosion is that it's created a whole new breed of irritating food snob: the salt snoot, who drones on about the difference between Fleur de Sel and flake, between unrefined French and Hawaiian red.

Recently some bloke approached me outside Holland Park Tube station to ask where they could get some Cayman Sea Salt. He even referred to it as 'the good shit' while looking around and wiping sweat from his upper lip.

A Selection of Cheeses

The cheese board is the alternative dessert choice available on the menus of most British restaurants. It comprises an assortment of fine cheeses, both soft and hard, several types of cracker, an unexplained digestive biscuit, some celery and four brown grapes.

The cheese board is the final course of choice for the retired headmaster or the recovering alcoholic.

Service Stations

Mock if you must, but British service stations provide rest and refreshment for millions of British motorists each and every year.

Remember: tiredness can kill. Objects in the mirror are closer than they appear. Take regular breaks from driving. Even if you have to pay £6.00 for a greasy cup of coffee and a three-pack of stale custard creams.

While driving home for Christmas last year I was nearly the last white man to die at the hands of the Apache.

I was doing 110 on the M5 between Taunton and Exeter. I'd missed my usual rest stop, Taunton Deane services. *Chants of the Native American Tribes* was on the CD player. The trippy incantations of the elders along with the lullaby rattle of the tin of dusty mixed-fruit travel sweets on the dashboard sent me into a ecstatic state of semi-consciousness. Only the intervention of my ancestors – Dragging Canoe and Little Big Chef – and dynamic stability control saved me.

Side Salad

Three rocket leaves, a tomato wedge, the world's thickest slice of cucumber and some oily French dressing – all served on a disturbing, shallow, kidney-shaped saucer.

You won't eat it, so don't order it.

Sitars and the Sledge: Restaurant Music Revisited

Last night I heard an Indian sitar version of 'He's the Greatest Dancer' by Sister Sledge in a curry house in Bromsgrove.

The bhangra version of the Sisters' famous disco beat forced me to bite my tongue and graze my gums on a sharp popadom.

For, whenever I hear the Sledge (or indeed the Pointers or the Degrees), I can hear – at a dog-whistle frequency – the subsonic chime of a cheap Brut Marie de Moy toast and the slurred homily: 'We're not so much losing a daughter as gaining a son.'

The Slice

The slice – minced beef and onion; chicken and mushroom; ham and cheese – is a modern British snack staple; the result of the zealous desire by Britain's bakers to combine the hermetic security of the pie with the eat-me-now convenience of the sandwich.

Microwaveable and ready to eat in an attractive lattice-pastry envelope. Not Suitable for Vegetarians. The slice. All served up with the dirty, metallic tang of the abattoir floor.

Small Fruit and Veg

Baby corn, baby new potatoes, tasty tenderstem broccolini; those midget cauliflowers the size of a premature kitten's head.

Just how much smaller can tomatoes get?

Yesterday I bought a honeydew melon the same size and weight as the miniature sponge rugby ball I got free in a Q8 petrol station during a prize giveaway timed to coincide with the 2001 Six Nations tournament.

Smoked Salmon

Recently, I dined in a musty silver-service restaurant – the kind of place where all the staff look like Roy Kinnear and shuffle about in shiny spats – and found myself seated near a party of well-fed, red-faced tourists from Munich.

From the Teutonic chatter I picked out one phrase; one phrase that, when spoken by the Kinnear-clone head waiter, had the Deutschland diners squealing en masse like it was reunification night all over again.

'Scottish smoked salmon.'

They couldn't get enough of it. All six of them ordered

thinly sliced smoked salmon served on toasted brown bread with a splash of lemon juice.

Funny thing about the Germans – along with the fact that all German men have big, red, wet lips, and that usually only the phrases 'Industrial Rock', 'Bayern Munich' and 'Hardcore Beer, Strudel and Leatherwear Festival' will excite them . . . Even more surprising was the disclosure that, in Germany, slices of Scottish smoked salmon still carried a premium food cachet; a lustre of luxury that they've long since lost in the UK.

Smoked salmon used to be a rare treat; a fish dish to savour. Now it's a cheap snack staple; nibble fodder served with cream cheese between slices of white bread, and sold in the supermarket cold cabinet. Smoked salmon is the new jumbo prawn.

Soda Bread

My mum seems to think that soda bread has mystical Irish powers, like the Blarney Stone, St Patrick's Well or that stupid drum thing that men with earrings play with a chicken bone in rural pubs and on promotional videos for the Irish Tourist Board.

It doesn't. It's vile, like chewing on a dusty Celtic verruca.

We don't live in stone huts or wear wolf pelts any more, Mother. I think the Middle Ages ended in the fifteenth century, sometime after the discovery of yeast.

Sorbet

Sorbet is ice cream for the slimmer, the show-off, the lactose-intolerant and the clean-palate obsessive.

It makes my teeth hurt. I do the Sensodyne shuffle to the bathroom.

Southern-Style/American-Style

Food from the Southern States of America: seasoned meats cooked over glowing coals. Rich gravies, yams, glazed hams, grits, squash, hot cakes and sorghum; pecan pie, banana pudding and peach cobbler.

Folks living south of the Mason–Dixon line call it 'soul food'. After eating it for several weeks you'll look like you've eaten Luther Vandross.

None of the dishes listed above are available at British restaurants offering Southern-style food, though the chef does have a certain knack with a defrosted seasoned drumstick, a double CD by the Nitty Gritty Dirt Band and a T-shirt with an airbrushed portrait of a white wolf wearing a Native American headdress, howling at the sky and lit by a ghostly prairie moon.

Every British supermarket chain has its own American-style food range: gunky, mushy, 100 per cent prime-beefed, cheese-topped, corn-flecked, chilli-flavoured tat with microwave Tex Mex wedge fries, authentic Arkansas coleslaw, stumpy corn on the cob with chilli butter and a Texan-style sour-cream-and-chive dip.

They're all packaged in finger-clickin' *faux*-hep Americana:

the stars and stripes; 1958 Cadillac Eldorados, drive-in diners, malted vanilla milkshakes and Wurlitzer jukeboxes. All as authentically American as Showaddywaddy or Russ Abbot draped up like a Teddy Boy on his *Saturday Madhouse*.

Speciality Bread

I can't cut bread in slices. If it isn't pre-sliced, I'm stuck. I can cut wedges of bread – I can cut wedges of bread like a professional. I just can't cut even slices. I need my bread pre-sliced or I'm not playing.

As a bread-slicer I just don't cut the mustard. Or, rather, I don't cut the honey-glazed and mustard-seed-topped knotted rye bloomer.

I'm sick of honey-glazed or -flavoured savoury foods – meats, breads, dips – and honey-and-lemon sauces. Who decided that everything should taste like Sugar Puffs?

I don't have time to slice bread in the morning. I don't even have time to shower – I've taken to rubbing myself down with lemon-fresh antibacterial kitchen wipes.

The clichés are correct. The wheel, the jet engine. That thing your gran calls the 'goggle box'. (She only has one for Aled Jones on Sunday nights and leaves it on when visitors come. How rude.) The SodaStream. The sliced white loaf. Milestone inventions all.

You can keep your fancy breads. Keep them and sell them off last thing on a Sunday evening – orange-stickered and marked down to thirty-nine pence.

Green-olive-and-pumpkin-seed loaf, sundried-tomato

rolls flecked with mustard seeds, onion-and-herb knot, sunflower-and-honey couronne.

They all taste the same. None of them come sliced. Even baps aren't immune: burger buns with cheese on top. Submarine rolls with stupid little seeds that stick in the teeth and scratch the gums.

Give us this day our daily cranberry-and-rosemary bloomer.

Speciality Chicken

Chargrilled chicken Black round the edges, this type of cooked chicken has a rich, smoky taste. It looks like it's been dropped on the garage floor and tastes like a damp 2B pencil.

Chinese chicken Battery-farmed fowl coated in a sweet, clotted, red MSG-packed paste.

Corn-fed chicken Surely this has to be against the law – force-fed chicken with the sickly yellow pallor of a dying alcoholic. Like dead former footballer George Best in his dog days.

Rotisserie chicken Melanoma-flecked poultry, cooked under a spotlight and on a spit. It's a carnival of grease; oily shrivelled meat turning slowly under a sun lamp, usually in the oil-slicked window of a fourth-tier chain convenience store.

Convenience stores that sell rotisserie chickens use the greasy, St Tropez-tanned bird as some sort of unique selling point – like a National Lottery booth with a chewed Biro on a fraying shoelace and a stack of invalid Thunderball forms; a small pick 'n' mix selection (all that's left is a compartment of bashed coffee fudge and three decapitated white-chocolate mice); a key-cutting/shoe-repair service; or a vending machine that dispenses egg-shaped novelty plastic 'prize' capsules.

Begging the question: which came first, the greasy rotisserie chicken or the novelty plastic egg?

Spork

The spork is that plastic fork-and-spoon hybrid used for impaling fast-food variety-meal coleslaw and wrangling slippery takeaway noodles.

Be careful when using the spork. I once lost a prong in a strip of Camden Market Chinese beef I was skewering and consequently chipped a tooth.

Spring-Water Bottles

I hate those bottles of spring water you get in top-class restaurants – ones shaped like Art Deco Parisian perfume bottles, made from patterned Chinese porcelain or fluted like a Viennese rose vase.

How much? £8.00, for a bottle of water?

There goes the taxi money.

It was a hot day. I should have bought a bottle from that man from Merseyside on the train – the one with the boil ready to burst on the back of his neck and the three shabby coolbags full of chilled tap water he was selling for £2.00 a pop.

Squash

No, it's nothing to do with that squishy butternut turnip thing that's *de rigueur* in middle-brow eateries. The squash I speak of is the concentrated fruit juice of yesteryear. I used to drink it after kite-flying or twenty-three-a-side summer-holiday football in the burnt-grass playing field in between the graveyard and the asbestos dump. I'd drink the fruity orange cup until my stomach bulged. I'd glug brightly coloured Quosh-brand lemon-and-lime cordial neat for that knockout fake-fruit fix and an instant sore throat, then rasp my excuses to Mum while scrubbing grass stains from my nylon tracksuit top with a wet chamois cloth that smelt like vinegar and our Vauxhall Viva.

Fruit squash is no more; it's been rebranded as 'hi-juice' and enjoys a one-sided *crush* on tennis – the world's most tedious sport; a ball game played by middle classes and Germans; a game that cannot compare with twenty-three-a-side football played on sloping fields, or flying plastic, psychedelically coloured kites shaped like birds of prey (especially if older lads were in the bushes aiming air-rifles and leering at rain-soaked *Razzle*s and *Swank*s).

Juices with bits, freshly squeezed refreshments and flavoured waters that aid rehydration have stolen cordial's thunder. Non-concentrated five-a-day-friendly fruit juices and EMO power pops hold sway with today's youth. They say, 'Squash is *soooo* gay!' as they swing their smoothies and update their blogs via Bluetooth.

It's a pity. Cordial had a strong citrus tang. You could vary the concentrate/tap water ratio and experiment. It

was science. It was packed with refined sugars that stripped
the enamel from your teeth.

Steak, French-Style

I crave steak at least once a week. Every seven days I salivate and drool for rare, bloody cuts of red-in-the-middle
beef.

I prefer it scarlet-hued and ruddy raw but I'll eat any
steak. I'll even eat a thin, charred strip of Scottish cow that
was butchered unethically in an urban abattoir, rendered
recognisable only by dental records, hopped-up on hormones
and served with a limp salad and a tinfoil-wrapped chive-
and-mayo-filled baked potato in a tatty West End steakhouse
with a *faux*-Hibernian theme, the overpowering smell of
disinfectant, freshly varnished dark-wood veneer, and 7-Up
rings on wine-red velour booth benches – shabby seating
which exposes flammable foam stuffing.

Perhaps it's an American-style steak, super-thick and
sizzling, cooked over coals and served on a bed of fries
with onion rings and Tex Mex chicken wings.

Maybe my weekly steak is a ten-centimetre-thick juicy
sirloin served with chunky gaucho-style chips in a
Uruguayan grill in West London with cowhide chair uphol-
stery and a clientele comprising affluent ex-pats from South
America on the run from a socialist uprising/military
junta/rampant inflation/currency devaluation, with deep
tans, gold watches, pressed chino slacks, smart sea-blue
shirts with the sleeves rolled up and lemon-coloured cash-
mere sweaters slung over their shoulders.

In this dining scenario the steak hardens and the gaucho chips cool while I spy on the steakhouse regular: he's on the run from the newly formed Patagonian People's Commission and their human-rights hearings. He's laughing at the paucity of decent extradition lawyers back home as he wolfs back vanilla pancakes with dollops of dulce de leche.

Perhaps the steak is a tiny 50-gram peppercorn rump sitting next to two chilli-lime jumbo prawns, three winkles, a lemon wedge and a wax-paper tub of seafood sauce in bright Miss Selfridge pink on the plastic surf-and-turf platter from a shiver-me-timbers seaside supper shack with a halfhearted pirate premise.

Three months ago I ate a bootleg T-bone from a locked larder in an illegal meat speakeasy. Two weeks ago it was a steak tartare from a Belgian beer house.

Steak tartare is raw, ground beef with onions. I didn't like the taste of it. It put me in mind of that Italian cannibal horror movie I'd seen the previous evening. I gave up on the raw diced-beef dish after one bite and hid the rest under a napkin.

Last week I fancied steak served in the Gallic way – in a rustic café with Art Deco tiling, accompanied by a wooden bowl of thin steak fries, side servings of garlic-slicked field mushrooms, oily onions and a bottle of spicy, peppery red wine.

The steak arrived, served by an elegant French girl; a French girl in the unattainable mould of movie goddess Catherine Deneuve or an elfin Jean Seberg in *À Bout de Souffle*. She smouldered, she sashayed nonchalantly on red silk pumps; I pictured her sitting outside a café on the

Champs-Élysées, sucking on a slim menthol cigarette, flicking through the *International Herald Tribune* and nibbling on the end of a dainty almond pastry.

She was dainty-pastry delicious. She was the first French female I'd seen in Britain for years who wasn't wearing a day-glo windcheater and retrieving a fold-out map of Central London from a neon backpack with a furry monkey keyring hanging off it.

The French steak arrived. It was colossal. It filled the entire plate. On first glimpse it appeared to be at least eight centimetres thick.

On closer inspection, the steak was slim – just a couple of centimetres. It was just topped with soft cheese and a quail's egg and smothered in a thick, yellow, white-wine sauce flecked with herbs.

I don't want thick sauce on my steak. I don't want it topped with poached eggs, sauce Gribiche or any other type of gunky gastro paste *à la Française*.

I scraped the sticky yellow gunk off my steak and it struck me that – apart from sustaining a stiff upper lip in stressful situations and queuing silently in the rain for a ride on the Nemesis at Alton Towers; not counting picnicking in multistorey car parks or fixing bayonets prior to charging a line of unarmed indigenous men, women and children – the archetypal British collective custom involves the wrinkling of one's nose, the angling of one's knife and the precise action of scraping sauces, pastes, stocks or soft-cheese toppings off portions of red meat, game or fish cooked in foreign styles.

Eating French food always involves the clandestine scraping of rich, cream-based sauces and toppings. This steak dish was no different. The French waitress walked over to ask, 'Is everything all right?'

I hoped she didn't spot the steak-knife separation of sauce and steak.

I am not xenophobic. My parents preached a strict no-bigotry policy so I toed the line and inherited no irrational prejudices. That's not counting the one time my mum damned the Wilson family two doors down – they had a metal detector, an instrument that Mum denounced as 'greedy' and 'immoral'. I've taken the same viewpoint on metal detectors throughout my life.

I don't care what race, creed or colour you are, but if you own a metal detector or any other beat-frequency oscillating device used for treasure-hunting in municipal football fields during the summer, well, in my eyes you're on a slippery moral slope. I'll stop you, write out some sort of moral citation and recommend that, given the eternal punishment for breaking one of the seven deadly sins, and the rarity of Roman coins in rutted rugby pitches, you're better off ditching the detector, bowing to your knees and muttering repentance to your God.

Yes, I'm pro-Europe. I'm an unabashed European. I salivate for spicy red wines, onion soups and those cheap little bottles of French beer my dad buys in the summer, and I frequently burn candles for French waitresses – this one in particular.

I cast her as 'Paulette', my neighbour's au pair in the as-yet-unfilmed culture-clash sitcom in my head. I dream that we go for a drive. It's sunny so I take the top down on a rakish racing-green convertible that splutters raspberry-style when it starts.

She says: 'Is zis – how you say? – having it off?'

[The studio audience explodes with laughter.]

I'm drinking tea; she's sitting at the antique bureau by the patio doors with a fake garden painted on cardboard in the background. 'What are you writing?'

'I am writing to my parents in Lille, *non*. It is ze – how you say? – French letter?'

[I gulp back tea and go bug-eyed.]

'I tell them I am – how you say? – with child?'

[I spit cold tea and mug a double-take.]

'*Non* – I mean, that I look after child, as au pair.'

[More uncontrollable audience laughter, whistles and applause over an end-of-show theme that re-imagines 'La Marseillaise' for the flute, adding a jaunty 'Rule Britannia' trumpet flourish at the end.]

'Is everything all right?'

Her words echoed and snapped me to reality.

'Perfect, thanks. I just don't like sauce on steak. Sorry.'

Yes, I'm a new model European citizen. Just don't cover my steak in cream-based sauces, soft cheeses or garlic pastes.

Merci.

Steak-and-Guinness Pie

You know that aisle in the supermarket – that misty, mystic aisle that no one ever browses. Not the aisle that sells tubs of rust-red shoe polish, wooden clothes-pegs, replacement shoelaces and wire wool, but that eerie, haunted aisle that sells nothing but poor-quality tinned meats:

stewing steak, beef and kidney cuts, stringy chicken-pie fillings in watery white sauces, tins of Scotch-beef bits for twenty-nine pence, braised Slovenian-gristle cubes, stringy chuck chunks and minced sow offal.

Well, that mystic aisle provides the main ingredient for the substandard meat, stout and soggy puff-pastry slop that passes for the steak-and-Guinness pie (with authentic jacket fries from the Old Country *to share*). It's the signature dish of Eire, another mystic isle, and it's served in every fake Irish pub in Britain (Tommy Flynn's, Paddy O'Shea's, Johnny 'Mad Dog' Adair's . . .) with the Cranberries on the video jukebox and a frizzy-haired banshee in a green sweatshirt (usually from Adelaide) behind the bar.

Hey, Tommy Flynn, remember: it isn't a pie unless it's entirely contained in pastry. Placing a roof on a casserole, like a flaky, buttery toupee, does not a pie make.

There is a British equivalent of the steak-and-Guinness pie. It's served in certain parts of Belfast and Glasgow. Bang the drum and don an orange sash for the steak-and-*ale* pie: it's a non-papist pastry with 100 per cent Fenian-free filling.

Stir-Fry

The bookshops are full of it: *The Ten Commandments of Stir-fry*; *Stir-Crazy*; *The Big Bumper Book of Stir-Fry*; *Stir-Fry: Now a major TV series*.

Mix up broccoli, beef, cashews, bamboo shoots, garlic, cashews, ginger, peppers, yet more sodding cashews. Served in a black-bean sauce that tastes like leaky Biro.

Stir-fry: it's not just a meal, it's a hobby – like keeping tropical fish, only with frozen snow peas and a lightly greased wok.

Stir-fry: it's a way of life. Like Buddhism or being into Marillion. Pass the oyster sauce and check the date on those water chestnuts.

I used to work with the most irritating woman in the world. We'll call her Sally-Anne. She'd constantly drone on about her ex (he was using her because his *X-Files* video box-sets, along with VHS copies of other shoddy science-fiction shows, were stolen while he was in New Zealand) and the fact that her sister was a practising white witch, and she would eat her lunchtime sandwich by holding it in both hands and nibbling on it – taking tiny bites like a hot-flushing church mouse (naturally, her lunch was a Boots meal deal). On a good day it could take her two hours to get through half a tuna-and-sweetcorn. Even more annoying than the ex talk and impressions of a field-mouse in repast was her constant stir-fry chatter.

'I think I'll go home, have a bath and make a stir-fry.' 'I had a lovely bok chow chicken while watching *Celebrities in a Submarine* last night.' 'It's orange pork with spring onions for me tonight. That was my ex's favourite. Can you believe he's still suing me over those *Star Trek: Voyager* videos.'

I haven't seen her around since she moved desks. Maybe she took voluntary redundancy. Maybe the ex beat her to death with Season One of *Deep Space Nine*. Maybe she choked on a cashew.

Stir-In Sauces

Jars of stir-in sauce make me gag. They require me to reach for a bucket, or for the washing-up bowl I keep next to my bed after a night out or bout of food poisoning.

Stir-in sauces rank alongside the five-minute stir-fry sauce as fake food for the smug culinary hobbyist.

Where's the pleasure or pride in heating up a jar of factory-sealed sweet-and-sour slosh, or in soaking battery-farmed chicken flesh chunks in an orange-hued sauce that tastes like rusty metal?

All the additional basil leaves in the world cannot make a stir-in sauce taste like an authentic regional dish. No matter how much mascarpone you pour on that penne pasta with the Italian-style sauce, you'll never erase the memory of that cancer-causing food-dye scare.

Suckling Pig

It's really a baby pig – a three-week-old piglet – with an apple in its mouth, stuffed with sage and served on a shiny silver salver. Roast suckling piglet is a dish that defines 'Epicurean'; an elite dish for deviant diners, or Caligula.

Don't let that put you off, though. The piglet didn't suffer any more, struggle any harder or squeal any louder than the contents of those breaded chicken nuggets or crumb-covered flipper-dippers you're stuffing your fat face with.

Summer Bites

Put that cream away and save that tube of soothing salve – 'Summer Bites' has nothing to do with mosquito marks. It's another audacious marketing concept that exists for supermarkets to sell see-through plastic 'jelly' sandals, budget badminton sets, bubble-blowers, paddling pools and disposable barbecues – all displayed on ratty Astroturf rugs opposite the tobacco booth (the booth where men in bad leather jackets buy cheap cigars with mellow flavours and students pay for cigarette papers with plastic bags crammed with copper coins) and underneath a corrugated-plastic sign in the shape of the sun that says:

Dine outside on our light summer bites; eat our gourmet minted lamb-burgers with goat's-cheese toppings while shooing away the midges. Picnic in a public recreational area and scoff lightly tossed salads containing hard-boiled-egg halves, field leaves, feta cubes, Italian dressing sachets and sliced black olives – all while keeping your eyes peeled for passing rainclouds and the peeping pervert who prowls the parks exposing his pecker (as profiled in the local paper).

Feast alfresco on our fresh, plump British strawberries in a rosehip-and-Chardonnay jelly while trying not to make eye contact with the vagrant by the bins: his matted beard is streaked with pale yellow – this is the kind of pale, banana-milk-tinged facial fur that only tramps and certain kinds of Central American squirrel monkeys possess – and he's rooting around for cigarette ends. What do they do with those cigarette ends? They're far too stubby to smoke successfully. Do they put them in a scrapbook or in an officially authorised album, like vagabond Pokémon? Or do they trade them *à la* Tramp Trumps? Quick, hide the hamper – he's looking our way.

'This pre-packaged exotic passion-fruit-and-zesty-lemon mousse is just delici . . . Oh, my God. I'm sure I saw a bloody big rat. He ran through the tall grass. You can't see him now – he's camouflaged against the soft spongy, melting Tarmac in the children's play area. Let's leave; it's put me right off the tuna niçoise and that really thin can of Shiraz spritzer.'

(See also Winter Warmers – the yang to Summer Bites' ying.)

Supermarkets

When I was growing up there was only one large super-market within eighty kilometres of our house – it was in Exeter.

There was a suburban Asda five or six kilometres away and one medium-sized city-centre Tesco, but my mum wasn't keen on the city-centre Tesco because it was where winos gathered during the day and it was 'too close to a public toilet'.

These days you're never more than spitting distance from a Tesco or Sainsbury's – an urban 'express' or 'local' – but twenty years ago we would regularly drive seventy-odd kilometres to shop at the supermarket in Exeter.

Exeter, compared to Plymouth, was a consumer's para-dise. Exeter was Plymouth's posh cousin; a cousin with moneyed parents who got a half-size snooker table on spindly legs from the catalogue for its birthday; a cousin with a pellet gun and a *Kick-Start*-style scrambler motorcycle and who was allowed to play out until nine.

Exeter had a pedestrianised city centre with cycle paths; a branch of McDonald's ten years before Plymouth got one and an undercover shopping centre – a real-life American-style mall with white and tangerine mosaics on its tiled walls, a Jessops for my dad, who loved looking at lenses, a Laura Ashley selling flowery furnishings for Mum, a couple of decent toy shops for myself and my sister, and a wooden cart in the middle of the walkway that sold coathanger sculptures, pom-pom animals and barley-sugar sticks from glass jars.

The mall's main attraction – the reason for our day trips – was a branch of Sainsbury's.

I was never quite sure why we'd take day trips to a supermarket; what did J. Sainsbury have that Asda didn't? I figured it must have something to do with the jars of 'French-style' mustard mayonnaise they sold there – Dad would buy about sixteen of them each time.

The whole experience would have the feel of a half-term treat. I'd eat a toffee apple in store and Dad would send the stick through at check-out – something that he'd never do in the local Asda.

It wasn't all about rampant consumerism, though. Despite taking our supermarket day trips at the beginning of the pre-packed sandwich era (the prawn-mayo sandwich had just been invented in a lab just outside Geneva and was ready to be unleashed on an unsuspecting Britain), Mum would make corned-beef-and-pickle pitta sandwiches and we'd eat them in our car while it was parked in the dingy multistorey car park opposite the Index Catalogue store.

The car-park picnic is a peculiarly British phenomenon. Remember to open the car door only to shake out Scotch-egg crumbs or the coffee dregs from your tartan flask. Open the door then close it quickly so you don't get overwhelmed by the dual odours of petrol and tramp's piss.

In the intervening years Tesco has opened three super-markets in Plymouth, and, in turn, Sainsbury's has opened two huge retail outlets; there's a Morrisons and a Somer-field, too.

Apart from a few luxury purchases they make in 'Mark-sies', my parents shop at Asda now, primarily because of their low prices, surprisingly tasty own-brand range and their marvellous chocolate trifle (really, you should try it).

I love Asda. I love its buzz and bustle: on a sunny Saturday lunchtime Asda has the busy rattle and clamour of a Middle Eastern bazaar. No spider monkeys or wicker pots, and a smaller rug section, but there are men hauling multipacks of crisps, sporting tattoos, huge gold earrings and black eyes.

For my dad, one of the surest signs that the world is going to hell in a handcart is the sight of a middle-aged man with one large gold earring shopping for crisps and cheap lager with his tribal-tattooed wife.

There are only a few things that have the potential to disturb my dad more than the sight of a grown man wearing an earring. Those things are: a coven of Satan-worshippers moving next door; tinned meats; owning a Sky dish; John Prescott becoming Prime Minister; and a hosepipe ban lasting fifty-two weeks a year.

'Say what you like about the Russians during the Cold War, but you never see any Soviet men with gold-plated ankle chains, hooped earrings and honey-blond highlights in their long hair.'

Supreme

Supreme: meat – chicken, pork or beef – in a thick, creamy sauce; a thick, creamy sauce made from condensed tinned soup. The recipe's on the label. Read the label. Burn the label to destroy the evidence. Pour the condensed soup on dry, chewy chicken fillets. Serve with a soggy sprig of something and fool your friends.

The 'supreme' suffix means nothing but it trips off the tongue. It's less gauche than 'deluxe' and more tangible than 'à la king'.

Incredibly, the labels on condensed-soup cans still suggest recipes for 'chicken supreme', 'pork deluxe' and the like. Pub and hotel menus still list dishes 'à la apricot' and 'à la king'.

'Voilà: chicken pieces supreme!' It's the sort of proclamation that I'd have made as a precocious eight-year-old after smothering a goujon in tomato sauce; affecting a French accent, curling a make-believe moustache at the edges and balancing the plate on one hand like a cartoon waiter.

'Stop showing off and eat your dinner, Martin.'

Surveys/Scares

TV Man's Dachshund Web-Cam Shame. TV Brunette's Drastic Diet. Coma Boy and Mystery Blonde. Screwdriver Man Hurts Mum. Swimming-Pool Fun. Toffs on Hard Drugs. Thugs Did This to My Daughter's Face. How Much Do Celebrities Really Weigh? Star Says: 'I'm Giving Up Men.'

Day after day British newspapers educate and inform the public on the issues and events that (supposedly) affect them.

In newsprint Britain, buried among the tales of courage and outrage, bravery and disgrace, incident, fury and atrocity, there's always at least one juicy front-page food scare.

Peanut Butter Causes Impotence. Maggots Found in Hospital Food. The Honey Monster is Lottery Rapist . . . Cashew Nuts Cause Tumours in Lab Rats.

(They're all made up, of course, but I made the last one up specifically to scare stir-fry fans because I hate them.)

Women's Body Shapes: Which One are You?

Sushi

Supermarket sushi: bland fish strips and chewy white rice; raw, refrigerated and served in fiddly plastic punnets that are impossible to open without hurting a finger. Dry strips of smoked salmon resting on top of hard, chilled rice rectangles; tinned tuna flakes and avocado wrapped in white-rice rings; unidentified orange bits in thin rice tubes;

omelette strapped to white-rice squares by means of sticky black-rice paper 'belts'; tubs of standard soy sauce; slivers of pink ginger; and green paste with a tiling-grout taste and texture.

In sushi bars the food is served exactly as above but at three times the price. It's well worth the money as the conveyor belt affords me the opportunity to concurrently crack the tops of passing crème brûlée with a fishy chopstick end and indulge in some feeble 'It's *The Generation Game*'-style jokes: tuna . . . oyster . . . egg . . . salmon . . . cuddly toy. You know the drill.

Sweetcorn

It's a maize hybrid. It's tuna's little helper. It's the small yellow lackey to the chicken-breast chunk. It laughs at their jokes and shines their metaphorical shoes. It's an all-round minion and lickspittle, sucking up to the big boys in a sea of fatty mayonnaise.

Tapas

Tapas: it's Spanish for 'nibbles'. Or something similar.

I'd never eaten tapas prior to the spring of 2006. In fact, my experiences with Spanish food had been entirely limited to a Menu Masters seafood paella and the odd ham-and-cheese omelette.

Why had I never tasted tapas? Maybe it's because – save for the three-minute microwave prawns-in-rice meal

– Spanish food has never been bastardised by the British. It's never been crammed in a meal-deal sandwich, sold in a service-station café or etched in faint white chalk on a blackboard menu in a smoky pub by a new-town roundabout.

Maybe it's because of the lack of melted-Cheddar or breadcrumb toppings, or the paucity of white-wine sauces and battered processed meats, but variations on Spanish cuisine are largely absent from our chest freezers and canteen menus.

Tapas dishes are small, shared snacks which, when combined and spread over an evening of slow, civilised drinking and intelligent, passionate conversation with *mucho* hand gestures and moustache-grooming, form a substantial meal.

I arranged to meet a friend for a whole evening of tapas. Between us we ordered eight or nine dishes: chilli kidneys, crab pancakes, fried squid, olives, octopus with butter-beans, and some other meaty-spicy-fishy stuff whose names I didn't recognise.

It was good food; a spicy feast. It sizzled on the tongue. It melted in the mouth. It simmered and bubbled in the piping-hot dishes.

It all came at once. It all started to fall apart – the idea of a Mediterranean meal in a calm, unhurried, un-British format; the slow-dining concept, the idea that the small portions would arrive slowly over three or four hours . . . It evaporated in the face of rapid service and the hectic Central London venue where a dozen other diners were waiting for tables and countless punters filed through the restaurant's dining areas, snaking through the tightly packed tables to get to the beginner's Latin dance class in the function room downstairs.

I ordered a lager. I picked at the dishes furiously. They were spread out on the gnarled wooden country-style table like a buffet: an exotic Andalucían buffet; a buffet with no puff pastry, cheese-and-onion rolls or pineapple and cheese chunks on cocktail sticks, but a buffet all the same. Buffet rules were applied: pile your plate, eat quickly and covet thine last nibble.

I tried to out-manoeuvre my friend Sarah for the last spiced kidney. She beat me to it. Bitch!

I mopped up chorizo sauce with crusty white bread, full-English-fry-up-style. I looked at my watch. I set myself a target: to finish the meal as soon as possible so I could nip to the Wheatsheaf for cheaper lager and projector-screen Premiership Plus.

I scoffed. I chewed frantically. I mixed dishes: one whole mouthful of octopus with liver, crab, sausage and spicy sauce. I grabbed chorizo and buttery squid chunks with my fingers. I wiped my mouth with the back of my hand and chased the food down with warm Carling dregs.

I ordered yet another beer and got all territorial over that last crab pancake in that vibrant salsa fresca.

Tardy Service

Leave without paying. You have my permission.

(See also 'There's No Way I'm Giving a Tip'.)

Taste of the Ocean

Several years ago, stalwart Scottish actor Brian Cox appeared in an ad campaign for a brand of frozen ocean pie. If I recall correctly, the ad was set in a lighthouse, Cox was backed by a red sun setting over wave-lashed rocks and wore a chunky Arran sweater. He dipped his fork into the prawn-and-cod bake (in a rich herb-and-cheese sauce with a creamy, grooved potato-mash topping; serves two), and intoned something in his plummy Caledonian burr about the fish pie tasting exactly like the ocean. He may even have been eating the pie with a coral-reef fork from half a large South Seas conch shell; I can't quite recall.

It was a superb piece of acting; my favourite performance in the overlooked category of Best Performance by a High-Profile British Thespian in a Convenience-Food Commercial since John Hurt whispered the immortal words 'broccoli rice au gratin' on behalf of Uncle Ben and his Instant Rice range.

You can never taste the sea in any type of food prefixed by 'ocean' (ocean pie, seaside surf-and-turf in a mermaid marinade, English Channel burger, King Neptune ocean sticks, lasagne de la mer, cod-and-sea-anemone bake au gratin), just a vague plankton aftertaste underneath lapping waves of ketchup or white-wine, brine and parsley sauce.

I love fish but don't try to sell me the ocean. I've tasted the ocean, having swallowed a bucketful of foamy brown Dawlish seawater back in 1983. I had stomach cramps for five days.

The one exception to this rule is the ocean-cocktail

sandwich – my all-time favourite guilty pleasure and the best-value lunchtime snack that your supermarket £1.49 can buy. Tuck into mashed fish sticks with gooey full-fat mayonnaise and a single piece of lettuce-on-the-turn, squeezed between medium-sliced brown bread. Eat with a squeeze of fresh lemon for the grimy, salty taste of the canal.

Tea Ritual

The tea ceremony was perfected by the warrior classes in seventeenth-century Japan as a way of refreshing themselves between meditation sessions and protecting goofy farmers from feudal lords with big fuck-off swords. During the precisely choreographed ceremony, participants focused on the profound beauty of a single object in the teahouse. Making conversation that enhanced the mood of serenity, they took time to savour every tiny action while sipping green tea, full of antioxidants and low in tannin to keep your teeth whiter.

The modern British tea ceremony takes place every half hour in the workplace's communal kitchen. Participants focus their attention on the shared refrigerator, appreciating Janet's lunch: last night's pasta shells with pesto sealed in yellowing first-generation Tupperware.

The communal refrigerator smells like strawberry yogurt, even though there's no strawberry yogurt in there. And that Five Alive has been in there since January 2003 – bad karma.

Those present at the modern tea ceremony take time to savour every aspect of daily life: 'Love those shoes –

are they from Office?' 'How was your weekend?' 'Mine was pretty chilled, actually.' 'I'm thinking of starting a curry club. Are you in? All the crew from operations have signed up.'

There's a huge, 750-gram tub of Nescafé Gold Blend instant granules with no lid. Someone put a wet spoon in there last Friday after stirring their coffee. Judy Yates from human resources sent an irate email around.

The collective stillness is broken by Greg, the junior project manager, who bites his lip and frets: 'I've got my peer-group assessment tomorrow and my line manager is always slagging off my workshop facilitation.'

Once the Zen calm is broken it can't be recovered easily. Amy (milky white in a Mr Men mug with two Canderel capsules) chatters on about her wedding plans. Tommy's proposed and they've set the date. It's in September 2012.

I'm very happy for you, but do we really have to hear about every detail – from the engagement drinks to the faceless Tommy's go-kart stag-do – for the next five years?

Tranquility is restored when the MD breezes in. Everyone bows respectfully. He's part of the twenty-first-century warrior class; a business-consulting Shogun, only without the big fuck-off sword. He's a coffee man with a generous biscuit budget and his own personal jar of Continental Gold.

Teetotal

I just don't trust people who don't drink. I once thought I trusted someone who was teetotal – a copy editor I worked with. I thought I could trust him until he wrote 'Someday you'll all be sorry' in my leaving card.

Terry's Chocolate Lemon

Terry's Chocolate Lemon was a shortlived experiment; a nice idea that didn't work. File it alongside the Milk Tray Bar – a large-format chocolate bar containing a dozen minute segments of the key Milk Tray varieties. It was edible, but you'd need a ruler to separate the varieties. One wrong move and your Lime Barrel burst prematurely all over your Turkish Delight.

You were much better off with a box of All Gold.

'Can I go to the second level – all these are rubbish?'

The Caramel Sack? The Cherry Cup? The Lemon Tuba? What shoddy milk-chocolate metaphors.

Oh, there is no second level.

TGI Friday

TGI-Friday is a chain of global steakhouses. It's where undemanding diners go to eat spicy Cajun chicken, scoff assorted frittered freezer fodder and celebrate special occasions. Bless.

If it's your birthday, you'll get a small iced sponge cake and 'Happy Birthday' sung to you by an Estonian art student.

Thai Food

Thai food is the noodle-splattered slop bucket of World Cuisine. Soups so thin and tasteless they'd shame a Dickensian poorhouse. Sliced chicken breast in a Crazy Glue sauce. Sugary peanut-butter-like satay sauces, duck dumplings and deep-fried canapés so stodgy and artery-endangering they wouldn't tempt a hungry Glaswegian. All washed down with piss-poor Thai beer: it tastes like supersaver shandy but it's brewed in bamboo casks by an ancient order of robe-wearing Zen monks, so £6.00 a bottle sounds perfectly reasonable.

Why is it that people who've been to Thailand or the surrounding regions have to mention the price of the food over there at every single fucking opportunity?

'Did you read that article about the war, Jez?'

'No, Ben, but I've been to Thailand. We hired mopeds, visited some temple ruins, fed wild monkeys and ate out every night – eight courses for thirty pence.'

'Lynn, I'm so sorry to hear about your mother. Savaged by a pack of wolves – it's such a terrible way to die.'

'Thanks, Anne. Did I tell you that we bought oyster noodles from a street vendor in the Kao San Road for less than the cover price of *Closer* magazine?'

The Thai-food anecdote: world travel's most economical souvenir. 'My friend went island hopping and all he/she brought me back was this miserable old yarn about the chicken nam prik noom served in a hollowed-out coconut for the equivalent of six British pence.'

If you wanted to hang out with hard-up backpackers and eat dinner for under a pound, you could have spent six weeks in Iceland (that's the budget freezer superstore, not the country).

Personally, I'd choose Iceland (the freezer superstore and not the country). It has a superior human-rights record and fewer gap-year moped fatalities.

Theme Restaurants

I once ate at the Planet Hollywood in downtown San Francisco. All the dishes had film-related names. I think I had the 'Terminator' club sandwich or the beef à la Ernest Borgnine: I can't quite remember.

Then there are the numerous bars and steakhouses, usually situated in Stourbridge, with an American-sports theme. They introduced to Britain culinary horrors like 'whet' chunky chips covered in bright-yellow processed American cheese, pricey gourmet burgers and chilli nacho platters. They display felt pennants, plastic replica Gridiron helmets and framed photos of Babe Ruth, Ty Cobb, Wade Boggs and other tobacco-chewing US sports stars with baggy pants and dopey names.

American sports bars started springing up around 1989, *circa* Kevin Costner in *Field of Dreams* and *Bull Durham*, and American Football as screened by Channel Four on Sunday nights (then, as now, there wasn't much choice on Sunday nights; just American Football highlights, *Songs of Praise* or suicide).

Ahhh, do you remember the American-sports craze? At the fad's height I had all the gear . . .

Around 1988 I was often seen in Plymouth city centre

in my yellow and green satin team jacket, my orange and turquoise Miami Dolphins Pony trainers and that officially licensed baseball cap/velcro wallet branded with the primary colours of the Kentucky Racoons franchise. It was a sartorial ensemble that would ensure that it would be at least fifteen years before I had a proper conversation with a real-life woman.

When in London you must eat at the music-themed Hard Rock Café on Hyde Park Corner. Choose from a delectable range of starters, main courses, sides and desserts. Dine among an Aladdin's Cave of rock 'n' roll memorabilia including Jimi Hendrix's Flying V, John Lennon's hand-written lyrics to 'Imagine' and Noel Gallagher's Union Jack guitar.

The Hard Rock Café trades on the premise that rock-and-pop memorabilia exist as twentieth-century versions of religious relics. Like the Image of Edessa, only signed in silver marker pen by the bass player from the J. Geils Band.

I don't know about you, but I wouldn't be interested in seeing Noel Gallagher's Union Jack guitar, even if the talentless Northern twat rode up to my table on a pink unicorn, draped in John and Yoko's dirty-hippie Toronto bed sheets, cradling his poxy UK-flag guitar and the embalmed head of St Thomas Aquinas.

I drew the male genitalia in blue crayon on Keanu Reeves' handprints outside the Planet Hollywood in San Francisco. The penis graffito (in a classic schoolboy-scrawling-on-bus-shelter rendering) was still there three years later.

'There's No Way I'm Giving a Tip'

The waitress wore a cheap gold ring on every finger – the gold-plated Claddagh on the middle digit of her left hand was turning green. The string at the rear of her apron didn't even begin to cover the waistband on her hitched-up cerise thong and the blotchy barbed-wire tattoo on the small of her spotty back.

'No one on this table ordered the prawn puri. What exactly is a puri anyway?'

The maître d' was called Clive and wore a name badge with three gold, gummy stick-on stars. He can't have been any older than sixteen.

'I'd assumed that the bread rolls and foil-wrapped butter pats were gratis.'

'Seasonal prices? Since when is chicken tikka seasonal?'

'Why do we always get the table next to the sweaty out-of-town businessman and the world's most obvious hooker?'

'When the waiters huddled and began to sing Happy Birthday en masse, I didn't know where to look.'

The waiter reeked of Vicks VapoRub and when the waitress walked by she wafted a sour summer-mists spray and cheap cooking wine.

By the time the slushy tiramisu that tasted of instant-coffee granules arrived, and sensing that there was no way he was going to receive a substantial tip, 'Antonio' had given up on the whole accent thing.

'The tenderness of the sweet-and-sour chicken strips was offset by the squeakiness of the bamboo décor.'

Tarnished napkin rings equals no gratuity.

The strolling accordionist had a malevolent stare, a shabby shuffle and an off-key take on 'Lady of Spain'.

Three Different Kinds of Cheese

A pub-grub menu staple: loaded jacket fries with *three different kinds of cheese*. Yes, count 'em, three different kinds of cheese!

Though we're not going to tell you which types they are.

Tip-Top

Fake cream from a tin. We weren't allowed it as children. Along with tattoos and *Noel's House Party*, it was 'common' and therefore forbidden.

To Go

I have a low tolerance for people who order to go and then consume their dirty food in front of everyone else. People who wave their stinking cheeseburgers around on public transportation or dribble grease from their minced-beef samosas on to platform seven at Victoria Station on a Friday night while waiting for the last train home to Twyford; tucking the slimy paper bag in the side of their arm rest when they alight at leisure-centre-upon-Thames. The fuckers.

This also goes for potato-crisp fiends caught licking their tacky, dusty, barbecue-beef-smeared fingers before grasping communal hand-rails or door handles, and anyone who eats those bright-orange cheesy Dorito chip things anywhere except in the privacy of their own homes.

I have a low tolerance, too, for those hasty individuals who, while returning home on public transport after a spot of record shopping, feel the need to unwrap their CD purchase on the Tube, throw the plastic cellophane on the floor and read the enclosed booklet – studying the lyrics to Coldplay, U2 or whatever middle-brow, middle-class, puny-fist-pumping, white-rock pile of worthy steaming shite they've bought in the HMV end-of-season sale as if it were a missing work by William Butler Yeats.

To Share

Another pub-grub menu staple: chicken wings, onion rings, cheesy potato boats, tortilla chips topped with melted yellow gunk – all served with sour cream and a barbecue dip. *To share.*

To share, you greedy fuckers, so don't even think of eating a whole platter yourself.

By listing the platter-menu option with the caveat 'to share', greasy chain pubs, smoky wine bars and steakhouses are obviously covering themselves against accusations of pandering to the glutton. Fair enough, although it's easily the most patronising and pointless promotional instruction this side of 'Yours to own on DVD'.

Toad in the Hole

Toad in the hole is a traditional British dish consisting of pork sausages set in a Yorkshire-pudding mix. Served with vegetable and gravy, it's a tasty meal with a fantastic name. A vivid name that conjures up images of fresh flippers sticking out of baked batter and a felt frog's throat cut midway through 'It's not Easy Being Green'.

Names matter. I will never own a Ford Focus or Toyota Picnic. My first-born son will be named Jerry Lee Lampen after my all-time hero – the piano-playing Killer of rock 'n' roll.

I'd never go out with anyone called Joan, Edith, Cath, Jules, Maude, Jo-Jo, Myra or Debbie.

I think the police would earn more respect from the general public if they rebranded themselves as the 'Crime Fighters'.

I once met a nice woman called Jayne. It's a sweet girl's name; like Jayne Mansfield or that unattainable girl from accounts. The first part of her personal email address was 'sparkly_jayne_diamond_glittergirl'. That really scared me and I told her so.

She didn't bother giving me her phone number.

Toasted Crusty Bread

Too crusty.

Tongue

Ox tongue: your grandparents serve it with British mustard, silver-skin pickled onions and tomatoes cut into flowers.

'Are you courting yet?'

'Gran, you're freaking me out. I'm only six. What's "courting"? Is it the same as "fucking"?'

'No, I don't know what "fucking" means. The big kids say it at school.'

'No. I don't want to try pig's trotters or pickled spleen, listen to Deanna Durbin's "Spring Parade" on wax cylinder or look at old photographs of men in hats. I don't care if Granddad did look like a young Spencer Tracy. Who the fucking hell is Spencer Tracy? Leave me alone to eat my Milky Way and watch cartoons in goddamn mother-courting peace.'

Tongue is a dirty little secret from the World War Two generation. Did you know that *swinging* band-leader Glenn Miller died in a Parisian brothel?

Have you seen the figures for the postwar increase in venereal disease?

Say no more: loose talk costs lives.

Trolley

I hate all food ceremonies: from the time-honoured yet ever-embarrassing birthday-cake sing-song to the sentimental Scotsman in checked skirt piping a boil-in-the-bag ball of oats, offal and sheep bits to 'Flower of Scotland' or a solo-album track by that woman in big red glasses that used to be in Fairground Attraction.

I also try always to avoid mobile food: courses that arrive on your table via a trolley. Flambéed meats cooked in Courvoisier next to you as you sit pretending not to notice. Charlotte Russe-style desserts dished out with deference and a squelchy sound by a pudding chef with a slippery silver serving spoon.

I dread the trolley and its squeaky wheels. Surrounding diners nudge, whisper and turn around to gape at the gauche spectacle of your baked Alaska being set on fire right next to your table, close enough to singe eyebrows or set shawls ablaze.

I was on a last-minute holiday to the Southern States of America a couple of years ago – Tennessee, Louisiana and the other one with the long name. I went on my own. I had a great time. I dined solo daily and rarely felt self-conscious. I wore a linen suit and took a book to the table – Faulkner, Steinbeck or Mark Twain, among others – and radiated insouciance: I'm a man of letters. I'm a serious diner. Fine dining is a daily necessity and not necessarily a social event. I eschew company and chatter while appreciating fresh fish and cooked meats.

I ordered the flambéed Bananas Foster at Brennan's in New Orleans – a speciality dessert made from bananas, fresh vanilla ice cream, brown sugar, cinnamon, rum and a banana liqueur. The waiter wheeled the ingredients next to my table on a trolley and set fire to the whole slushy-bananas-and-booze mess. Everyone stared. People pointed. A girl whispered to her guardian. I'm sure she said, 'Why is that man eating on his own, Mommy?'

I turned bright red and hid behind my book – a predictable murder mystery set in the world of horseracing, published by Pan Paperbacks with a cover photograph of blood-splattered racing silks.

Tropical

In Britain, any food or drink – be it a concentrated juice, cordial or sugary carbonated fizz – containing lemon, lime, pineapple or mango is tagged as 'tropical'.

It's important to note that other items included in the taxonomy 'tropical' are tuberculosis, typhoid, tularaemia, tropical storm Arlene, steel-drum bands on *Blue Peter*, and the entire recorded output of Pato Banton, Shabba Ranks and both Chake Demus *and* Pliers.

Tuna-and-Pasta Bake

I left my hometown of Plymouth in the summer of 1997 (in the middle of the night, when no one was looking), moved north and rented a comfortable one-bedroom flat on my own in Chiswick, a leafy, well-heeled part of West London, full of young, well-off couples, shops and boutiques selling nothing you would possibly want – just stuffed olives, essential oils (they couldn't have been that essential; I'd lived quite happily without them for twenty-three years), scented candles, organic soaps and osese-wood candlesticks, hand carved in West Africa.

Having never had to fend for myself before, I didn't try

cooking anything too fancy. I relied mainly on fish-and-chip suppers, watery ready-meals for one and cans of new-wave soup (this was the year in which the snotty, punk upstart carrot-and-coriander set the broth clock back to year zero, crushing those bloated bisque dinosaurs minestrone and cream of mushroom).

The one meal I'd always make from scratch was a tuna-and-pasta bake with breadcrumbs. It was a classic bake 'n' take recipe that covered all the bases of middle-brow British nosh. The use of poor-quality, starchy white pasta shells meant it was a shoddy appropriation of a foreign cooking method. The recipe required huge quantities of melted Cheddar cheese and its main ingredient came from a squat little can. It was topped with bland breadcrumbs and eating it was a slightly more enticing prospect than outright starvation and gut rot.

God only knows why I ate it three nights a week for my first two years in the big city.

Why was that dubious story about the broom cupboard selling for the half a million pounds in the London evening paper every night? Was it the same cupboard each time?

Why did all the damn pasta shells stick together? I'd put oil in the pan. Why did the sauce taste like sulphur? Why were there about 8,000 Southern-style fried-chicken shops in South London alone? Why were pubs in the Borough of Westminster charging £9.45 for a Big Ben Burger? Why did that one low-rent Dixie-Fried-Chicken franchise in Brixton display the Confederate flag in its window? Was it run by racists? If so, why was it staffed with Somalis? Will the South (London) rise again? Did it sell Ku-Klux-Koleslaw?

Why was it that every time I sat down on a London

Underground train the person sitting next to me was highlighting passages in a book about Jesus?

V

Denotes Vegetarian option.

Veal

Veal is the meat of calves – calves raised by artificially restricting their muscle growth by rearing them in confined, cramped spaces.

Even though I occasionally enjoy a portion of veal, I must admit that it's a cruel and inhumane process that puts this rich meat on our plates . . . Or, more accurately, on the plates of regular veal-eaters: overweight Austrian businessmen and wheezing, ruddy-faced South African police chiefs.

Even more distressing than wilful animal cruelty and factory farming is the use of calfskin to make criminally naff leather goods.

Does one more animal have to die in the cause of yet another misshapen jacket made from leather (leather that's rugged-yet-soft with a generous padded lining)? Does the world need one more black-leather-bound, hand-stitched backgammon board or rust-red, grain-textured key-holder-and-wallet gift set? Can we, as the free-spending classes, survive without another mottled-tan blouson bomber with 'F-16 Tomcat Pilot' painted on the back in weathered white ink?

The leather jacket was once a symbol of youthful rebellion. Now it's a convenient method of identifying serial sex attackers or men who spend whole weekends in do-it-yourself superstores.

The true Golden Age of the bad leather jacket was the early nineties, when the dying days of the speckled-taupe, padded-shouldered bomber overlapped with the inexorable rise of the mottled-tan blouson style with the silky, ancient-map-of-the-world lining.

When shopping, seek out garments with the six-pronged, occult-esque 'Real Leather' symbol.

See our ladies' styles in soft Italian calfskin with batwing fringes. How about durable, distressed cowhide for the rugged look or soft, buttery leather for the fashion-conscious?

Stop this cruel and brutal trade!

Veggie Burger

Vegetarians are served badly in this area. The veggie burger is that deep-frozen, defrosted and deep-fried, multicoloured mosaic of rancid vegetable scrapings.

Very Berry

Oh fuck off.

More preserved fruits in sugary syrups, fruits-of-the-forest redux in compotes, shakes, smoothies and pie fillings.

Wagon Wheels

A mallow-and-jam biscuit with a chocolate-flavoured coating, shaped like the wooden cart wheel on a covered wagon in a Western movie. The Wagon Wheel dates from a time when boys played Cowboys and Indians, watched John Wayne films on rainy Sunday afternoons and aspired to the heroic Western ideal.

If biscuit-makers were market testing an aspirational mallow-and-chocolate lunchbox filler on youngsters today it would be shaped like a Nokia 6125, Linkin Park, a crack pipe, Kool Moe Dee or a Premiership footballer's nine-in-a-bed sex romp.

Water

Drink two litres of water every day?

No. Don't. It's just not worth it. You'll bloat up like some kind of tropical puffa fish and people will point.

Weddings

Wedding food: puff-pastry sausage crescents, fillet of salmon with lemon-and-herb butter, roast sirloin of beef with Yorkshire pudding, market vegetables and rich pan gravy. The menu works out at £42.00 a head including floral centrepieces, spotty service from the Youth Training Scheme and a sensible seating plan that keeps Uncle Andy away from the children's table.

Sounds lovely, but the last few weddings I've been to have been New Age mockery of the blessed ritual. Couples designing their own rings etched with sacred symbols originating from Phoenician artisans; Yohji Yamamoto white-silk deconstructed-hoop-skirt wedding dresses; string quartets playing avant-garde works by Louis Andriessen at the reception . . .

Vegan wedding cake and tapenade? I want an ox-tongue buffet, a Dexy's-centric disco and at least one fifty-something male relative with a Teddy Boy hairstyle.

Welsh Rarebit

Cheese on toast: it's Welsh rarebit to those in the know. It's the perfect British rainy-day lunchtime snack – quick, cheap, easy to prepare, wholly customisable and brand independent.

It's a national icon. I'd like to commission a portrait. I'll take a whip-round and hire an airbrush artist to paint a tribute in the style of an eighties high-street print – like the ones Athena used to sell of bright-eyed black panthers peering out from jungle rushes, unfeasibly large quadruple-stacked beefburgers with dripping ketchup, and sexy, leggy female androids. Beneath it, in angular graffiti-style 'bubble' lettering, I'd like the following: 'CHEESE ON TOAST'.

Eat it at lunchtime or at 2.00 to coincide with that *Rockford Files* repeat. Make it with medium-sliced white loaf and grated Cheddar cheese for even toasting. Grill it till the cheese bubbles and the bread turns dark brown.

Serve with relish or sweet pickle. Eat standing up while looking at the window – passing the time till Parcel Force deliver those catalogue clothes – or daydream-admiring James Garner's checked jacket and slacks and wondering if it's possible to buy copies made from modern materials.

If you're using pre-sliced supermarket cheese squares, get a grip. No wonder you can't find a rewarding job; and it's no surprise that the highlight of your day is melted cheese on white bread and an episode of that home-grown daytime drama set in a small-claims court. No matter how little your Income Support is, do not eat cheese on toast at night as well as at lunchtime. It will induce sweating, shivering and weird, vivid dreams about Jessica Fletcher from *Murder She Wrote*.

I had cheese on toast in a silver-service chophouse in the City not too long ago. The toast was crusty white bread; the cheese came melted and mixed with full-cream milk and chopped rosemary in a small silver dish. The idea was to spread or pour the cheese on the toast yourself. It was called not cheese on toast but 'Parson's Delight' or something similarly rural. The guidebook that recommended the chophouse used the word 'bucolic', which sounded to me like a stomach complaint.

I don't trust any dish that requires an element of self-assembly: curries bubbling away on metal hotplates in the middle of the table; crispy-duck pancakes from Peking where there's never nearly enough shredded duck and the last three, anticlimactic pancakes are filled with thin cucumber strips and fatty, clotted plum sauce.

Back at the chophouse and a stringy trail of congealed cheese linked my plate with the small silver bowl. The snotty cheese threads criss-crossed the linen and weaved a fatty path through the condiments. My lunch-meeting co-worker ordered the steak. Neither of us was on expenses – I was a good £15.00 down on the deal and my white cuffs were marked with waxy melted cheese.

White-Wine Sauce

It was the era of the three-day week – donkey jackets, power cuts and BBC Two plays set in Northern factories that featured Antony Sher or Colin Welland in brown overcoats; an off-screen carnal act that lasted thirty-six seconds, followed by a female factory worker putting her cardigan back on; at least one subplot about an abortion; and a 'slow' character called Maurice who, after constant teasing by the bawdy shop-floor girls, would freak out and throw himself into a piece of heavy machinery.

Then it would end – no music over the closing credits; just silence and a shaky camera close-up of Maurice's hand, hanging limp and lifeless from the grinder/press/loom/sheet-metal stamper: BBC MCMLXXV.

Yes, in those dark days before the *Observer* Food Monthly and Marks & Spencer's Gastropub range, the only glimpse of a brighter, more sophisticated manner of dining came from the occasional gooey Chinese take-away and chicken, cod, sole or plaice cooked in a creamy white-wine sauce.

It was the answer to every problem in the seventies – stringy chicken breasts, spoilt cod; bruised haddock; over-long TV comedy sketches with poor punchlines set in train compartments; the Middle East oil crisis; dull Progressive Rock; England failing to qualify for two successive World Cup Finals . . . Drown it in half a bottle of Black Tower, sprinkle on some dried parsley and put it out of its misery.

Cooking with alcohol? It was the ultimate in decadence – unparalleled culinary luxury in the days before goat's cheese, plum jus and shallots. And the best was yet to come.

The best came in the eighties, when jumbo prawns, cod pieces and chicken strips started appearing on British menus coated in beer batter.

Beer batter? Cooking with beer? It was like something off *Falcon Crest*.

'Who Do You Think You Are – Egon Ronay?'

When I mention to friends, family and casual acquaintances that I'm writing a book about British food culture they all say the same thing: 'I hate all those TV chefs. Are you going to write about those bloody celebrity chefs?'

Well, no. I'm not going to write about them. That's far too obvious. And, besides, I wholeheartedly approve of the whole celebrity-chef phenomenon. And if the mere mention of the celebrity chef or superstar saucier, their book-to-TV tie-ins, personally endorsed stainless-steel cookware sets or first-round voting exit on ITV2's *Celebrity Tank Squadron* makes you want to puke, consider, if you will, the following scenarios and send praises to Almighty God in heaven for the era of the TV chef.

You're at a family wedding. Uncle Terry, he of the rapidly receding Teddy Boy quiff and tin of twelve miniature Café

Crème cigars in his back pocket, is brandishing his compact Canon camera like Walter Santesso in Fellini's *La Dolce Vita*. A black padded camera bag is slung over his shoulder, creasing his rented suit and holding his filters, light meters, telephoto lens, tripod, tub of Vaseline and well-thumbed copy of *Amateur Photographer*. So your impish cousin John – the one with the head caked in gel even though his hair is cropped so close that it doesn't need any styling – blurts out, in an effort to rain on Uncle Terry's delusions of photographic adequacy, 'Who do you think you are, Uncle Tel – David bloody Bailey?'

You're back at your parents' for the weekend, showing off your brand-new 500-gigabyte MP3 player, Sony PlayStation portable player or George Foreman lean, mean, Bluetooth, wi-fi grilling machine. Your mum, to whom every piece of new technology looks like 'something off *Star Trek*', comments with polite bemusement, 'Oooo. Does it make the tea as well?'

'You've been printing out that document for hours. What is it – *War and Peace*?'

Let's get this straight, John: David Bailey is no longer the most famous photographer in the world. I'd rank David Lachapelle, Annie Leibovitz and at least two dozen others above him. I'd even list above him the female photographer I once went out with – the one who reckoned that her house was possessed by the mahogany carving of an African deity; a carving that her lodger had bought for £4.00 at a car-boot sale at Tripes Farm near Orpington. She rang me at 3.00 on a Sunday morning to tell me she'd seen a raven in her back garden and was thinking of calling a 'holy man'. Yes, she actually used the term 'holy man'.

I told her never to contact me again.

And, Mum: please ditch the whole *faux*-naïve 'making the tea' shtick. The idea that the pinnacle of modern compact technological achievement is a machine that can make the frigging tea is so passé it makes cousin John's perma-gelled grade-two crop with the slicked-down ringlet fringe seem fit for the cover of *Gentleman's Quarterly* (maybe David Bailey can take the sodding picture).

And I bet none of you have even read *War and Peace*.

Everyone: stop using these ridiculous, borrowed *bons mots*; quips more creased and rented than Uncle Terry's ill-fitting hound's-tooth patterned suit.

The rise of the celebrity chef, then, has at least given us some alternatives to the standard borrowed witticism when the cousin Johns of the world are confronted by someone who fancies themselves as a bit of an epicure. In such circumstances and in the age of the popular culinary know-how and confident cathode-ray charisma of today's TV cooks and celebrity chefs, the knowing wag should no longer feel tied to the weary epigram: 'Who do you think you are – Egon Ronay?'

Window Seating

'Look: that restaurant is full – it must be good.'

'No. Look closer: it's practically empty. It's just that the diners have been forced to sit in the window. Strolling strangers can stare at diner's fried-squid and side-salad starters and they, in turn, can watch strolling strangers spit on the street – it's a fair swap.'

It's the old 'sit them in the window' scheme. As an optical illusion, it's dismal. Like the trick with the spinning card on a piece of string that makes the bird-in-cage picture, the silhouetted mirror-image faces where the neutral space resembles a candlestick, or that hair-thickening bald-spot spray sold in the back of Sunday supplements.

Wine

Wine. It's made from grapes. Appellation d'Origine Contrôlée. It makes your head go THUMP THUMP THUMP and leaves an aftertaste, sometimes indistinguishable from bile, at the back of your throat.

A few months ago, I fell over in an off licence. I hadn't been drinking; I just lost my balance and staggered over on to a case of Chablis, breaking two bottles and my mobile phone.

It was OK, though. It was an accident so I wasn't charged for the bottles and I was due an upgrade anyway.

As a kid I fell over in shops all the time, usually in the shops that Mum and Dad dragged me to; shops that displayed doe-eyed Lladro angels and folksy-yet-intimidating handwritten signs that read: 'Nice to handle, nice to hold, but if you break it we say "sold".'

A few months ago I knew nothing about wine. I could plot my wine education on a simple graph, drawing a short straight-line trajectory over five sequential dots:

1) The glass of alcohol-free Shlöer grape juice I'd drink with roast dinners every Sunday between the ages of eight and fourteen.

2) The odd glass of Sauvignon Blanc with a meal as a teenager. You could unblock a drain with it, yet I'd swirl the glass like one of those old kings contemplating a good mead; kicking off the chain-mail in the wake of a muddy, bloody battle: 'Mmmm. Nice nutty aftertaste. Bring on the lutes and the jester.'

3) Three mini-bottles of Chardonnay on Transatlantic flights – plus the three spare I'd squirrel away in my carry-on bag (having wrapped them in the complimentary travel socks so they wouldn't clank together suspiciously through immigration) to drink while watching *Die Hard 2* in Spanish when I got to the hotel.

4) The occasional measure of vinegar-sharp chain-pub Riesling sold only by the glass, as if it were served on some sort of siphon system from Alsace or the gent's. And . . .

5) Back to the non-alcoholic grape juice because it didn't give me headaches.

It's a trajectory that pops, drops off and falls flat to the floor like the cork on a bottle of fizz from the former Yugoslavia.

After the off-licence tumble, I decided to learn all about wine – to suss out regions and vintages with the merest whiff of fermented grape. I yearned to know which blends to buy, which vineyards are set in rolling, sun-licked hills, and which grape fields are located next to *autobahns*, *autostradas*, *autopistas*, *autoroutes* or antifreeze factories on the river Rhine.

Is it acceptable to add lemonade to half a glass of Château du Cèdre if you have to get up early the next morning and are 'taking it easy' tonight?

Which wine does one drink with red meat, stuffed game,

fresh fish, barnacles in Thousand Island sauce or one of those delicious frozen roast-beef meals served in a large Yorkshire-pudding 'bowl'?

Craving the mysteries of the vine, the grape and the secret of getting the last drop of salty Australian white from the bargain box of vino blanc at Christmas (open the cardboard box, take the silver-foil bag out, squeeze the last drop from the plastic tap, then take the tap off, cut the silver-foil bag down the middle with scissors and lap up the remaining drops), I enrolled in an eight-week series of wine-appreciation evening classes.

I've been wary of evening classes ever since I signed up for an instructional course on book illustration in 2002.

I'd been told that the classes would prepare me for a career in illustration which would earn me £££'s, improve my artistic skills and render me irresistibly attractive to scores of attractive, eligible, watercolour-savvy, pencil-slim, arty women in Quality Street-style bonnets and floral dresses with baskets between the handlebars of their bicycles.

In reality, I paid £250.00 to listen to a cocky pavement-chalk artist 'deconstruct' children's-book illustrator Quentin Blake.

I hate the lazy modern method of cultural criticism and analysis – as practised in the dull arts sections of Sunday newspapers, on Radio Four biographies or *South Bank Show Special*s – where an artist's work can be evaluated only by comparing it to someone else's; using variations on 'Without Alfred Hitchcock there would have been no Steven Spielberg' or 'The animated triumvirate of Pixie, Dixie and Mr Jinks were heavily influenced by Fred Quimby's mid-period *Tom and Jerry* theatrical shorts'. I also abhor the lazy critical conceit that dictates that everything – music, films, books, performance art, layered mousse desserts – have to be like something else (Little Richard, Howard Hawks, Les Dennis and Dustin Gee) 'on' something (acid, smack, Dry Blackthorn Cider).

I knew within five minutes of the first class that I'd spent £250.00 for sixteen hours of 'Without *Winnie-the-Pooh* illustrator Ernest H. Shepard there would have been no Meg-and-Mog books. He was like like John Tenniel on Mogadon. Now see if *you* can draw a weasel in a top hat.'

Besides, there were only four other people enrolled in the illustration class: two mature male students from overseas (there, I reckoned, on the off-chance of a still-life nude); a woman with a homemade Fimo brooch pinned to her shawl who wanted to immortalise her cats in coloured pencil; and a man in his late twenties called Ian who sketched dragons and balloon-breasted, sword-wielding barbarian warrior maidens wearing bronze bikinis and winged headgear.

I peered at Ian's sketchbook and 'deconstructed' his work as Wagner meets the Games Workshop via *2000AD* magazine in heavy charcoals.

My deconstruction of the fantasy doodles took ten seconds and cost considerably less than £250.00. It did not appear in a Sunday paper's culture supplement.

One of Ian's sketches was of a robot dragon – light 3B shading had given him a credible metallic sheen and the wings were attached with rivets. He had suggestively wrapped the dragon's spiked tail around a warrior woman in pointy pewter Playtex and tight bronze hotpants. I edged my chair away from his.

'I see you like dragons. Have you heard that song . . . ?'

'Which song?'

'"Puff the Magic Dragon". Peter, Paul and Mary.'

He edged his chair away from mine.

I stopping going after two weeks. I wasn't learning anything and had started dreaming about dragons. Using a fictional illness as my excuse, I phoned in sick the following week and pressed for a full refund. They refused at first, citing 'the rules', but eventually gave in when I (fingers crossed behind my back) pleaded poverty and stressed the continuing cost of my dialysis care.

Subsequently, I didn't hold high hopes for the social aspect of the wine-appreciation course at the community centre. It cost £180.00 – even less than the shoddy illustration lectures – and when I arrived the room at the community centre was in a right mess: there was the overpowering smell of sweaty feet and the Kempo karate class hadn't even put the tables and chairs back after their belt-grading ceremony.

I was early so I caught the end of the karate examination. For about thirty seconds it made me want to take it up. I'm always early. Usually, being early for a business meeting, a job interview, a wedding, birthday party or any other social occasion means I have to walk round the block four times, stroll to a coffee-shop to buy a black coffee I don't want, then to a newsagent's to buy spearmint gum to take the coffee taste from my tongue. It usually takes me a good twenty minutes to find a newsagent's.

This time, being early meant I had to watch the karate and meet Anthony – the wine expert and lead lecturer – and make wine- and traffic-related small talk while I helped him lay out the tables, chairs, wine-tasting spittoons and course literature – the latter comprising a single side of A4 on wine terminology, the same on responsible drinking, and some flyers for the advanced brandy course in September.

Anthony didn't look like a wine expert. Where were the bow-tie and the knitted tank top?

Wine experts always wear bow-ties. I closed my eyes and reimagined Bacchus, son of Zeus and the Roman god of wine, with a sack-cloth bow-tie, combination tunica-tank top, red Roman nose, broken blood vessels on the surface of his skin and slurred speech patterns.

Eyes open: Anthony didn't wear a bow-tie. He was young, smartly dressed and had the air of a family solicitor or pleasant pensions advisor in a television advertising campaign.

He worked behind the counter in a wine shop; a high-end, specialist wine shop. A wine shop that sold nothing but expensive wines, champagnes, cognacs and vintage ports; certainly it didn't sell six-packs of fruit-flavoured spritzers or cheap cigars.

The students arrived. Two couples in their forties; an old boy – odds-on an ex-major – in a bow-tie; and two women straight from the office – one of whom placed a furry pencil-case on the desk (the other was a small American in a small trouser suit; another microchip-commercial ex-pat).

Anthony perched on the table at the top of the room, trendy-teacher-style, and invited introductions from the class.

'Let's go round in a circle. Give us your first name and one fun fact.'

She loves skiing. He once played the trumpet on a session with Basement Jaxx. The woman with the pencil case is scared of the green gel in the children's film *Flubber*.

One couple have just got back from their honeymoon: mild 'awwws' from the room. The American woman is from 'Cincinatti, Ohio.' Andrew the major type fought in Korea in the early fifties – a fact that draws less interest than Kim's fear of *Flubber* or the perky couple's Caribbean beach wedding. Such are modern social concerns.

I was last. Inspired by the karate demonstration and belt-grading ceremony, I weighed in with: 'I'm Martin. I can kill a man with my bare hands.'

Misjudged.

'The karate . . . Before this . . . The martial-arts class . . .'

I pointed to the door and turned red.

And so the class began. Anthony was glad the group was a small one: too many people on these courses and they can feel like seminars rather than 'hands-on' classes. He gave us an enthusiastic overview of wine production and his own personal wine-education trajectory: grape juice with lemonades; wine-bar chardonnay; three years working in various Continental vineyards; hitchhiking through Europe helping small grape-picking peasant communities battle feudal vineyard-owning, claret-swigging overlords, *Seven Samurai*-style. He's worked for a Southwest London wine importer since 2003.

He also told us not to be afraid of the screwcap or the British Riesling. Don't dismiss German wines – they're fine with puddings and for filling Bavarian pastries. He explained the difference between vintage and non-vintage. I can't remember the difference, but that can be put down to my short attention span rather than the quality of the instruction.

I can never concentrate when I'm out in the evening; all I can think about is how I'm going to get home, where the nearest cashpoint is, whether or not there's anything to eat when I get back – cereal, a tin of salmon or half a jar of peanut butter.

At the wine class all I could think about was what time we were going to finish, how long it would take me to get home and whether I'd catch the beginning of the late movie – usually a revisionist Western with counterculture overtones from the seventies starring Dennis Hopper which is always lousy so I switch over to the late-period Chevy Chase flick on BBC One; one in which he gets his biggest laugh by referring to someone as a 'dingleberry' or 'numb nuts'.

And then the tasting started. He took four bottles of red from a carrier bag and then spent five minutes caught up in panicky fumbling for the receipt; first in the carrier bag and then in his pocket, wallet and sports holdall. He eventually found the receipt and produced some large wineglasses.

I made a note to get some of those large wineglasses. The only wineglasses I have were a gift from my parents and have strawberry plants printed on them in glazed transfer form. I've tried to scratch them off but to no avail.

Everything my parents own involves floral patterns – from the framed watercolours that decorate their staircase to their kitchenware and linen. My wineglasses are part of a range called 'Strawberry Fayre' and have sticky smears on the base where the pricetag wouldn't peel off properly.

Anthony poured from the first bottle of wine, just quarter-filling the glasses. (At home, I fill my Strawberry

Fayre glasses to the brim.) It's a Merlot from Chile. Everyone breathed it in before sipping and swilling.

Anthony invited us to swirl the wine round in our mouths, to rinse around like mouthwash, to make faces if necessary. Then we had to spit it out.

I'm terrible at spitting. It won't come out in a small, neat ball of spittle; all I can ever do is spray or dribble and drool slowly.

Men are supposed to know how to spit. Women might not know this, but whenever a man uses a public urinal he's expected to gob into the bowl. It's a territorial thing that says, 'I'm a man using a public urinal. Don't get too close. I just want to urinate and get out. I probably won't even wash my hands. I'm scared of the liquid soap.'

I didn't risk spitting out the wine from a distance, even though the idea of spraying either the newlyweds, the pencil-case woman or the American ex-pat in the trouser suit with nutty, berry-like Chilean Merlot with the rich coral colour was pretty appealing.

Like my dad eating spaghetti, I lowered my head to the bowl so I didn't spray wine over anyone when I spat it out.

We chased the Merlot with Pinot Noir and some kind of Cabernet. I just couldn't tell the difference. Everyone else could taste the robust, oaky grapes. All I could taste was the 14.5 per cent alcohol and the after-coffee spearmint gum I chewed while watching the karate.

That's when I realised that I didn't want to know all about wine. Wine is dull. People who are into wine are dull. They wear bow-ties and know how to spit.

When tasting wine, there are no berries, blackcurrants,

black peppers or reasons to bring a pencil-case. Wine has no grip, spice, blood-type-like density. It's just alcohol from 13 to 14.5 per cent.

I didn't attend the class the next week. I had something else on. I phoned Anthony and apologised. He said, after promising to post the refund cheque first thing the next morning and wishing me the best of luck with my treatment, that I was in his 'prayers'.

Winter Warmers

It's a marketing term applied to pullovers, socks, slippers, knitted sock-slipper hybrids with rubber-speckled soles and even shawls; powdered chocolate drinks for slimmers in single-serving sachets, ethnic stews with couscous or rice. Northern hotpots or British stews with dumplings and lashings of glutens. Casseroles and soups thick with lentils, beef stocks, more glutens and artificial, gel-based thickening agents.

Feel free to apply the Winter Warmer tag to both shepherd's and Cumberland pies. They're pretty much the same thing – the same minced-meat and vegetable filling, the same gravy. Different potato-topping texture, though: wave-like grooves topped with Cheddar cheese on the Cumberland verses peaked mini-mash-mountains on what I call 'shep's pie'.

The Winter Warmer label is usually applied to pub-grub sausage-and-mash dishes. Menu options with greasy gravy, defrosted pork, apple and herb sausages and some sort of chive-streaked creamy potato mash.

I can just about accept the warming properties of pub-grub sausage, onion, gravy and mash – as long as the sausages are of a standard shape and not wound round in one whole, unnatural, pig's-tail-like circular pork link. That's disturbing meat. That's meat that's curled, dog-turd-like in a hypnotic loop. It's evocative of the heated coil element on a pensioner's faulty portable fire – another potential health hazard and so-called Winter Warmer.

(See also Summer Bites – ying to Winter Warmers' yang.)

Wood-Fired Pizza

Big fucking deal.

Wrap

Sandwich wraps. We never had any choice in the matter. They appeared, suddenly and without warning. Why didn't we, as a nation, organise our own million-man march, demand a referendum or, at the very least, write a stern letter to *Which?* magazine?

I'm talking about the wrap. The chicken-tikka wrap, the 'old-fashioned' egg-mayonnaise wrap, the mint-yogurt-chicken model, the American-style hickory-steak and sweetcorn version.

The wrap has no history; it's a snack without a past that now takes up 50 per cent of the supermarket space allocated to the lunchtime trade. Who is responsible for this tasteless, low-carbohydrate, tubular, honey-ham-filled atrocity? Who buys this nacho-chicken-and-Chinese-sauce-filled sack of shit?

Zest

Zest is the rind of a citrus fruit. It's also another intangible quantity; a certain spice, a flavour and piquancy, to induce appetite, get juices flowing and stomachs rumbling.

I'm still looking for food with that kind of zest. I'm still hungry and still can't taste any nuts and berries in the house wine – just fermented grape and maybe dishwasher tablets.

'Zesty lemon-flavoured' dishwasher tablets and fruits-of-the-forest room spray from a Unilever subsidiary.

I haven't discovered anything about myself. I haven't been on any journeys, exorcised any personal demons, improved myself, grown as a person, found 'closure', learnt any weighty life-lessons or secured the secret of the perfect soufflé.

I haven't overcome any obstacles or personal tragedies and I still don't live in North London with the aromatic wife I met on an illustration course and our newborn son Kye.

Though he wouldn't be newborn now; we'd be weaning him off the unethical powdered Nestlé milk and on to the solids: rusk biscuits, mashed-up buffalo mozzarella or 'Baby's First Butternut Squash'.

I *have* now been to a dinner party, though that was terrible. I made a fool of myself and lost a Marcello

Mastroianni cufflink on the way home. I'm never going to another one. I would consider going to a black-tie ball, should anyone want to invite me.

I saw Bev and Chris, my dinner-party hosts, in the supermarket during my Saturday-evening shop three weeks ago. They were browsing olive oils in the Continental Larder with their children, Sophie and Jake. I abandoned my trolley in the middle of Sunkist Alley and left the store empty-handed. I stopped for petrol, bought six Lotto tickets and ate cereal with cold milk when I got home.

The pedometer offer has finished. For breakfast I'm currently eating honey-flavoured wheat rings for the sticky sugar fix and one of six collectable flicker-stickers of prehistoric creatures. I only need the mammoth for a full set.

Or is it a mastodon?

I am still looking for food, drink or dining experiences with a certain zest; and I still never know what to eat on Saturday nights.

Chicken, turkey or scampi in breadcrumbs. A combination Cajun-peri-peri steak – juicier than non-diluted orange cordial, thicker than a large-print hardback copy of *War and Peace*, topped with French-style crème fraîche and soaked in white-wine sauce. None of the above hold any appeal. I'd rather go hungry and spend my money on scratchcards.

Food seems to have merged together in my mind: baked cod and curly frites; sea-bass fish fingers and goat's-cheese rissoles. All wrapped up in filo pastry. All indistinguishable from each other; all mixed up with a hummus-and-Maris-Piper mash mix; flavoured with coriander and four other spices that no one can name; topped with fruit-flecked roulade; available smoked or un-smoked, matured until it turns the colour of *Our Finest* liquid soap, and served in a wicker basket, hand-woven in the traditional method in the last working mill in Britain.

I can't eat out. I'm sick of snotty waiters, slow service, gushing water features and irritating diners on adjacent tables. The glass turntable on my new microwave is broken. The noise is unbearable; I have to leave the room when reheating risotto.

But don't let me put you off your food.

Tuck in. Enjoy. Eat heartily and drink sensibly. Raise a glass to me. Head down to the supermarket for pre-washed salad, a selection of small fruit and veg and emergency meringue nests. Get yourself down the local Irish pub for a glass of German dessert wine or a lamb-shank casserole with a flaky-pastry 'lid'.

And would you like to see the dessert menu?

A NOTE ON THE AUTHOR

Martin Lampen was born in Plymouth, Devon, in 1973. Now living in London, he works as a freelance design consultant on high-profile media projects. Martin is also the creator of the incredibly successful website www.bubblegum-machine.com, which eulogises catchy-yet-long-forgotten pop music, meaning he receives thousands of emails per year from Belgians enquiring about Mungo Jerry B-sides.

A NOTE ON THE TYPE

The text of this book is set in Linotype Sabon, named after the type founder, Jacques Sabon. It was designed by Jan Tschichold and jointly developed by Linotype, Monotype, and Stempel, in response to a need for a typeface to be available in identical form for mechanical hot metal composition and hand composition using foundry type. Tschichold based his design for Sabon roman on a font engraved by Garamond, and Sabon italic on a font by Granjon. It was first used in 1966 and has proved an enduring modern classic.